We'll All Be Murdered in Our Beds!

We'll All Be Murdered in Our Beds!

The Shocking History of Crime Reporting in Britain

Duncan Campbell

First published 2016 by
Elliott and Thompson Limited
27 John Street
London WC1N 2BX
www.eandtbooks.com

ISBN: 978-1-78396-133-7

9 8 7 6 5 4 3 2 1

A catalogue record for this book is available from the British Library.

Typesetting: Marie Doherty
Printed in the UK by TJ International Ltd

Contents

Introduction

'Wherever God erects a house of prayer,' wrote an early crime reporter called Daniel Defoe, 'the Devil always builds a chapel there; And 'twill be found, upon examination, The latter has the largest congregation.'

The same applies to the news – stories of crime and the underworld have, for centuries, attracted the largest of readerships. But how did people become so interested in all those devilish miscreants – the bandits, the highwaymen, the murderers, the outlaws, the gangsters, the robbers, the cat-burglars, the conmen, the getaway drivers, the men and women who broke all the rules?

The Bible described how Adam and Eve were caught stealing forbidden fruit. Was that the first crime report? Was their banishment the earliest coverage of a criminal sentence, and was the killing of Abel by Cain the original murder story to whet the appetite of the reading public?

Crime reporting has been a staple of news since the first newsbooks, chapbooks and broadsides, as the early forms of the press were known, were sold in the wake of public hangings centuries ago, some of them initially read aloud for the benefit of the illiterate. From the capture of the highwayman, Dick Turpin, and the execution of the great escaper, Jack Sheppard, in the eighteenth century, to the hunt for Jack the Ripper and the scandal of child prostitution in Victorian England, to the Brides in the Bath murders during the First World War, the Old Bailey trial of the Kray twins in the 1960s and the funerals of the great train robbers in the 2010s, the fascination with the transgressive has remained unabated.

Some themes are constant. 'Crime in England this century has increased 400 per cent, in Ireland 800 per cent and in Scotland above 3,500 per cent,' *Blackwood's Magazine* told its readers in 1844. The causes were clear. Big cities were partly to blame because 'restraint of character, relationship and vicinity are lost in the urban crowd' but there were other culprits: 'the employment of women has destroyed the familial bond, emancipating the young from parental control.' Twenty years later, another factor in the growth of crime was spotted by *The Times*: 'under the influence of philanthropic sentiments and hopeful policy we have deprived the law of its terrors and justice of its arms.' A century and a half on, panic about lawlessness, dismay at the behaviour of the young and criticism of over-lenient punishments still provide a backdrop to the coverage of crime.

Why such interest? Why does the old news-desk motto, 'if it bleeds, it leads', still hold true? The writer Thomas De Quincey, in his famous satirical essay 'Murder Considered As One of the Fine Arts', published in *Blackwood's Magazine* in 1827, wrote of how he came across the case of John Williams, accused of killing seven people in east London in what were known as the Ratcliffe Highway murders: 'in came the London morning papers, by which it appeared that, but three days before, a murder the most superb of the century by many degrees had occurred in the heart of London'. In a postscript published in 1854, De Quincey added: '[E]very day of the year we take up a paper, we read the opening of a murder. We say, this is good, this is charming, this is excellent!'

Charles Dickens, in a letter to the *Daily News* on 28 February 1846, on the subject of the death penalty, noted that 'there is about it a horrible fascination, which, in the minds . . . of good and virtuous and well-conducted people, supersedes the horror legitimately attracting to crime itself, and causes every word and action of a criminal under sentence of death to be the subject of a morbid interest and curiosity.' He felt that such reports were published 'because they are read and sought for . . . it is in the secret nature of those of whom society is made up, to have a dark and dreadful interest in the punishment at issue.' A decade later, in his poem 'Bishop

Blougram's Apology', Robert Browning returned to the theme: 'Our interest's on the dangerous edge of things./The honest thief, the tender murderer,/the superstitious atheist.' And an interest in dark and dreadful criminals and far from tender murderers has been cited as one factor in increasing literacy in Britain in the wake of the Education Acts of 1870 and 1880, when the press reported every detail of the wicked offenders and their progress to the scaffold.

Newspapers themselves pondered on the fascination and sought to justify it in different ways. 'This appetite of the mind for particulars of great crimes and criminals has been stigmatised as vulgar,' said the *Daily Telegraph* in 1881, after running tens of thousands of words on the case of a murderer called Percy Lefroy Mapleton, who killed a man in the first-class carriage of the Brighton to London train. 'It is only vulgar in so far as it is universal, the common attribute of every age, people and clime.' The Athenians, it was suggested, were just like us because they were thrilled by Sophocles' *Oedipus the King* and the fact that he had killed his father and married his mother. The paper concluded that 'public attention dwells on the life story of a great criminal as it hunts out the moral of a literary or pictorial satire. In both cases the analytical faculty stimulates the intellect to an exhaustive inquiry.' Well, up to a point. But certainly the ways in which crime is reported over the centuries, the language used, the judgments made, the prejudices revealed, create their own rich history.

Crime is, in many ways, the prism through which we see society and its anxieties and phobias. What are the most egregious offences? How should they be punished? Are offenders bad or mad? In 1910, a young Home Secretary, Winston Churchill, made a speech in which he explained: 'the mood and temper of the public in regard to the treatment of crime and criminals is one of the most unfailing tests of the civilisation of any country.' Crime reports are a running commentary on those unfailing tests. And the crimes reported deal with the most visceral emotions – hate, love, greed, desire, fear, jealousy, anger, revenge, redemption, compassion – and shine a light on a nation's attitudes to sex, race, gender, religion, property, wealth and power.

A day in a magistrates' court provides as illuminating a snapshot as any lengthy think-tank report or ministerial briefing on the state of education, immigration, unemployment, drug use, alcoholism, mental health and popular culture, not to mention policing, the criminal justice system and the failures or successes of government policies. Nor is it a grim beat; the phrase 'gallows humour' did not come from nowhere. Life and death. Human nature. Drama. As Mitchell Stephens noted in his book *A History of News*, 'criminals and their victims, even given the heavy-handedness of most crime coverage, may be the most fully drawn characters in the news'. And as Edgar Wallace, himself a crime reporter before becoming the best-selling author in Britain, remarked: 'My experience of crime reporting taught me a great deal about humanity that has been very useful to me.' No wonder the television channels overflow every day with fictional and non-fictional criminals and detectives.

Is it a British thing? Murder certainly seems to be, despite – or perhaps because of – the fact that our murder rates are low and detection rates high. The title of this book comes from a catch-phrase uttered by a character called Minnie Bannister in the 1950s BBC radio comedy series *The Goon Show*. Everyone laughed when Minnie said it, not least because no one thought there was a possibility of it ever happening to them. 'Death in particular seems to provide the minds of the Anglo-Saxon race with a greater fund of innocent amusement than any other single subject,' wrote Dorothy L. Sayers in 1934, in a preface to a short stories collection of mystery, detection and horror. She was writing about its fictional portrayal but murder and its detection and punishment has been responsible for the sales of countless newspapers. The abolition of the death penalty in 1965 was blamed by at least one Fleet Street editor for the subsequent decline in the sales of evening papers.

Reports of crime have been accused of both fuelling fear by highlighting the horrific and of glamorising gangsters by treating them sometimes as likeable rogues. Wallace did not subscribe to the idea of the romantic criminal: 'Criminals are stupid, treacherous and dull people. The only interesting criminals are those I write about in my books.'

Nevertheless, many bad boys and girls in history have been painted in a favourable light. The comedian and director Mel Brooks, in his majestic comedy routine The 2,000-Year-Old Man, recorded in 1961, plays the part of someone who has lived to this incredible age and met everyone from Jesus Christ to Joan of Arc. He is asked by an interviewer, played by Carl Reiner, if he ever met Robin Hood. Of course, he had. Was it true, asked the interviewer, that he robbed the rich and gave to the poor? 'No, he robbed everybody and kept everything!'

Crime reporters have, of necessity, had a symbiotic relationship with both police and criminals throughout history. All sides have had reason to embellish and exaggerate their deeds: the criminals to justify or explain their acts, the police to make it look like they are successful and even-handed, and the reporters to impress with their inside knowledge. The hardest three words for any journalist to say remain 'I don't know'.

The crimes and the punishments reported over the years are often shocking – from Dick Turpin holding an elderly man's bare buttocks over a fire to force him to reveal where his money was hidden in the early eighteenth century to the debonair John George Haigh dissolving his victims in acid in the 1940s. Shocking, too, is the relish with which some crimes and punishments were reported and shocking sometimes in the preconceptions, prejudices and ignorance displayed. But there have been great acts of bravery and fine writing; from Dickens in the *Daily News* to W. T. Stead's exposé of child prostitution in the *Pall Mall Gazette* and the campaign that led to the jailing of the killers of the black teenager, Stephen Lawrence.

My first exposure to this world was through a magazine called *True Detective*, at a time in the 1950s when I should have been reading more wholesome fare, like *The Eagle* or *The Children's Newspaper*. I started to swap Agatha Christie and genteel country-house murder for the grainy black-and-white photos of real crime scenes and detectives called Bob or Jim rather than Hercule or Miss Marple. Sometimes in the background there would be a chap with a notebook. A crime reporter. What a job!

In the same decade, the famous and far from bashful Superintendent Robert Fabian – Fabian of the Yard, as he liked to be known – wrote *The Boy's Book of Scotland Yard*; girls were presumed not to be interested. In it he informed any curious nippers that '[behind] a scarcely noticeable green door is a room with men playing cards, perhaps, or reading or just smoking and chatting . . . They are the crime reporters of the national newspapers . . . They more than anyone else are the link between you, the public and the police. You want to know what the police are doing. You can't go and see for yourself but you can read about it in your newspaper.'

I met my first professional criminal, a charming fraudster who had studied economics at Jesus College, Cambridge – or so he said – in Perth prison in 1962 when, as part of a team of cocky schoolboys, I debated with prisoners whether going to the moon would be a good idea. I interviewed my first chief constable in 1965, a legendary character called Wee Willie Merrilees – five inches too short for the police but given a special dispensation – who was one of the Most Unforgettable Characters in the *Reader's Digest*. One of his coups as a police officer was an operation in which he had hidden himself in a pram disguised as a baby to catch a molester active in Edinburgh at the time. Was this my first lesson in the old-school rule of journalism – 'too good to check'? He also told me, chillingly, how the police in the thirties had cleared up the 'homo problem' in Edinburgh by rounding up the clientele of the city's few gay bars and putting them on a non-stop *Flying Scotsman* to London.

Down in London, in the dark days of the seventies, I saw some detectives cheerfully lie to ensure convictions – and then saw them again years later in the dock themselves. I also called 999 a few times myself in response to nearby screams and violence, and was always impressed by the fearless way young, unarmed police men and women leapt from their vans to grapple with a violent bully.

I soon learned another important journalistic lesson: never assume. Not everyone fitted the stereotype. I got to know a former armed robber – he gave it up because he found prison so boring – who was an early beneficiary of the Open University. One night in the pub I noticed that he was reading

Virginia Woolf's *To the Lighthouse*. I mentioned this to another OU-graduate armed robber who replied dismissively: 'Not her best.' And I met a detective who knew as much about Harold Pinter, Bob Dylan, the French impressionists and Native American battle plans as any critic or historian.

And the job? Is it as exciting as it is portrayed in plays and films like *The Front Page* or in Edgar Wallace novels? One of the first cases I covered in any detail was a 1970s double-murder trial at the Old Bailey. Two men, both professional criminals, had been accused of killing two others, the body of one of the victims being cut up and dumped in the Thames, thus leading to this being known as the Torso Murder case. I had been told there was something dodgy about the case and indeed there was. The trial took six months and it had everything: the prison informer; the detective nicknamed 'the Old Grey Fox'; the accusations that the defendants had been 'verballed up' (compromising words attributed to them by the police); the gilded barristers from the other side of the tracks; the relatives of the living and the dead; the conflicted jury; the different verdicts; the furious protests from the dock. Many years later the informer admitted to me in a bar in Brighton that he had made his evidence up. The two men were eventually cleared but only after spending more than twenty years behind bars.

Hanging round the Old Bailey, gradually getting to know the participants from both sides of the fence – and the people who wrote about them – was an apprenticeship. The windowless press room in the bowels of the Bailey has barely changed over the years, although the gents next to it is now a prayer-room – prompting the observation from one old crime reporter that, not for the first time, people are found in there on their knees.

Most crime reporters, current and retired, would not have swapped the job for any other. As the old police recruiting slogan had it: 'Dull, it isn't.' Unlike many other forms of journalism, there is often a beginning, middle and end. A crime. An arrest. A trial. A sentence. But there is so much more in between: who are the people involved, the perpetrators and the victims? What were the motives? There is always a story within the story.

It's about people at their best and worst, their bravest and most cowardly. Human and inhuman nature. I have met a woman who spent six years trying to confront in prison the man who murdered her daughter and who found a kind of peace as a result, and I have met a man who, at the time, was only staying alive so that he could kill his daughter's killer once he finally emerged from jail. I have seen a murderer acquitted, leaving the court sniggering at the jury's gullibility and heard later that he now wanted to confess because he had been unable to sleep properly ever since.

The crimes being reported have changed. My earliest efforts as a student journalist in the 1960s were about abortion and homosexuality, both then against the law, although soon to be legalised. The drugs squad in the Met police at that time consisted of one cheery sergeant. Throughout the second half of the last century, the main reports of professional crime concerned organised robberies. Such highly-planned events still happen in this century – as the theft of an estimated £14 million from safe-deposit boxes in Hatton Garden over the Easter weekend in 2015 demonstrated – but are much rarer.

Acquisitive crime through the internet has started to replace them and public opprobrium has shifted from the 'ODC's – the ordinary decent criminals – to the legal chancers, the bankers, tax dodgers and financial wide boys. It was not Robert Browning but Bertolt Brecht who was worth quoting: 'What is robbing a bank compared to founding one?' The fortunes of the family firms that ran crime in Britain half a century ago (the Krays, the Richardsons and others) have mirrored what has happened to British business. They have been replaced by often faceless multinationals anxious to avoid the limelight.

There have been changes, too, for reporters over the years. The earliest reports in this book were often anonymously written, by clerics or lawyers or authors. By-lined journalism did not become standard until the last century. And until the last few decades of the twentieth century crime reporters were almost uniformly male and white.

Journalism has changed in other more dramatic ways, firstly through the arrival of radio and television and more recently with the decline of the printed press and the attendant growth of the internet and online news. Reporters have responded to the digital revolution much like Eastern Europeans to the collapse of the Soviet Union: some embraced the new world with evangelical fervour, others muttered about the loss of a simpler, more ordered world. The speed of the internet is now a major factor. Rumour used to be halfway round the world before Truth had got its boots on; now Rumour, given wings by Twitter and others, has been twice round the world while Truth is still in its pyjamas.

Major trials, with a very few exceptions, are no longer covered in detail. When they are, reporters are expected to tweet details from the court, constantly under pressure to update, whereas in the past there was time to talk to the detectives, lawyers, witnesses, defendants. Deadlines come by the minute rather than by the day. Much of the writing on crime comes now from a commentariat, selectively picking second-hand details of cases to reinforce an argument or fuel a panic.

Some traces have lingered through the centuries. In 1728, John Gay based his character Macheath, in *The Beggar's Opera*, on Jack Sheppard, the most written-about criminal of his day. Can Gay ever have imagined that a song, 'Mac the Knife', based on this creation, would one day be the favourite melody of one of Britain's most notorious gangsters, Ronnie Kray? Public executions at Tyburn or Newgate in London or the Grassmarket in Edinburgh are no longer a staple for crime reporters, but did Dickens and other writers distressed by the mob's enjoyment of such events ever imagine that millions would one day be watching beheadings on tiny screens?

This is, inevitably, a selective, personal and rough history, from the early days of crime reportage in the seventeenth century to the legal and moral journalistic turmoils of the twenty-first century. While it is mainly in chronological order, there are many overlapping themes, such as the coverage of drugs, of 'femmes fatales', of the changing relationships between journalists and police and criminals, of the language of crime reporting. There will be errors and omissions, to which I plead guilty now in exchange for a shorter sentence. The bibliography at the back of the book lists the essential volumes that will give the interested reader much greater detail on many of the characters and subjects explored.

1

Not So Ordinary

The First Professional Crime Reporter

G o to the fourth floor of the British Museum, turn right past the earnest American students staring bemusedly at Michelangelo's cartoon, 'Epifania', and you will find the Department of Prints and Drawings Study Room where material not on general display is stored but made available by a sweetly helpful staff. Amongst this treasure is 'The Idle 'Prentice Executed at Tyburn,' by the artist William Hogarth. The engraving was the penultimate one of Hogarth's twelve-part series, *Industry and Idleness*, created in 1747, which charted the progress of two imaginary apprentices, one industrious and ambitious, the other, idle and dissolute. While the first one, Francis Goodchild, works hard, marries well and eventually becomes Lord Mayor of London, the other one, Thomas Idle, gets in with the wrong crowd, hangs out with prostitutes, becomes a highwayman and murderer, and by the eleventh drawing of this morality tale, is being taken to the scaffold to be hanged.

Hogarth's engraving shows the condemned man on his way to Tyburn – what is now Marble Arch – as a mob, full of pickpockets, drunks and wastrels, gathers to watch the execution. The atmosphere is one of ribaldry and excitement, like a crowd that has spent too long in the pub on its way to a football match. Thomas Idle is in a carriage, his coffin beside him, being hectored by a Wesleyan priest. But who is the bewigged figure staring out of the carriage immediately preceding him?

This is the Ordinary of Newgate, the chaplain of the prison where the condemned men and women spend their last days. He will have already interviewed the miscreant about his life and sins and he is on his way to the scaffold to report on his end. He will then publish his account which will be bought in its thousands by the growing number of literate Londoners, many of whom would read it out loud to those who couldn't. He could claim to be the first professional crime reporter.

Look carefully at the picture and there, in the foreground, is a woman with what looks like a pamphlet in her hand entitled 'The last dying Speech and Confession of Tho' Idle'. She is selling what is essentially a pirated account of the apprentice's life and death as she already knows that the public appetite for crime is as gluttonous as the rakes whom Hogarth will portray in his other famous drawings; no one will mind that she could hardly have access to Idle's dying speech when he is clearly still alive. Already there are rival accounts of the deeds of villains, despite the Ordinary's apparent monopoly of the condemned.

So who was the Ordinary and how did he help to set in train the enduring fascination of readers with the dangerous edge of things?

We need to go back to the previous century, to the 1670s, when Charles II was king of England after the restoration of the monarchy and the Anglican church was established as the official religion amidst rumours of a 'Popish plot'. The capital was just recovering from the Great Plague and the Fire of London and organised religion had a power and authority unimaginable in Britain today, so it was natural that the role of writing about criminals and their punishments should be the responsibility of a man of the cloth who could draw a handy Christian moral from each wasted life.

Newgate had been a jail, in various forms, since the twelfth century and would be so until the beginning of the twentieth. Its proximity to the Old Bailey meant that it held the most notorious – and newsworthy – of the city's offenders. London at the time had a population of around half a million and was internationally notorious for its high levels of crime, so the Ordinary essentially had unfettered access to the leading villains of the day. The reports by the various holders of the Ordinary's office ran from 1676 to 1772 and are one of the main sources for our knowledge about crime during that period. They were Anglican chaplains although, after 1735, Catholic, Jewish and Methodist prisoners were also given access to preachers from their religions. The Ordinary's role was both to record the final thoughts of condemned prisoners and to write a potted biography of how they had strayed.

Who was his audience? Literacy was growing apace. Most of the male gentry could read and around half of the middle classes and merchants and just under a third of the poor were literate; it has since been estimated that only around 10 per cent of women of all classes could read at that time. There was also a fear of what was seen as growing criminality, with London regarded internationally as a hotbed of dangerous villainy. This combination gave the Ordinary a substantial potential readership. At the time he was logging his reports, thanks to the so-called Black Act passed in 1723, there were more than 200 crimes punishable by death and, although many were pardoned for minor offences, these penalties remained until sweeping reforms took place a century later. Almost every public hanging was attended by a large crowd, strongly suggesting a large audience hungry for further details.

The Ordinary was, to a certain extent, keeping a public record, but he and his rivals were essentially in the business of commercial crime reporting. While the most notorious criminals were known to the public via ballads or rumours, the Ordinary was for the first time providing detailed information for a reading public and thus provided his readers with accounts of the lives of more than 2,000 executed criminals.

The Ordinary addressed his audience in the first of his publications thus: 'Reader, wherein canst thou more experience thy self for the ordering of a good Conversation, than by seeing the follies of those, who either by their own idle or extravagant living are forced to seek out those ways and means, which either are destructive in themselves, or purchase shame and destruction in their end?'

Or, put another way, what better way to pass the time than to chat about some terrible crime and learn the details of its perpetrators and its victims? More than 350 years later, readers may not have been addressed in quite such candid fashion but the rationale is the same: how entertaining to have a conversation about a terrible crime that has not affected one in any way, how comforting to read of perils affecting others, how reassuring to learn of the decadence of the offender and how satisfying to know of their punishment.

The very earliest of the Ordinary reports, on the confessions and executions at Tyburn on 17 May 1676, told of the fate of Henry Seabrook, Elizabeth Longman, Robert Scot, Edward Wall and Edward Russell, and was 'published for a Warning, to all that read it, to avoid the like wicked Courses, which brought these poor people to this shameful End'. Longman was described as 'an old Offendor, having been above a Dozen several times in Newgate: Some time since she was convicted, and obtained the benefit and favour of Transportation, and was accordingly carried into Virginia.' However, Longman was not suitably contrite and made her way back to both England and her stealing ways. She was asked if there was a reason why she should not suffer the death penalty and claimed that she was pregnant. 'But being searched by a Jury of Matrons, they found no such thing; so that she was carried with the rest into the Hole, and ordered for Execution.' No bleeding hearts there.

In those very early reports, there is another story that, centuries later, will seem all too familiar. 'There was a French Man also tryed for a Rape; pretended to be Committed on his Maid-Servant, upon the Tryal she gave Evidence that she was one Morning about her business, and her Master arose and as she said took her Virginity from her, being askt what she meant by that, she answered her Maidenhead; but it appearing to the Court, that she had not acquainted any one of it till three days after it was pretended to be done, nor had not accused her Master for it till above three weeks after, he was found not Guilty, and so acquitted.' The maid-servant was not believed simply because she had waited three days to report the rape and the Ordinary makes it clear where he stands by suggesting that she had 'pretended' it had happened.

In his book *The London Hanged*, Peter Linebaugh suggests that the prominence of women described as prostitutes who were executed may

4

be confusing as the Ordinary, being a clergyman, was very moralistic and applied the label to most of the condemned women. Certainly the Ordinary spared nothing in his dismissal of even the most minor female offenders. A very active pickpocket, Mary White, known as 'Mary Cut-and-Come-Again' because she snipped off the pockets of her victims, was hanged for stealing an apron and described by the Ordinary as 'the queen of the blackguards, pilferers and ballad-singers'.

Better known of the condemned women was Mary Young, alias Jenny Diver – who would appear as such in John Gay's *Beggar's Opera* – and who was, according to the Ordinary, 'thought to be one of the most artfullest Pick-pockets in the World'. She was nothing if not inventive and had procured a pair of false hands and arms so that her real hands could get to work undetected. She had already been transported to America not once but twice, both times managing to bribe her way back to London and continue her wicked ways. She was hanged at last, however, aged forty-one.

There were ten holders of the office in the eighteenth century and one of the most prolific was Paul Lorraine, who held the office from 1700 till his death in 1719. It was he who expanded the format and turned his accounts into what was essentially an entertaining periodical done in the style of what in a modern newspaper is called a 'backgrounder', the longer article published at the end of a major trial, full of biographical details of the guilty man or woman which have not featured in the trial itself. While the Ordinaries were much mocked by satirists, their accounts remain fascinating and instructive.

Some of the condemned prisoners refused to cooperate on the grounds that the Ordinary was charging between 3d and 6d a copy and thus making a fat profit of around £25 an edition, or £150 a year (which would be roughly £30,000 today), out of their misery. One of them, John Allen, was even called to account in 1700 and accused of extorting money from convicts 'under pretence of procuring them reprieves or pardons'. It was also suggested that he promised to get people bail in exchange for money and even to omit one condemned man from his account so as to spare his family embarrassment. Some prisoners made a point of handing over their own confessions and stories to the printers, thus cutting out the middleman and ensuring that the hanged man's version was at least his own.

The appetite for tales of crime was clearly huge. In his essay on the subject, in *Crime in England 1550–1800*, Peter Linebaugh noted that the Ordinary's accounts 'enjoyed one of the widest markets that printed prose narratives could obtain in the eighteenth century'. Not surprisingly, the Ordinary faced increasing competition from freelancers but the writers who entered this competitive trade by the 1740s had to labour anonymously, relegated from the more genteel literary world. Nowadays they would probably describe themselves as hacks. One of the Ordinary's regular printers was John Applebee, who soon realised what a lucrative market this was. He duly employed his own writers, known as 'Mr Applebee's garreteers', to produce rival versions, for which he would pay a small fee to the condemned men; a very early example of criminals being paid by the press.

Amongst this anonymous number was Daniel Defoe, who found fame with *Robinson Crusoe*, and whose other freelance work at the time supposedly included a biography of Duncan Campbell (no relation), a deaf-mute Scottish soothsayer who told the fortunes of fashionable London but was sometimes accused of being a charlatan. Defoe, in *Moll Flanders*, makes clear his disdain for the Ordinary: when a minister is treating Moll sympathetically in Newgate, she observes that 'he told me he did not come as the Ordinary of the place, whose business is to extort confessions from prisoners, for private ends'.

The format varied little over the years. Anyone interested in the misdemeanours and morals of the period can study them in detail as they have now been helpfully and meticulously compiled at oldbaileyonline.org. The Ordinary may have been a man of the cloth but he was happy enough to witness grotesque punishments inflicted on accused men. In 1721, a highwayman, William Spiggott, was arrested and, as Tim Hitchcock and Robert Shoemaker recount in *Tales from the Hanging Court*, refused to plead to the charges so was subjected to the press – the placing of a massive weight of 350 pounds on his chest as he lay spreadeagled and naked on the cell floor with only a cloth to cover his 'privy members'. Even then, he would not confess. The Ordinary, Thomas Purney, wrote that, 'I there prayed by him and asked him why he would destroy his soul as well as his body by such obstinate kind of self-murder.' Another 50 pounds was added to the press after which Spiggott obligingly agreed to plead.

One of the Ordinary's most remarkable cases was that of James Maclaine, not least because it coincides with the arrival of other publications covering crime. Maclaine came to London from Ireland in 1743, married into a fortune, squandered it on gambling and met up with a dishonest apothecary called William Plunket, who steered him to a life of robbery. The Ordinary would later describe the attraction of crime for Maclaine who was 'doatingly fond of gay clothes, masquerades, etc at which he made a very gay and impudent figure'. The pair became notorious for the robbery in Hyde Park of Horace Walpole, son of Robert Walpole, the former Prime Minister. Their victim escaped with a graze under his eye from a pistol shot and the loss of his watch.

Walpole placed an advertisement offering a reward to which Maclaine cheekily replied, explaining that he had not meant to injure him and seeking the reward. He also wrote a letter to the *Daily Advertiser* in which he claimed that the gun had gone off by mistake. This use of the media by someone on the run was to set a pattern that continues to the present day, whether those contacting reporters are escaped train robbers or people who feel they have been wrongly accused. Maclaine was finally arrested after robbing the Salisbury Flying Coach and held in the Gatehouse, where he was visited by many members of fashionable society. Even after his inevitable sentence to death, he was again visited by hundreds of admirers, to the amazement of Walpole, who in a style repeated by many a tut-tutting columnist over the centuries, confessed himself astonished that 'the prints that are published of the malefactors' were much more flattering than anything accorded, say, a distinguished general.

Nearly a century after the first Ordinary reports, the same moral tone predominated as his role came to an end in 1772 – and, according to

Robert Shoemaker, professor of eighteenth-century British history at the University of Sheffield, Newgate was the only prison in Britain known to have had ordinaries who wrote up accounts of convicts' lives and executions for public consumption. The *Newgate Calendar* then took on the role of crime reporter to the condemned. The *Calendar* was a monthly compilation put together by the Keeper of Newgate and described in its first edition in 1773 as containing 'interesting memoirs of the most notorious characters who have been convicted of outrages on the laws of England'.

Volumes of the *Calendar*, often lavishly illustrated, were published until 1826 and found a ready audience amongst an increasingly literate working-class. The last of the Ordinary reports, delivered by assistant ordinary John Temple, tells of five condemned men who had stolen items ranging from a pair of silver knee-buckles, valued at four shillings, and eight pairs of silk stockings, valued at thirty shillings. Temple concluded by stating that he hoped that the executions and words of contrition would 'prove a means to stem the torrent of immorality and vice, by which multitudes of the unwary, and especially our thoughtless youth, are brought to their untimely end'. Parents were urged to prevent their offspring from reading books that would inflame their minds with lewd ideas, as young people, 'from a vain affection of their own importance', spent too much time 'associating indiscriminately with profane and immoral persons, especially such as multitudes of the public houses in this extensive metropolis abound with, where their natural propensity to vice occasions them to be unthinkingly carried down its lethiserous stream, until ruin overtakes them'.

Elsewhere in Britain, meanwhile, the lethiserous and deadly stream had been flowing strongly and amongst those plunging cheerfully on horseback into it were the highwaymen of legend, with no shortage of writers anxious to record their deeds.

2

A Highwayman Came Riding

The Arrival of Celebrity Criminals

While the Ordinary was carrying out his painstaking work, a different style of crime reporting was establishing itself. The nation was witnessing the creation of the 'celebrity criminal', a genre that would last to this day, and it encompassed both the burgeoning 'broadsides' – the newspapers of their day, printed initially on one side only – and the work of some of the finest writers of the period. This glamorisation came about both as a result of contemporary reports and of romanticised, semi-fictionalised accounts produced subsequently by authors. During the early part of the eighteenth century, three of Britain's most famous – or notorious – criminals were operating: the thief and master-escaper, Jack Sheppard, who was executed in 1724; his nemesis, the thief-taker Jonathan Wild, who died on the scaffold the following year; and, perhaps the best-known of the three today, Dick Turpin, who met his end in 1739.

Perhaps it is no coincidence that their rise to notoriety coincided with the careers of three of Britain's greatest writers: Daniel Defoe, John Gay and Henry Fielding, author of *Tom Jones*. Defoe put the growing criminality and its press coverage in context when he wrote about the crime wave that followed the 'South Sea Bubble' in 1720. This was the catastrophic investment scandal involving the South Sea Company, which had rights to trade with South American countries – hence the name – and corrupt politicians. It led to ruin for the huge numbers who had unwisely invested.

The American writer Aaron Skirball credits Defoe as the 'wily old newspaperman' whose coverage of Wild and Sheppard 'enthralled a kingdom and birthed a genre'. He concluded that Defoe gave us the celebrity criminal, who has since been seen so often in literature and on film in the shape of highwaymen, wild west outlaws, train robbers and Mafia bosses. The broadsides played their part in this, writing of daring robbers, escapers and highwaymen much in the same way as a twentieth-century press would later do of Soho and East End gangsters, great train robbers and jewellery thieves, with that intoxicating cocktail of disapproval, fascination and exaggeration.

'On a sudden we found street robberies became the common practice,' wrote Defoe, who spent time in prison himself for publishing a religious tract, 'conversation was full of the variety of them, the newspapers had them every day, and sometimes more than ever were committed; and those that were committed were set off by the invention of the writers.'

One of the writers accused of invention was 'Captain' Alexander Smith, who had started a trend that was to continue for the next three hundred years, of detailing both exploits and the early lives of criminals. Smith, who may have awarded himself the 'captain' title, was a prolific recorder of the seamy side of life. His 1714 publication was called 'The History of the Lives of the most noted Highwayman, Footpads, Housebreakers, Shoplifts and Cheats of both sexes, in and about London, and in other places in Great Britain for above forty years past'.

Smith promised readers 'most secret and barbarous Murders, unparallel'd Robberies, notorious Thefts, and unheard of Cheats'. His official rationale was that, by reading in detail the shocking lives and fatal ends of criminals, people would be deterred from crime. He made big claims for his work, saying his accounts were not taken from the Ordinaries but were the 'first impartial Piece of this Nature which ever appeared in Europe.' He apologised to readers for some of the oaths and curses he recorded but explained that he was only doing so to paint the criminals 'in their proper colours, whose words are always so odious, detestable and foul that some, as little acquainted with a God as they would be apt to conclude that Nature spoiled 'em in the Making by setting their mouths in the wrong end of their bodies.' He stressed that he was not exposing these 'offending wretches with any design of making them sport and ridicule of vain idle fellows who only laugh at the misfortunes of such dying men but rather revive their manifold transgressions for a means to instruct and convert the wicked and prophane persons of this licentious age'.

His accounts are entertaining. Writing of the Cambridgeshire high-wayman Ned Bonnet, who was executed in 1713, he reported how he had robbed rich young gentlemen students whom he found in a brothel and, because they gave him some trouble before handing over their money, made them strip naked, tied them to their horse, and sent them into Cambridge for the entertainment of the crowd who were 'hallooing and hooting' after them. Smith used his reports to bring moral messages to his readers. In his account of the murderer and highwayman, William Holloway, from Staffordshire, who blamed alcohol for his crime in 1712, saying that he had been 'in drink' and unaware of what he was doing, Smith concluded: 'thus we may evidently see the fatal consequences of drunkenness which odious vice is now become so fashionable'. Taverns and alehouses were 'academies of sin'.

The reports tell us about both the modus operandi of criminals and the class system of the time. Smith's writing on women criminals also demonstrates the different standards by which female offenders were judged in the press. Mary or Moll Raby, who operated under a number of aliases – much easier in those pre-photo, pre-fingerprint days – was convicted of robbing Lady Cavendish in Soho Square in 1703 and Smith adds that she had given herself up to 'whoredom and adultery' and, before she was hanged, admitted other wickednesses including 'Sabbath-breaking and swearing, drinking, lewdness, disposing of stolen goods and harbour-ing of ill people'. Smith reported that on one occasion she sneaked into a house in Downing Street and hid under a bed while the residents and their dog dined in the same room and she became so nervous that she 'discharged herself . . . which made such a great stink that it offended the people who supposing it to be the dog turned him out' and left the room, allowing Raby to steal the bed linen. On another occasion, Raby supposedly stole a pearl necklace off the sleeping landlady of a Wapping inn and swallowed the pearls. When the landlady woke and accused Raby of the crime, she allowed herself to be stripped naked in a private room to prove her innocence.

Anne Holland, a pickpocket who had five aliases, was described by Smith as being 'very clean-skinned, well-shaped, having a sharp piercing eye' but this only meant that she attracted many a man 'under Cupid's banner' which led to her inevitable decline: 'if once a woman passes the bounds of modesty she seldom stops till she hath arrived at the very height of impudence'. Her courage on the scaffold in 1705 – cursing the judge for his 'hard heart' – did not impress Smith, who was sure that her soul would be delivered into 'less merciful hands' than if she had repented.

The first of the trio of 'celebrity villains' of the period, Jack Sheppard, was a wily thief and master-escaper and it was his skill in the latter capacity that captured the public's imagination. The sneaking admiration in the press for the escaper has lasted to the present day as the great train robber, Ronnie Biggs, demonstrated when he went over the wall at Wandsworth prison in 1965 and remained a folk-hero for many thereafter. Sheppard's reputation was confirmed by the 'History of the Remarkable Life of Jack Sheppard and the Life of Jonathan Wild Thief-taker General of Great Britain and Ireland', which is often attributed to Defoe, and was supposedly published as 'a warning to young men'. We learn of one of Sheppard's four spectacular escapes in 1724 that 'it has been allow'd by all the Jayl-Keepers in London, that one so Miraculous was never perform'd before in England'. But the writer noted drily that Sheppard 'returns like a Dog to his Vomit' and is soon caught again and executed that same year, much to the fury and dismay of the public who crowded onto the streets as he was taken to the gallows.

Sheppard's celebrity was such that the printer and publisher John Applebee, whose *Weekly Journal* specialised in crime tales, paid him a retainer of eight pence a day as he awaited his end, in order to secure his exclusive story. The *Journal* portrayed him as a dashing character in 'a handsome suit of Black, with a Diamond Ring and a Cornelian ring on his finger'. Henry Mayhew later noted, in *London Labour and the London Poor*, that, 'Of all books, perhaps none has ever had so baneful effect upon the young mind, taste, and principles' as the one on Sheppard; he suggested that young Londoners were more familiar with it than the Bible.

Jonathan Wild, who gloried in the title of 'Thief-taker General', played on both sides of the law although his nickname – still used in the twentieth century by some senior police officers anxious to be portrayed as tough on crime – refers to his function of arresting miscreants in the pre-police era. He operated in London as a successful gangster and, by the 1720s, had a profitable criminal empire. The expanding press had fuelled a fear of crime and Wild took advantage of this and the absence of any organised police force; the Bow Street Runners did not arrive until 1749 and a proper Metropolitan police force until 1829. Wild used the newspapers to his own ends, placing advertisements in them which advised anyone who had been robbed to come to his Lost Property Office which was handily placed in the Old Bailey. There he would agree a fee for finding the stolen goods and the victims would return a few days later to pay the money and get their property back.

Gerald Howson, in his biography *Thief-taker General: The Rise and Fall of Jonathan Wild*, calculated that between 1714 and 1724 Wild was responsible for the punishment by hanging, transportation, branding or imprisonment of up to 150 people. He was brutal even to those close to him, as the *Tyburn Chronicle* reported of Mary Milliner or Molyneaux, a prostitute who became Wild's wife: 'she had some time so provoked him to wrath that he swore he would mark her for a bitch, and thereupon drawing his sword, he cut off one of her ears – this occasioned a divorce'. Because of his reputation as a dodgy double-dealer his demise was widely celebrated by the poor. Here is how the *London Journal* reported it: 'so outrageous were the mob in their joy to behold him on the road to the gallows, who had been the cause of sending so many thither; that they huzza'd him along to the Triple Tree.'

Dick Turpin made up this triumvirate of villainy. Central to the myth surrounding him was the idea that he would always be one step ahead of the law, and the press played a major part in this. *Reid's Weekly Journal*, in May 1737, reported: 'the people about Epping Forest say he will never be taken till a proclamation offering a reward for apprehending of him and give the reason, that as he has declared he will never be taken alive but he will kill, or be killed, and it will be dangerous to attempt it'. His robbery of a farmer called Joseph Lawrence in 1735, carried out with others, was particularly brutal, with the elderly victim having his trousers pulled round his ankles and his bare buttocks held over the fire to force him to say where his money was. James Sharpe in *Dick Turpin: The Myth of the English Highwayman*, notes how Turpin became a romantic character when he was in reality a thug.

In July 1737 the political periodical *Common Sense* had already objected to the way Turpin was being portrayed. How could it happen, the publication asked, that a 'fellow, who is known to be a thief by the whole kingdom shall for a long time rob us, and not only so, but to make jest of us, shall defy the laws and laugh at justice'? This was to set a theme for the coverage of professional criminals – as opposed to murderers – over the next three centuries: horrified fascination at the skill and daring followed by stern disapproval that they were even being written about.

When Turpin was finally arrested, the *General Evening Post* of 8 March 1739 described how 'a great concourse of people flock to see him, and they all give him money. He seems very sure that nobody is alive that can hurt him, and told the gentleman that used to hunt with him, that he hoped to have another day's sport with him yet . . . He is put every night into the condemned hold, which is a very strong place.' The reports of the time pointed out that even then the criminals were complaining that the press had got them wrong. 'Turpin confessed himself to be really the man so infamous for his robberies in the south part of England, tho' he denied many facts father'd on him in the public prints.'

After Turpin's execution in 1739, highwaymen featured less prominently in the press, with only four showing up in *The Newgate Calendar* compendium from 1750–61, being outnumbered by notorious murderers or, a new breed, forgers. What is remarkable is how Turpin was later mythologised, due in no small part to an embroidered and imagined account of his life by the prolific nineteenth-century writer, William Harrison Ainsworth, who created this fantasy highwayman: 'rash daring was the main feature of Turpin's character. Like our great Nelson he knew fear only by name.' The appetite for tales of derring-do remained unabated. As Kevin Williams noted in *Moral Panics, Social Fears and the Media*, readers of the triweekly *Whitehall Evening Post* were treated to a regular fare of 'footpads stealing watches, wigs and purses from passers-by; of highwaymen haunting the heaths and roads of London . . . of gangs creating sham disturbances in order to commit hit-and-run robberies.' This led to the baleful conclusion in the paper, voiced in 1749 and echoed over the decades, that 'there is no Possibility of stirring from our Habitations after dark without Hazard of a fractured Skull.'

3
Killing Times

How Murder and the Noose Made the Front Pages

I n 1779, Martha Ray, the mistress of the Earl of Sandwich, was shot dead on the steps of Covent Garden theatre by a besotted young clergyman called James Hackman, who then tried to kill himself. For the press of the day, it was a murder to die for: a spectacular public setting, a beautiful victim, a fallen clergyman, an adulterous member of the aristocracy and illicit sex. While the reading public had until then been fascinated by the adventures of highwaymen, robbers and escapers, for the next few centuries it would be the coverage of murders, trials and executions that provided crime reporters with the richest of tapestries.

Hackman, besotted with Ray, who apparently did not return his affection, had written a suicide note and put it in his pocket before he set out on his mission with two pistols. He was convicted within days at the Old Bailey and executed shortly afterwards. However, then as now, the public setting, the love triangle, the involvement of such a rakish member of the aristocracy as Sandwich, guaranteed that all the newspapers, which were just starting to flex their editorial muscles, would be ravenous for copy on the case. Ray was something more than just a mistress; she had borne Sandwich nine children, five of whom survived, and she would seem to have won the unrequited love of Hackman, whose suicide note to his brother-in-law reckoned that 'the world will condemn me, but your good heart will pity me.'

Many of the news reports of the time did indeed pity Hackman, an early demonstration of the crime story as human drama. Even James

Boswell, the biographer of Dr Johnson, entered the fray as a crime reporter, offering his account of the affair to the *Daily Advertiser* and penning a piece later for the *St James Chronicle* in which he wrote of Hackman: 'he loved Miss Ray with all his soul, and nothing could make him happy but having her all his own'.

The press accounts were remarkably frank, even by today's standards. *The Gazeteer*, decided that 'love could not be the impulse,' and passed on the rumour that 'Miss Ray was satiated with the vicious enjoyment of splendour and desirous to enter the Temple of Hymen with a man who had given every proof of affection; but that there was some barrier to prevent the union, and she absolutely refused to marry him, though in the hour of reciprocal tenderness she had promised.' The *St James Chronicle* concluded that the murder 'was occasioned by an unhappy Passion which the Prisoner had entertained for the Deceased'.

Murders were not uncommon but their coverage depended then, as now, on their newsworthiness. As John Brewer writes in *Sentimental Murder: Love and Madness in the Eighteenth Century*, his fascinating study of the case, 'a similar crime of passion committed by a drunken labourer who killed an impoverished girlfriend – the London courts handled many such cases – would have merited only a line or two, if that, in the London newspapers.'

Although the Martha Ray case set a template for murder coverage to come, it was far from being the first such report. A century earlier, in 1624, a newsbook alerted readers to 'The crying Murther: Contayning the cruell and most horrible Butcher of Mr Trat'. The newsbook, small in shape and up to 28 pages long, would normally cover just one subject such as a particularly gory murder while the broadsides were more like our idea of a newspaper, complete with sensational headline. Poor Trat, the curate of a Somerset church, had been attacked on the highway by three men and a woman, who killed him, cut him up and then boiled his limbs to disguise their crime. Readers were spared no detail: 'these butchers, with their hands already smoking in blood, did cut up his carcass, unbowel and quarter it; then did they burn his head and privy members, parboil his flesh and salt it up'. Three and a half centuries later, in 1983, readers of the daily press would learn how a former soldier called Dennis Nilsen had par-boiled the heads of many of his dozen or so victims in a pot on his stove in his north London home. Regardless of the century, gruesome killings have always made news.

Mitchell Stephens, in his *History of News*, suggests that from as early as 1575 the most interesting murders made it into print in England: 'The journalists who were feeding the early printing presses learned what all journalists have learned: that crime news is prime news.' He cites the killing in 1613 of Sir Thomas Overbury, a court adviser, who was poisoned in his Tower of London cell after angering the Countess of Essex over her plans to dump her husband and marry her lover. Four people were executed for the murder although the Countess's life was spared by James I. Historian Matthias Shaaber located fifteen separate accounts of the murder and executions. As Stephens concluded: 'no crime in England before the development of the newspaper appears to have received more attention from the printing press'. The enterprising father-and-son printers, John and James Catnach, who were based in Seven Dials in London, capitalised on this public fascination with crime by publishing many confessions and tales in the early part of the nineteenth century.

Judith Flanders, in *The Invention of Murder*, her terrific examination of the British fascination with violent death, quotes Thomas De Quincey as to why readers were so attracted to such tales and notes that 'it is like hearing blustery rain on the windowpane when sitting indoors'. She credits one John Thurtell, a bungling murderer who bludgeoned to death William Weare, a well-known gambler, in Hertfordshire in 1823, with being the subject of the first 'trial by newspaper', thus inadvertently founding newspaper fortunes, such was the appetite for reports of his case. The Thurtell case certainly exercised the daily press in a way that would have their editors hauled in front of the judge today for contempt of court, *The Times* leading the charge with completely unsubstantiated tales. After Thurtell's conviction, *The Observer* announced a special execution edition at twice the paper's normal size – and twice the price.

Obviously some murders were more newsworthy than others. But when a Suffolk molecatcher, Thomas Marten, discovered the rotting remains of his daughter hidden under hay in his barn in the summer of 1828, he was unwittingly a part of the genesis of a new style of crime reporting. The murder of twenty-four-year-old Maria Marten led to a famous trial and execution and it introduced us to the work of James Curtis of *The Times*, seen by some as a key figure in the history of crime reporting.

The Red Barn murder, as it became known, captured the public imagination. Maria Marten had three illegitimate children by three different men, the last of them by William Corder, the member of a wealthy local farming family. She had then supposedly gone to London with Corder and, Thomas Marten told the inquest into her death, held in the Polstead village pub, that Corder had assured Marten that he had wed his daughter and that she was safe and well in London. Suspicion immediately focussed on him. There were local reporters on hand for the inquest and their appetite was whetted. They were soon joined by James Curtis, who made his way by foot from London to the village, a distance of more than 50 miles. No claiming fanciful expenses on taxis in those days.

When Corder appeared in the courthouse of Bury St Edmunds charged with the murder, the reporters had to fight their way through the crowds outside to the press benches. Such was the interest in the case that people erected ladders outside so that they could see inside the court and guards had to be stationed at the Red Barn to stop souvenir-hunters. Into this frenzied scene came Curtis to take the story of a sad, local, 'domestic' murder and bring it to a national audience in a style to be much copied over the years.

Paul Collins, the American writer and academic, in an article for *The Believer* magazine, argues that Curtis could claim to be 'quite possibly the most knowledgeable crime reporter that had ever lived'. One reason for his success, Collins suggests, is that he was an insomniac, not sleeping more than three or four hours a night. He also had enviably swift short-hand skills; he even wrote a primer called Shorthand Made Shorter. He had the reputation of having covered every major Old Bailey trial and every execution during his career. When he arrived in Polstead, he not only interviewed all of Corder's acquaintances but the man himself and even sat beside him at his trial. Out of this came his book, *An Authentic and Faithful History of the Mysterious Murder of Maria Marten*, which has been likened to Truman Capote's *In Cold Blood* for its detail and descriptive passages.

He described the victim as having 'a handsome face, a fine form and figure, and, moreover, a superior address, accompanied with a modest demeanour – for innocence and purity then lodged in her breast – with such advantages and attractions, it cannot excite much surprise that she should have been beset by admirers' and he followed the case through to its end, reporting the execution at Bury. The case won a wide readership outside of *The Times* with more than a million copies of Corder's 'last dying speech and confession' being sold.

Another figure seen as advancing crime reporting in the period was James Fitzjames Stephen, a jurist and later a judge who wrote for a variety of publications, most notably the *Saturday Review* and the *Pall Mall Gazette*. 'If my body ever had a call to anything by the voices of nature,' he wrote, 'I have a call to journalism.' He often covered murders, pointing out in his book, *The Criminal Law of England*, what he saw as the difference between horrific killings and an occasion when 'a man in a fair duel shoots another for seducing his sister'. Young lawyers, writing anonymously, often doubled up as reporters in this period, as Judith Rowbotham, Kim Stevenson and Samantha Pegg point out in their book *Crime News in Modern Britain*: 'lawyers, judges and journalists mixed and met in the social milieu of the London clubs'.

And if Curtis and Stephen had their admirers as crime reporters, they would never be quite able to compete with another contemporary who was equally fascinated by the subject.

4
A Twist in the Tale

Charles Dickens, Crime Writer

He was a 'roystering and swaggering young gentleman' and one of the most cunning pickpockets in London before he fell foul of the law and was transported for stealing a silver snuff box. This was Jack Dawkins, better known as the Artful Dodger in *Oliver Twist*. But while Dawkins was a fictional character, his creator, Charles Dickens, who had worked as a court reporter and had learned shorthand, was more than familiar with the reality of crime in London and would play a crucial role in how it is reported to this day.

His good friend George Augustus Sala said that what most tickled Dickens's fancy was the latest play, 'the latest exciting trial or police case . . . and especially the latest murder'. And he became a good friend of William Harrison Ainsworth, who made his fortune by writing about Dick Turpin and Jack Sheppard. As a journalist, Dickens edited *Bentley's Miscellany*, a general-interest monthly and, briefly, the *Daily News*.

He often wrote of his visits to London prisons and, whenever he was travelling, always sought to visit the local jails whether in the United States, Scotland, France, Italy or Switzerland. He witnessed at least three and probably more public executions, and attended many trials. In 1845, he attended a beheading in Rome – 'ugly, filthy, careless, sickening' – where the severed head ended up on a pole. In his book *Dickens and Crime*, Philip Collins traces his subject's fascination with criminals and police: 'he always had a journalistic flair for seeing and interviewing, instead of reading, speculating or cogitating'. He was, in today's terms, an old-school reporter rather than a commentator, basing his observations on direct experience whether of the jails, the courts or the gallows.

He described the boy prisoners he met on one visit and their 'terrible little faces . . . not a glance of honesty – not a wink expressive of anything but the gallows and the hulks, in the whole collection. As to anything like shame and contrition that was entirely out of the question.' Dickens noted that the naughty boys were quite gratified at being the subject of curiosity and saw themselves as an essential part of the Newgate show. 'We never looked upon a more disagreeable sight,' he concluded. He pursues this theme in his 1868 essay 'The Ruffian', where he asks: 'why is a notorious Thief and Ruffian ever left at large? . . . I demand to have the Ruffian employed, perforce, in hewing wood and drawing water somewhere for the general service, instead of hewing at her Majesty's subjects, and drawing their watches out of their pockets.' The cost for keeping someone in Pentonville in 1848 was £36 a year, which irritated Dickens when a farm worker had to get by on 12 shillings a week.

But Dickens did not see savage punishment as the solution. Here he is in 1851, in his magazine *Household Words*, commenting on two child offenders whose heads barely reached the top of the dock who were sentenced to a whipping for stealing a loaf of bread: 'Woe! can the state devise no better sentence for its children? Will it never sentence them to be taught?'

He did not limit his reporting to the British penal system and was an interested visitor to foreign jails. In 1842, as Anthony Babington records in *The English Bastille*, he was shocked by what he found on a visit to a penitentiary near Philadelphia, where he discovered that every prisoner had a black hood drawn over his head on admission and was kept in a cell which he never left until his sentence was completed: 'I looked at some of them with the same awe as I should have looked at men who had been buried alive and dug up again.'

While seeking inspiration for the part of the magistrate in *Oliver Twist*, he gained access to the police court at Hatton Garden, where sat a notoriously harsh and bad-tempered magistrate called Allen Stewart Laing on whom the novel's Mr Fang would be based. It was a satirical paper, *Figaro in London* (much like today's *Private Eye*), that ran the most sustained campaign against Laing and his tough and unfair sentences, leading to his removal from office. Dickens noted the importance of the court reporters because 'enough fantastic tricks are daily played [in the courts] to make the angels blind with weeping; they are closed to the public save through the medium of the daily press'.

A common theme for Dickens and his contemporaries was criticism of the vast disparity of punishment between courts, much as today. Dickens was fascinated by and friendly with the police, notably detectives, with whose arrival in British fiction he is often credited. The Metropolitan Police and Dickens started out together – the police force being set up in 1829 by Sir Robert Peel, at which point Dickens was a brand-new crime reporter of seventeen. It is interesting, in the twenty-first century, at a time when police are discouraged from dealing with crime reporters, to recall the seventh of Peel's nine principles of policing: 'To maintain at all times a relationship with the public that gives reality to the historic tradition that the police are the public and that the public are the police.' In other words, the police should not regard themselves as separate from the rest of the population.

Writing in *Household Words* on the subject of the recently formed Detective Police, Dickens is dismissive of their predecessors, the Bow Street Runners, whose reputation, he suggests, was partly due to unprincipled crime reporters: 'continually puffed besides by incompetent magistrates anxious to conceal their own deficiencies, and hand-in-glove with the penny-a-liners of that time'. The Runners had been formed in the 1740s by another writer, Henry Fielding, author of *Tom Jones*, who was also a London magistrate, and his brother, John, but came to be regarded with suspicion and were disbanded in 1839; the 'penny-a-liners' were the hacks of the day.

Dickens was often expansive in his admiration of the police, who responded by allowing him unprecedented access. He must have been one of the earliest reporters to have been, as it were, embedded with them, travelling into criminal redoubts and spending a night at Bow Street police station. Such practices are now common throughout the world as the police have realised that allowing someone to see how they work often leads to sympathy and understanding; the danger, as with war reporters embedded with regiments, is that the journalists 'go native' and, flattered to be trusted, inevitably side with the people who are looking after them and might be tempted to ignore their flaws.

Dickens found the detective force to be well trained and systematic and 'is always so calmly and steadily engaged in the service of the public that the public really do not know enough of it to know a tithe of its usefulness'. He invited the entire detective force to parties at *Household Words* and was fulsome in his praise of their character, as they were men of 'unusual intelligence . . . generally presenting in their faces, traces more or less marked of habitually leading lives of strong mental excitement'.

The execution of the valet François Courvoisier in 1840 for cutting the throat of his employer, Lord William Russell, was watched by around 40,000 people. Dickens was among them, having hired a room to ensure a decent view. The preceding trial, according to the broadsides of the time, was a popular one with 'the court besieged at an early hour by numbers of ladies and gentlemen fortunate enough to obtain tickets from the undersheriffs'. The Duke of Sussex secured himself a seat and the author William Makepeace Thackeray was amongst other spectators at the hanging, declaring himself afterwards to feel ashamed and degraded by the experience. Writing later in *Fraser's Magazine* in 1842, Thackeray concluded that, 'I have been abetting an act of frightful wickedness and violence performed by a set of men against one of their fellows.'

Much later Dickens recorded in a letter to the *Daily News* that at the hanging he had seen 'no sorrow, no salutary terror, no abhorrence, no seriousness; nothing but ribaldry, debauchery, levity, drunkenness and flaunting vice in fifty other shapes. I should have deemed it impossible that I could have ever felt any large assemblage of my fellow-creatures to be so odious.'

It was an issue he returned to in other reports of executions, most notably perhaps that of Frederick and Marie Manning, the husband and wife hanged in 1849 for murdering the wife's lover. Again he shared his thoughts with the *Daily News*: 'I hold that no human being, not being the better for such a sight, could go away without being the worse for it.' Marie Manning, a Belgian, was fearless and rude during her trial, accusing England of being 'base and degraded' and devoid of a decent legal system. It is often suggested that she became the model for Hortense, the wild Frenchwoman in *Bleak House*, played so memorably by Lilo Baur in the BBC television adaptation in 2005.

Bleak House also contains Inspector Bucket, widely believed to have been based on Inspector Charles Field with whom Dickens embedded himself, as he recorded in 'On Duty with Inspector Field' in 1851. The Inspector also featured prominently and admiringly in *The Times* of this period and was a regular dinner guest of Dickens. 'Saint Giles's clock strikes nine. We are punctual,' wrote Dickens. 'Where is Inspector Field? . . . Inspector Field is, tonight, the guardian genius of the British Museum. He is bringing his shrewd eye to bear on every corner of its solitary galleries, before he reports "all right".'

The death penalty continued to trouble his thoughts and he quoted with approval Edward Gibbon Wakefield, the author of *Facts Relating to the Punishment of Death in the Metropolis*: 'Whoever will undergo the pain, of witnessing the public destruction of a fellow-creature's life, in London, must be perfectly satisfied that in the great mass of spectators, the effect of the punishment is to excite sympathy for the criminal and hatred of the law.' He noted that out of 167 convicts under sentence of death, only three had not been spectators of executions. *The Times* viewed Dickens's objections to public executions unfavourably. In a leader on 14 November 1849 they stated that 'it appears to us a matter of necessity that so tremendous an act as a national homicide should be publicly as well as solemnly done.'

In fact, Dickens lived to see the abolition of public hanging in Britain, with the last execution in 1868 of Michael Barrett, who had been convicted of being part of a Fenian plot to blow up Clerkenwell jail and help his comrades escape. Local residents let rooms for spectators and realised that this was their last chance for a bonanza and increased the prices accordingly:

£10 for a small room on the second floor. The *Telegraph* reported one shop-keeper resisting all offers – 'I haven't fallen so low as to let my windows to see a fellow-creature hanged' – and then pondered in an editorial: 'A generation hence it will be well-nigh incredible to our children, that, in the midst of the reign of good Queen Victoria men and women should have been publicly strangled in a narrow lane connecting two of the most populous thoroughfares in the British metropolis.' Although public hanging ended, journalists were able to attend executions. When the murderer Charles Peace was hanged in 1892, four reporters were present to take notes of his last words: 'I know that my life has been base and bad.'

As Dickens and Thackeray were agonising over public hangings, a newspaper was being launched which capitalised on the public's fascination with crime and punishment. The first edition of the *News of the World* was published in 1843 and featured murder, kidnapping, rape, embezzlement, fraud, theft, abortion and arson. 'Extraordinary occurrence – much sensation was created in Lambeth' was the headline over the tale of a 'very handsome' servant girl raped and dumped, alive, in the Thames; 'Diabolical attempt at Incendiarism' was how the arson of a flour mill was reported.

Over the next 160 years the paper would provide its readers with details of every crime imaginable and its rivals with a template of what Britain rather fancied for its Sunday breakfast. The popular press, aided by the lowering, in 1836, and the eventual abolition, in 1855, of stamp duty on newspapers, was on its way, replacing the broadsides, chapbooks and newsbooks of the previous centuries.

Dickens, meanwhile, with his creation of the 'Artful Dodger', gave every reporter of the future a handy phrase to encapsulate that dangerously seductive mixture of bravado and shamelessness that would personify the high-profile career criminal. And for all his concerns about both crime and punishment, Dickens was not to have such a profound effect on the law as another author and newspaper man who was soon to take centre stage and paint an even more disturbing – and non-fictional – picture of the nation's underworld.

5
From the Maiden to the Ripper

How Muckraker-general
Changed Crime Reporting For Ever

'All those who are squeamish, and all those who are prudish,' were warned not to read the series of four articles entitled 'The Maiden Tribute of Modern Babylon', which appeared in the *Pall Mall Gazette* in July 1885. They were the work of a driven and fearless man, William Thomas Stead, who is often described, with justification, as the father of investigative journalism in Britain.

The articles were the culmination of months of work by Stead and exposed the vast but hidden trade of under-age prostitution in Britain. To show how easy it was to buy a girl, Stead immersed himself in the world of the brothel, arranged the purchase of a thirteen-year-old and then wrote about it. For this, he was eventually arrested and charged under the Offences Against the Person Act of 'unlawfully taking Eliza Armstrong, aged thirteen, out of the possession and against the will of her father', and, after a colourful Old Bailey trial, he was jailed for three months. A more profound effect of his investigation was that the age of consent was raised from thirteen to sixteen. While Dickens embedded himself with the police and observed, Stead decided to go further and expose.

Stead was much more than a campaigning journalist infuriated by the indifference of his fellow-citizens to the exploitation of young women. He was also an anti-war campaigner who was nominated for the Nobel peace prize, a staunch defender of Oscar Wilde, an imaginative novelist, a champion of the bicycle as a force for redemption and a committed believer in the ability of the dead to correspond with the living.

He had no doubt about the importance of the press and its power to change and, as he saw it, improve society and he espoused the notion of 'government by journalism' and was driven by an almost evangelical zeal to change society for the better. He saw God as his 'Senior Partner' in their joint endeavours and had the loftiest of ambitions in his chosen career: 'God calls . . . and now points . . . to the only true throne in England, the editor's chair and offers me the real sceptre. Am I not God's chosen . . . to be his soldier against wrong?' He suggested that a newspaper had an almost religious duty: 'we have to write afresh from day to day the only Bible which millions read'. Following an early career on the *Northern Echo* in Darlington, he felt impelled to head south after learning that English girls were being sent to Brussels as prostitutes: 'If I have to write it, I shall have to plunge into the depths of social hell and that is impossible outside a great city.'

While he made allies and enemies with the campaigns he undertook – from his opposition to the Boer War to his espousal of international peace conferences – and received mockery and approbation in equal measure, it was the 'Maiden Tribute' series that was to define him and to set a marker for what can be achieved by deeply-researched exposés of crime. The impact of his work is felt to this day.

Stead's journalistic triumph came as a result of being approached by the City Chamberlain, Benjamin Scott, who asked for his assistance with the Criminal Law Amendment Bill, which would raise the age of female consent, as a way of tackling the abuse and prostitution of girls. At his prompting, Stead investigated, was horrified by what he discovered and decided to campaign on the issue, working alongside, amongst others, Bramwell Booth, son of the Salvation Army founder William Booth.

Shocked by the scale of the practice of forced prostitution and the failure of parliament to address it, he embarked on his campaign to wake up the nation. He found the world of the brothel both fascinating and horrifying. 'O, Bramwell, it is killing me – the Devil's work,' he told his friend. 'I have just interviewed a brothel-keeper who has undertaken to procure for my abuse two English girls of thirteen or fourteen, warranted virgins. Price £5 per head.'

Interestingly, Stead was not the first distinguished writer to note the scandal of child prostitution in London. 'In the Haymarket, I noticed mothers bringing their young daughters to do business,' wrote a visitor to the capital some two decades before the *Pall Mall Gazette* investigations. 'Little girls about twelve years old take you by the hand and invite you to follow them.' The year was 1862 and the visiting writer was Fyodor Mikhailovich Dostoevsky, in London a few years before the publication of *Crime and Punishment*.

Stead's research, which involved interviewing brothel-keepers, pro-curers, prostitutes, roués, missionaries, doctors, politicians and welfare workers, took months and led him to houses of disrepute across London and in the country. One of his sources was an experienced detective who told him that buying young virgins was a well-established part of the trade. Stead responded that the very thought of it was 'enough to raise hell'. 'It is true,' responded his policeman friend, 'and although it ought to raise hell, it does not even raise the neighbours.' Another interviewee was an MP, identified as George Cavendish-Bentinck, by the American academic Grace Eckley, in her detailed study *Maiden Tribute: A Life of W. T. Stead*. He supposedly laughed in response to Stead's questions and said : 'I doubt the unwillingness of these virgins. That you can contract for maids at so much a head is true enough. I myself am quite ready to supply you with 100 maids at £25 each, but they will all know very well what they are about.'

The techniques to persuade gullible young women to come to London were many: a hint of an offer of marriage from a brothel-keeper dressed as a parson, the promise of work as a lady's maid, a chance to see the sights of the big city. Some of the girls whom Stead interviewed had been given laudanum or 'black draught' to put them to sleep. Many of the accounts of how vulnerable girls were approached and entrapped have echoes in the twenty-first century in the grooming and abuse of girls of a similar age in scandals exposed in Rotherham, Rochdale, Derby and Oxford, many of them being plied with drink and drugs to break down their resistance.

It finally led to the lengthy series of articles which ran over four days. It is worth studying in some detail, not just for the revelations of the mighty hypocrisy of Victorian Britain, but also for the florid prose and evangelical tone. The title of 'The Maiden Tribute of Modern Babylon' – whether it meant any more to Stead's nineteenth-century readers than it does today is a moot point – came from the Greek myth that Athens, after a disastrous campaign against Crete, was obliged every nine years to send to Crete seven youths and seven maidens who were thrown into the Labyrinth of Daedalus, where they would be devoured by the half-man, half-bull Minotaur, who was, as Stead informed his readers, 'the foul product of an unnatural lust'.

The articles were punctuated with dramatic headlines, some of which were used on the placards that advertised the special editions of the paper and which understandably caused something of a sensation on the streets of London, not to mention record sales for the paper. One such was 'The Violation of Virgins', which, Stead explained, was a subject 'upon which even the coolest and most scientific observer may well find it difficult to speak dispassionately in a spirit of calm and philosophic investigation'. He made clear that he had an aim in mind. London exhibited 'all the vices of Gomorrah, daring the vengeance of long-suffering Heaven . . . But the sojourn in this hell has not been fruitless . . . My purpose was not to secure the punishment of criminals but to lay bare the working of a great organisation of crime.'

On the second day of the series, Stead continued with an explanation of how the trade functioned: 'people imagine that the brothel fills itself. That is a mistake. It is recruited for as diligently as is the army of Her Majesty, which is perhaps one of its greatest patrons.' He quoted one brothel-keeper as saying business was bad and telling Stead: 'I have been very slack since the Guards went to Egypt.' He found one procuress who was well versed in the law and age of consent and kept up to date on the matter by studying the court cases in the *Weekly Dispatch* and *Lloyd's*, which she spent the best part of her Sunday reading. Stead even tried some dark humour to make his point, comparing the protection of the grouse which could not be shot before 12 August and rules about fishing with the lack of protection for a thirteen-year-old girl who could legally be seduced for 'a bag of sweets, a fine feather, a good dinner, or a treat to the theatre . . . sufficient to induce her to part with that which may be lost in an hour, but can never be recovered'. He concluded that 'the law ought at least to be as strict about a live child as about a dead salmon'.

As the series progressed, Stead revealed that one of the most ingenious methods of entrapping girls was for a procuress to impersonate a Sister of Mercy. Such 'sisters', dressed in full habit, would meet young Irish Catholic girls arriving at Euston station and tell them that the Lady Superior had sent her to take them to safe lodgings. She would then whisk them through the streets of London to the brothel where they were shown their bedroom and abandoned to their fate. Stead alerted readers to the fact that many of the prostitutes' clients were from the highest echelons of society including the owner of a well-known store who treated his staff 'in much the same aspect as the Sultan of Turkey regards the inmates of his seraglio, the master of the establishment selecting for himself the prettiest girls in the shop'.

In the final episode, Stead explained that he had been 'a night prowler' for weeks. He had gone, he wrote, in different guises to places like St James's Park, the Serpentine, Leicester Square and the Strand, Mile End Road and the area round the Tower of London. He concluded that 'if there is one truth in the Bible that is truer than another it is this, that the publicans and harlots are nearer the kingdom of heaven than the scribes and pharisees who are always trying to qualify for a passport to bliss hereafter by driving their unfortunate sisters here to the very real hell of a police despotism.' What was interesting about his coverage was this criticism of the police, whom he accused of taking advantage of their position to fill their own pockets.

At the heart of the series was his successful attempt to purchase thirteen-year-old Eliza Armstrong to prove how easy it was to do so. The girl was spirited away to France and a safe house there through the offices of the Salvation Army before being returned to England. It was this act that led to his arrest.

The articles caused a sensation and, perhaps for the first time, established the journalist in the role of campaigning and inspirational hero. But, as W. Sydney Robinson's biography, *Muckraker*, explains, not everyone agreed that Stead was justified in his actions. While the *Methodist Times* argued that it was what 'Christ Himself would have done' and Queen Victoria supposedly 'sympathised very keenly', *The Times* dismissed Stead as a 'self-elected guardian of morals'. Cartoonists mocked him as 'the man with the muck-rake' and as suffering from a 'swollen head' to rhyme with Stead.

In August, Stead capitalised on the interest generated by the articles by holding a conference on the Protection of Girls of which his own paper reported that he received 'a most enthusiastic reception, the meeting rising and waving handkerchiefs and cheering loudly'. The paper noted the many cheers and cries of 'shame' and said of Stead that 'he desired women to expect men to be as moral as themselves; next that men should think of themselves as moral as women; and, third, that the seducer of the innocent girl should be regarded as worse than a murderer.' A Hyde Park demonstration followed, attended by, according to Eckley, an estimated 100,000 to 150,000 people anxious to support his 'social purity' campaign. In the same month, parliament finally voted to raise the age of consent. Stead's mission was accomplished.

But now the law swung into action against him and he was charged under the Offences Against the Person Act of 1861 with four associates, including the procuress and Stead's friend, Booth. It was the establishment's revenge. The trial started on 23 October 1885 and Stead honourably protected his sources on the grounds that he had promised them secrecy and acknowledged that he had been, '[D]rinking champagne with the mistress of that brothel, and telling her lies about what I wanted, as I had to, otherwise I would have been summarily ejected; I felt, after getting her confidence in that way, I could not go and expose her personally.'

After three hours of deliberation, the jury returned with a guilty verdict. Stead was jailed for three months, a penalty he wore as a badge of honour throughout his life, even arriving at his office on the anniversary of his imprisonment every year, proudly wearing his prison uniform. Here was an early example of a journalist prepared to challenge the police, to protect his sources, despite pressure to reveal them, and to go to jail for a principle. His stance set an important ethical precedent.

From Holloway prison he continued to edit his paper and took pleasure in writing to bishops and cardinals on prison-headed note-paper. He was released on 18 January 1886 and gave an address at Exeter Hall in the Strand that evening to a standing-room-only crowd of five thousand.

No wonder that Stead felt that the future of the newspaper was as a moral guardian. He defended 'sensationalism', of which he had been accused, on the grounds that, '[W]hen people object to sensations they object to the very material of life. Sensationalism is a means to an end . . . For the great public, the journalist must print in great capitals, or his warning is unheard.' This was pioneering stuff and led many newspapers in the years ahead to run deeply researched investigations, although not always with such obvious success.

In stark contrast to the investigative diligence embodied by Stead in exposing child prostitution was the unresearched and speculative coverage by the entire press of what became known as the 'Jack the Ripper' murders in 1888. No murderer has had a greater effect on the way crimes are reported, not least because there is still no certainty as to his identity.

Stead's own coverage of the Ripper murders was a mixture of horror and condemnation. He mocked the Chief Commissioner of the Metropolitan Police, Sir Charles Warren, for not finding the killer and, in a satirical column, mischievously suggested that Warren had asked the killer in future to leave his calling card on the body of his victim. He also saw the murders as an illustration of the vast divisions in society and an example of upper-class indifference to the sufferings of the poor.

In December 1888, Stead ran a front page story by 'one who thinks he knows' on the 'Whitechapel Demon's nationality and why he committed the murders'. This was an entirely speculative piece which suggested that the killer was a French practitioner of black magic whose abominable practices required a 'certain portion of the body of a harlot'. Eventually the *Pall Mall Gazette* concluded that 'Whitechapel is becoming so blasé with murder' that a fresh killing 'hardly caused a ripple of emotion in the East-end murderland'.

The Times meanwhile reported on the first Jack the Ripper killing on 10 August 1888: 'it was one of the most dreadful murders anyone could imagine. The man must have been a perfect savage to inflict such a number of wounds on a defenceless woman in such a way.' Both the national and local press speculated wildly on who the murderer might be. Initially, the murders were the work of the 'Whitechapel Fiend'.

In his magisterial work, *Jack the Ripper and the London Press*, Professor L. Perry Curtis Jnr of Brown University – we are indebted to American academics for much of the historical research on British crime – points out that the press created a male suspect who was swarthy, black-bearded, black-coated and 'foreign looking'. Early suspects included a Jewish butcher or slaughterhouse man, two doctors and a Russian secret agent whose plan was supposedly to undermine and destabilise Scotland Yard. *The Times* reported in July 1889 that the attacks were taking place in an area 'principally occupied by foreign Jews'. Much of the coverage was sensationalist, anti-semitic and inaccurate.

Then, on 27 September 1888 the Central News Agency received a letter addressed to 'Dear Boss' and claiming to be from the killer. It was signed by 'Jack the Ripper'. Some of the suggestions as to Jack's identity were vague – others specific enough to invite a libel action from the wrongly accused. A Jewish bootmaker, John Pizer, was named by *The Star*, prompting the innocent man to demand damages. *The Star*'s editor, Ernest Park, invited Pizer to the newspaper's office and persuaded him to accept £50 in damages and cannily helped him get the same amount from others who had libelled him.

Despite this being the supposedly prudish Victorian era, much of the coverage of the injuries sustained by the victims was considerably more graphic, not to say pornographic, than daily newspapers would publish today. *Reynolds*, a Sunday newspaper, called the death of the first victim, Mary Ann Nichols, 'too horrible to describe or even hint at', although the police surgeon Rees Llewellyn was then quoted as saying that 'she was ripped out just as you see a dead calf at the butcher's'.

Sales of the London press soared and there was a strong strain of judgmental moralising about the victims because of the nature of their profession, something that would be echoed a century later in the coverage of the Yorkshire Ripper murders. The *Evening News* of 1 October 1888, covering the murder of Elizabeth Stride, sent their reporter to the morgue where he saw that the victim's lips were 'thick, the upper one especially so, with that sort of double fold often noted on lascivious women'. She was, he concluded, after a voyeuristic description of the body, 'undoubtedly debauched beyond all respectability'.

It may also have been the first occasion when the press employed the practice of hiring private detectives – as the *News of the World* did in the twenty-first century in the hacking scandal that laid them low – in an effort to beat the police at their own games. The *Evening News* reported that they had hired two private detectives from a firm in the Strand to track down the killer. The paper promised 'the most startling information that has yet been made public . . . and the first real clue'. The detectives found a greengrocer called Matthew Packer who had sold grapes to Stride just before her murder and described her escort as being stout, of medium height and looking like a clerk. Nothing came of it.

What is interesting is how disrespectful the press was at this time to Scotland Yard, constantly berating them for their ineptitude until they finally secured the resignation of Sir Charles Warren. It was probably not until the campaign against Sir Ian Blair in the twenty-first century that a Commissioner was pursued from office in quite the same way. Scotland Yard was blamed for the deaths, both as a result of their failure to police the Whitechapel area properly and for their detectives' incompetence.

Curtis notes the huge volume of coverage which lasted for four or five days after each murder and a further two days after each inquest: 'the sheer quantity of the *Daily Telegraph*'s coverage (72 columns over 24 issues) may help to explain why it boasted the highest circulation (300,000) of any morning paper in London.' The *Sunday People*, only launched a few years earlier in 1881, covered the Ripper case extensively, under the leadership of their savvy editor, William Madge, and thus ensured its commitment to the coverage of crime over the next century and a half.

What was now clear was that there was a fantastic market for detailed reports of crime. What was also clear was that there were the first signs of unease about the newspaper-buying public's fascination with the subject. In 1886, the *Pall Mall Gazette* polled its readers as to what was 'the worst English newspaper'. The prize went to the *Illustrated Police News*, a weekly which specialised in graphically illustrated coverage of crime in all its most gruesome and dastardly forms, sparing the reader no visual details with such tales as 'A father strangles his wife and child and afterwards hangs himself', and 'A girl shoots a man dead at a ball for treading on her foot and declining to apologise'. The *PMG* sent a reporter down to interview the *IPN*'s proprietor, George Purkess, who accepted the award with 'great good temper, not to say complacency', cheerfully admitted it was a sensationalist paper but argued, as would many before and since, that it steered people away from committing crime. The *PMG* told Purkess priggishly that 'the popular impression is that your paper makes for criminality, that many of your patrons are apt to believe that they will have attained to the heights of heroism and glorification when their portrait appears in *Police News*.' Given the way the *PMG* had profited from Stead's sometimes lubricious descriptions of vice, there was more than a whiff of hypocrisy to the award.

The *Illustrated Police News* was indeed a remarkable publication and the antithesis of Stead's investigative ideal. Founded in 1864, it advertised itself as providing news of all the courts and 'the lives and trials of celebrated criminals of all nations who by atrocious deeds have rendered themselves notorious'. In its first year, it covered the trial of a young German tailor, Franz Muller, who was charged with the murder on a train of a banker called Thomas Briggs, who had been found by the railway tracks in east

London, and was taken to a nearby pub where he was declared dead. Muller fled to America, was arrested in New York where he was found to be in possession of a gold chain and hat belonging to Briggs. Sent back for an Old Bailey trial, his public execution was attended by 50,000 people. The *IPN* saw it as 'the greatest criminal trial of modern times'. Significantly, it was the first murder on a train and, in the days when there was no corridor between compartments, the press reports created an inevitable panic for travelling passengers.

The *IPN* had no reporters as such, lifting their stories from other papers and adding their speciality, the graphic illustration. By 1877, it was selling 300,000 copies a week, occasionally reaching double that, as in their reports on Charles Peace, the legendary burglar who was immortalised by the *IPN* in 1879 with a fascinating illustration of his head from a phrenologist's point of view: his brain is shown to contain some thirty little compartments, a wonderfully compelling piece of nonsense that claimed to demonstrate the phrenological theories of the time.

In 1895, the *IPN* featured a grim tale headlined 'Boys Murder their Mother. Revolting Crime at Plaistow.' It was the kind of story which would have been front page news in any century. Two boys, Robert and Nathaniel Coombes, aged thirteen and twelve, were accused of stabbing to death their mother, Emily, after she had smacked one of them for stealing food. They left her body in her bedroom and went to Lord's to watch the Gentlemen v Players match, pawned some property and were playing cards with a neighbour when relatives found them two weeks later. *Lloyd's Weekly Newspaper* – in a censorious article jauntily reprinted in the *IPN* – suggested that the two boys 'have been greedy devourers of sensational literature; indeed that have been found in the house all kinds of penny dreadfuls and blood-curdling narratives'. Robert was found guilty but insane and his brother cleared. By the end of the First World War, the *IPN* had become pretty xenophobic and was blaming an increase in crime on 'the pernicious teaching of the Teuton criminal'.

Challenged by the expansion of the popular press, which had had a new lease of life with the abolition of excise duty on paper in 1861, and their more detailed coverage of crime, the *IPN* finally folded in 1938. Linda Stratmann says in her book, *Cruel Deeds and Dreadful Calamities*, 'love it or deplore it, the *IPN* tapped into a universal need for news of startling events and its legacy is still seen in the news media of today'.

No doubt noting the popularity of *IPN*, the *Daily Mail* was launched in 1896. As Matthew Engel points out in his book *Tickle the Public*, the *Mail* was lucky to launch in the same month as two great murder trials. The first was that of Amelia Dyer, sometimes described as Britain's first serial killer in that she was suspected of killing many of the babies whom she was given to mind. Her victims, as the paper informed its new readers, were 'the most helpless of God's children . . . and nothing in the ghastly record of (past) monsters of crime touches our heart with quite the same thrill of wrathful sorrow'. Dyer was convicted and hanged. The other trial, for a murder in Muswell Hill, north London, culminated in a spectacular brawl in the dock when one defendant – 'eyes flashing like a wild beast . . . his brawny throat exposed' – attacked another and had to be pulled off him by six constables.

Meanwhile, from his editor's chair, William Thomas Stead watched the expansion of the mass media and the continued interest in crime. He continued to take a high moral stance, not least in support of Oscar Wilde, who had been jailed for two years for gross indecency in 1885 and whom Stead met in Paris in 1900. Stead 'greeted him as an old friend. We had a few minutes' talk and then parted, to meet no more, on this planet at least.' He noted that 'if Oscar Wilde . . . had ruined the lives of half a dozen innocent simpletons of girls, or had broken up the home of his friend by corrupting his friend's wife, no one would have laid a finger upon him.'

Stead died on the *Titanic* – which he described in his final missive as 'a splendid monstrous floating Babylon' – on his way to lecture in the United States. He supposedly behaved heroically at the end, giving up his life-jacket and assisting women and children into life-boats, and although there are various accounts of his last moments, there are none that reflect badly on him. The family tombstone in Preston pays tribute to 'journalist, champion of defenceless womanhood, apostle of universal peace'.

6

From Bodysnatching to Bodysnatching

Crime Reporting North of the Border and the Man Who Couldn't Have Enough of a Good Murder

Scotland has a different legal system from the rest of Britain and its own national press, which has always found crime a rich source of material. Two of Scotland's greatest novelists, Sir Walter Scott and Robert Louis Stevenson, used real crimes as the basis for some of their fiction, so it is no surprise that there is a long history of Scottish crime reporting from the eighteenth century onwards. For his novel *Heart of Midlothian*, Scott took the real story of Isabelle Walker who, in the 1730s, was sentenced to death in dubious circumstances for killing her child. Her sister, Helen, then made her way to London by foot, carriage and cart to seek a pardon – and was successful.

She appears as Jennie Deans in Scott's novel. Robert Louis Stevenson's better-known work, *Dr Jekyll and Mr Hyde*, is often said to have been based on the story of Deacon Brodie, like Stevenson a native of Edinburgh, whose case provided the early broadside writers with much rich material and led to a flowering of crime writing in Scotland.

Deacon (the title given to the president of a trade guild) William Brodie was an upright cabinet-maker and respectable citizen by day, and a reckless robber by night, often burgling the premises of his own acquaintances to cover his debts, gambling problems and erratic domestic arrangements. He was caught, tried and executed in 1788 and is still commemorated by a pub named after him on the Royal Mile in Edinburgh. The *Edinburgh Advertiser*, one of the many publications which covered his case, observed that, 'Mr Brodie's behaviour during the whole trial was perfectly collected. He was respectful to the court and when anything ludicrous occurred in the evidence he smiled as if he had been an indifferent spectator.' Brodie was an admirer of John Gay's *Beggar's Opera*, which was often performed in Edinburgh, and the *Advertiser* noted that, as he prepared for his end, 'Brodie seemed to take the character of Macheath as his model and the day before his death was singing one of the songs from the *Beggar's Opera*. This is another proof of the dangerous tendency of that play which ought to be prohibited from being performed on the British stage. It is inconceivable how many highwaymen and robbers this opera has given birth to.' Clearly the *Advertiser* took an early stern line on the glamorisation of crime by the media.

As for the execution, the paper reported that 'it is not a little remarkable that Brodie was the planner, a few years since, of the new invented gallows on which he suffered'. Brodie bade his farewell to the world 'in a handsome suit of black clothes and had his hair powdered and dressed with taste'. The *Edinburgh Evening Courant* reported on his end and gave an early example of the press's sneaking admiration for the daring criminal: 'his crimes appear to be rather the result of infatuation than depravity; and he seemed to be more attracted by the dexterity of thieving than the profit arising from it'. The *Courant* also reported on the furious battle between the publishers of an original version of the trial, rushed out at speed, and two pirated versions, which mirrored the often angry disputes in London over competing reports in different publications of executions and criminals' confessions. Again, there are resonances with the rivalry of tabloids nearly two centuries later in their efforts to sign up witnesses, victims and even criminals involved in a notorious case.

Four decades after Deacon Brodie had excited the readers of the *Advertiser* and the *Courant*, came the case of Burke and Hare. William Burke and

William Hare were the two bodysnatchers who realised there was good money to be made in supplying corpses to the emerging medical school in Edinburgh and duly despatched sixteen unfortunates to the morgue before they were caught.

The description of Burke on trial carried in a contemporary broadside is quite flattering. He was 'one of the most singular characters ever consigned to the scaffold. He was considerably superior in education to his own class of his countrymen, and was just possessed of so much knowledge as should make the recollections of a series of murders drive him to the borders of despair.' He was praised for keeping his nerve and the reporter noted that 'he even laughed and attempted to talk over the murder of his victims with as much indifference as a shopkeeper would over his losses in trade, or the good bargains he has made'.

On the other hand, Hare, who had turned King's Evidence to save his own skin, was described as having 'all the outward appearance of a ruffian, drunken, ferocious, and profligate, and appears to have been the more deeply designing of the two'. Burke was credited with being brighter and thus the one 'that always went out to prowl for victims, and to decoy them to their destruction'. The fact that Hare escaped hanging did not please the crowd, as it was reported that 'Hare's wife was set at liberty lately, and in crossing the Bridges, was recognised by some person who had seen her in jail. A crowd soon gathered round her, and pelted her with snow balls and other missiles; and had not the police promptly interfered in her behalf, the ungovernable rabble that beset her would have quickly executed summary justice both on herself and the sickly infant she bore in her arms.' Here the reporter delivers a moral message that 'it is to be hoped, that the populace will not allow a commendable detestation of crime to lead to acts of outrage, which the law must punish with the same rigour in her case as in that of any other child of sin and misery that breathes under its protection'. Again, R. L. Stevenson echoed real life in his short story 'The Body Snatcher', and the Burke and Hare story has since been turned into a number of films.

The broadside report of the execution of Burke in January 1829 was given in fastidious detail: 'At an early hour, the spacious street where the scaffold was erected, was crowded to excess; and all the windows which could command a view, were previously bespoken, and high prices given for them.' Burke was brought overnight by coach from the Calton Hill jail to the scaffold and the account makes clear that the authorities did not want him to linger there too long: 'when he presented himself on the Scaffold, the crowd, to their shame . . . gave three triumphant cheers, which were heard at a great distance'.

Prior to the trial, broadsides containing their supposed confessions were widely on sale and the press whipped up excitement, with the *Caledonian Mercury* of 5 January 1829 carrying a supposed statement from Burke in which he confessed his crimes and described how he had killed his victims by getting them drunk and then suffocating them. Owen Dudley Edwards, in his book *Burke and Hare*, commented on the coverage of the period: 'The press in 1828–29 gave better value for less money, since they had only line drawings and better caricatures to fill a small part of pages nowadays smeared by tabloids with visual images as nauseating as possible. They were much more literate and their condescension was much less offensive that the illiteracy which the modern pressman likes to hang round the necks of his wretched readers.' Dudley Edwards suggested that the journalists 'raced in and out of the West Port to scribble down facts, half-facts, rumours, alcoholic ramblings, vague recollections and straightforward invention from anyone they could find'. The reports from Scotland were eagerly regurgitated by a fascinated English press.

As Thomas Ireland suggested in *The West Port Murders*, published in 1829, 'blame has sometimes been cast upon the periodical press for raising popular excitement by exaggerated statements'. He noted that 'the offices of the newspapers published on that day were beset by eager purchasers and the presses kept constantly at work could scarcely supply the unceasing demand'. An extra 8,000 copies of Edinburgh newspapers alone in addition to the normal run were sold during the week of the trial, although 'the citizens of Edinburgh are by no means bloodthirsty'.

Scotland's most notorious crimes had no more diligent recorder than William Roughead, who had trained as a lawyer but was to find his metier as the reporter of the major murder trials of his native land from the end of the nineteenth to the middle of the twentieth century. Amongst his criminal mementoes was a portion of the skin of Burke, which he kept in a snuff-box, and a mahogany cupboard made by Deacon Brodie.

Roughead, born in 1870, was known as 'the murderer's albatross' because anyone charged with unlawful killing, if they glanced around the court and saw his familiar, bald, rotund figure sitting, pen poised, would know that the gallows might well be awaiting them and the details of their life and crimes would eventually become one of the collected reports of this prolific writer. As a seventeen-year-old, he was first attracted to murder cases by reading a volume entitled *The Book of Remarkable Trials and Notorious Characters* by Captain L. Benson, which he found in his uncle's bookshelves. He was then, as he put it later in his essay 'Enjoyment of Murder', 'taken captive by the Captain, I sat absorbed in his entrancing pages, so admirably and aptly illustrated by the grisly humour of Phiz, until I was chased to bed'.

He was soon seduced away from legal practice by the trial of Jessie King, a baby-farmer from Stockbridge in Edinburgh who was convicted of killing three infants whom she had been paid to adopt. He followed the case while surreptitiously nibbling on digestive biscuits when he should have been in his dull solicitor's office. From 1889 onwards, he was a familiar figure in court for almost every major murder trial. Although he occasionally ventured south, he was happiest covering cases in Edinburgh or Glasgow, despite the fact that he often felt that there was a shortage of decent murders in his native land compared to its southern neighbour: 'We have in Scotland a really good murder about once in five years . . . [England] more favoured in matters criminal, boasts one a week.' And he made a distinction between the two countries: 'no mere English malefactor is, to my mind at least, a patch upon the kindly Scot, whose crimes in common with the national products, whisky and haggis, have about them a distinctive flavour . . . English Sunday papers have a brand new murder in well nigh every column.'

When he died, Roughead left his books, letters and papers to the Signet Library in Edinburgh, where they are faithfully kept in the Commissioners' Room and provide a veritable treasure trove of material. One case that he wrote about in great detail was the so-called Arran murder, in which a young Englishman called Edwin Rose was found dead, buried under a pile of boulders on Goatfell, on the isle of Arran, in 1889. He had last been seen in the company of a man who called himself John Annandale, although his real name was John Laurie, a pattern-maker from Glasgow, who was soon identified and fled his home. The Glasgow newspapers were full of 'The Arran Murder' as it became known and *The North British Daily Mail* even published a letter from the wanted man in which he denied responsibility for the murder and blamed it on 'two men' they had supposedly met at the top of Goatfell. 'If things go as I have designed them,' he added enigmatically in his letter, 'I will soon have arrived at that country from whose bourne no traveller returns.'

Laurie wrote again, still on the run three weeks after the body had been found, to the *Glasgow Herald*, proclaiming his innocence but saying that because he was a 'ruined man' he had no intention of giving himself up. The papers at the time were spoiled for choice in terms of murder coverage as Jack the Ripper was being hunted in London and an American woman, Florence Maybrick, was on trial in Liverpool for poisoning her husband with arsenic extracted from fly-paper. Laurie was eventually spotted by a police constable and caught hiding under a bush, having given himself a superficial throat wound with a razor. He now admitted robbing Rose but denied killing him.

When Laurie stood trial in Edinburgh, the *Scotsman* estimated that some two thousand people tried to enter the court. He was convicted by a majority, with eight voting for guilty and seven for not proven, a verdict which is not available in English courts and is referred to, with some cynicism, as 'we know you did it but we can't prove it' or 'not guilty, but don't do it again'. The *Scotsman* of 27 November carried an interview with Laurie's father – an early example of relatives of murderers being pursued by the press – who told their reporter that 'he knew that his son had some little peculiarities but he had never shown any sign of vice and the thought that he could possibly be a murderer altogether unmanned him'. Laurie died in Perth prison in 1930.

Roughead enjoyed mixing with the big literary names of the time. Arthur Conan Doyle, originally from Edinburgh himself, was an admirer and dined with Roughead at the North British Hotel. Conan Doyle was in Edinburgh because both men were much involved in the case of Oscar Slater, who had been wrongly convicted for murder and was eventually freed partly through their work. In 1925, Roughead entertained himself in London with a group known as the Crimes Club and heard a talk on the Oscar Wilde case at which one of the other guests was Conan Doyle. He also lunched with John Buchan and dedicated one of his books to him; showed J. B. Priestley round Edinburgh; and was friends with Scottish writers like Sir Compton Mackenzie, author of *Whisky Galore*, and Eric Linklater. Ludovic Kennedy recalled being introduced to him as a boy: 'it was like meeting God'.

Roughead was proud of being told by Henry James that 'you write so well'. The latter signed off a letter to him: 'I rest my telescope on your shoulder and am yours, all gratefully, Henry James.' But he was modest about his gifts in comparison to some of his contemporaries: 'Unlike Edgar Wallace and other men of real genius I boast but a piddling talent,' he wrote to his friend in the United States, the writer Edmund Pearson.

In his fine biography of Roughead, Richard Whittington-Egan explores the transatlantic friendship – almost a mutual admiration society – between Roughead and Pearson, who had written the definitive work on the American woman, Lizzie Borden, puzzlingly acquitted in 1893 of the axe murders of her parents. The letters act as a revealing diary of his thoughts on the business of crime writing. Pearson wrote jokingly on 16 September 1924, from New York, that 'it is a matter of great regret that you feel yourself unable to come to Fall River and pursue your plan as to a suit for her [Lizzie Borden's] affections. That was further than I thought of going: I did see some of her petticoats, waving in the wind, but lost the courage to go nearer.' Pearson signed himself as 'friend, admirer and assistant toiler in the same vineyard.'

'All I claim to do is to tell a tale of crime well and truly,' was how Roughead described his role. He described his style as 'plain simple food' with 'no psychological sauce to whet the appetite'. And he confessed himself fascinated by his subject: 'murder has a magic of its own, its peculiar alchemy'. He professed that 'they say that even of a good thing you can have too much. But I doubt it. True, such good things as sunbathing, beer, and tobacco may be intemperately pursued to the detriment of their devotees; yet, to my mind, one cannot have too much of a good murder.'

Roughead defended the genre of reporting murder cases against that of crime fiction. Writing in his introduction to the non-fiction book *Twelve Scots Trials* in 1913, he said that 'the fact that they were real men and women, who sinned and suffered in their day, and whose stories are unfortunately true, is alone enough to alienate the fiction-loving public . . . although the fitness of my rascals to adorn a tale may be questioned, their ability to point a moral is beyond dispute.'

Although Roughead lived through the notorious period of Glasgow's gang wars in the 1920s and 1930s, it was not a world to which he seems to have been attracted. Gang warfare, although violent, did not often result in Roughead's speciality – the murder trial. But as early as 1916, the *People's Journal* was warning its readers of the 'hooligan menace' on the streets of Glasgow and naming the leading gangs as the Beehive Boys, the Death Valley Boys, the Ging Gong and the Bell On Boys. The *Glasgow Herald* reported that one gang shouted 'we are the Redskins' as they went into battle and added the names of the Billy Boys, the Cowboys and the Baltic Fleet (from Baltic Street) as the active outfits, along with the Ping Pong, the Hi-Hi and the San Toy. These gangs always had much more imaginative names than their English counterparts. By 1935, the *Sunday Express* was suggesting that Glasgow was on its way to becoming another Chicago: 'The gangsters have come to Britain. Glasgow, second city of Empire, frankly acknowledges their reign of terror. A thousand young men – not forty are more than thirty-five – rule the poorer class districts.'

As we shall see, English papers would follow suit with the Chicago analogy in the 1950s.

In his book *City of Gangs*, Andrew Davies noted that there was no shortage of advice from the press on how to deal with the issue. In the *Sunday Post* in June 1930, under the headline 'How I Would Deal with the Glasgow Gangsters', an anonymous professor of psychology suggests forming a Foreign Legion like the French so that 'on the frontiers of India or among the sands of Mespot the hooligan would soon get all the discipline he needs'. At the same time, a 'special investigator' for the *Evening Citizen* was telling its readers that, as far as the police are concerned, the problem was solved, suggesting that the police knew the names and addresses of all the gangsters: 'how it is done is a secret that must not be given away'. This indicated that the relationship between police and crime reporters at the time was close.

But in 1936 Billy Fullerton, leader of the Billy Boys, decided to give his side of the story to *Thomson's Weekly News* (later the *Weekly News*), albeit writing under the pseudonym of 'Bill Fulton'. He was introduced to readers as 'powerful a personality in his own sphere as the Al Capones and Spike O'Donnells of the USA'. This was quite a step for a newspaper to undertake in the 1930s and eventually, in 2009, it would become an offence to pay criminals for their stories; in the meantime, crime reporters on both sides of the border would act as ghosts for both criminals and detectives.

Fullerton used the serialisation to paint himself and his gang in a more flattering light. Dealing with the allegations that they essentially ran a protection racket, he explained to readers: 'Shopkeepers give willingly each week. Don't think of it as a form of blackmail. The money they pay is for protection against other gangs.' He suggested that there were still, despite the best efforts of the police, around 1,500 active gang members in Glasgow and recounted a recent battle in which 300 had taken part using razors, broken bottles, hatchets and knives: 'although there were many casualties, none of the injured went into the infirmary. Past experience has taught the gangster that to land in the infirmary is to risk landing in jail. So, unless he is very seriously injured indeed, he just goes home and patches himself up with sticking plaster.' The world was captured in *No Mean City*, the classic 1935 Glasgow gang novel by H. Kingsley Long (himself a journalist with the *People*) and Alexander McArthur.

A perceptive observer of the media's fascination with crime was James Cameron, one of the outstanding journalists of the last century, who recalled the early days of his career with the *Sunday Post* in Scotland in the 1930s. 'I acted as journalistic amanuensis to an eerie creep who was contributing a series called "Secrets of the Mayfair Vice Rings", who conscientiously established his bona-fides by attempting to seduce me on the top deck of a green tram,' he wrote in his memoir, *Point of Departure*. One of his tasks was, at the conclusion of a gruesome murder trial, 'to call on some distracted or avaricious mother up a close in Lanark or Motherwell and guide her hand through an article entitled "Why My Boy Should Not Be Hanged".'

One of Cameron's colleagues had a very close relationship with the duty sergeants in Glasgow police stations and was thus able to track down every serious attack in the city. 'He was by the far the busiest of our little crew. Throughout the night, his voice provided a running obligato . . . "Aye, Jock boy, good, good; to the effusion of blood, eh; that's no bad at all . . . do your best lad; try and get me a wee slashing in the Gorbals; it's a thin night for the town edition."'

Another criminal who cast dark of clouds over Scotland in the 1950s was the American-born serial killer Peter Manuel, who shot and bludgeoned at least seven people to death, and probably another two, before he was caught, tried and hanged in Barlinnie prison in 1958. Before it was known who was responsible, the killer appeared in the press as 'the Beast of Birkenshaw' and Manuel appears to have taken some satisfaction from the coverage he received and his ensuing notoriety.

It was not until 2009 that his fascination with his own image in the press was fully revealed. That year, a poem he had written while in prison during the trial was finally released from the papers of his former prison governor. The *Daily Record*, which covered the story, noted that 'with the ability of a headline writer he [Manuel] tries to write his own epitaph in his poetic confession as he variously calls himself "The foulest beast on earth" . . . "A reptile in disguise" and the "rat of Birkenshaw".'

The Manuel case reminded newspapers that there remained a big market for crime.

The late Paul Foot, who started his career on the *Record* in Glasgow in the 1960s, recalled being initiated into what he was told was a regular feature of Scottish journalism: the court brawl. In an article many years later, in *The Journalist's Handbook*, Foot recounted how he had been told that a deal had been made with the lawyer of a man who was about to be released from a murder charge, the case having been found 'not proven'. He was surprised to see that five other reporters in three cars had been designated to meet the man as he left court. 'The surprise vanished in the street outside the court,' recalled Foot. 'The *Scottish Daily Mail* and the *Scottish Daily Express* also had three cars there. Their reporters were also under the illusion that the defendant's lawyers had done a deal with them.'

What transpired was a mighty battle between the rival papers followed by a car chase through Glasgow, with the bewildered ex-defendant being grabbed from one car at a traffic lights and hauled into another. The *Record* did not get their man. The following day there was inquest at the paper to see what had gone wrong. Not enough cars? Had the lawyer been underpaid? Should they have fought harder?

Later at a meeting of the local branch of the National Union of Journalists there was an eventual agreement between the warring parties that such an event should not happen again. Such a battle is unthinkable today although this may have more to do with the decline of tabloid sales and the consequent deep cuts in the staffing of newsrooms.

Crime reporters in Scotland faced other problems. In the 1960s and 1970s, the rise of Arthur Thompson, often described as 'the Godfather' and head of the 'Tartan Mafia', was followed diligently in the press in Glasgow but reporters had to be wary because Scottish criminals had learned that there were other ways to intimidate than with a razor or a gun. 'In my days as a writer we always referred to Arthur Thompson as a businessman,' veteran crime reporter Stuart 'the Bullet' McCartney told the *Scotsman* in 2002. 'We couldn't call him anything else. His criminal record was minor and he would almost certainly have sued if we had libelled him. Yet everyone knew what he did.'

Thompson died in 1993 and by then bodysnatching, in all its forms, had come to an end. But the pioneering way in which Roughead covered murder cases and the basis of real crime for memorable fiction, exemplified by Scott and Stevenson and modern authors like Ian Rankin and Val McDermid, meant that the Scottish contribution to crime writing (in both fiction and non-fiction) was both major and enduring.

7

From Brides in Baths to the Cleft Chin Murder

Crime Reporting During Wartime

The judge was summing up in one of the most sensational murder trials Britain had ever seen but his mind was elsewhere. 'Since last August, all over Europe, sometimes in England, sometimes on the seas, thousands of lives of combatants, sometimes of non-combatants, have been taken daily with no warning and sometimes with no justification.' Mr Justice Scutton was addressing an Old Bailey jury in June 1915. 'Yet while this wholesale destruction of human life is going on, for nine days all the apparatus of justice in England has been considering whether the prosecution are right in saying that one man should die. It is quite right that it should be. In England, in this national crisis, we try to carry on business as usual; we hope with confidence for victory as usual and we are determined to maintain justice as usual.'

It was the Brides in the Bath case. George Joseph Smith, a petty criminal and bigamist, was accused of murdering three of his wives in order to profit from their life insurance policies. The war had broken out the previous year and, far from being over by Christmas as had been optimistically predicted, was already responsible for the losses of the lives of tens of thousands of young men. So who cared now about domestic murders when every day brought news of deaths at the front?

The reporter and author Philip Gibbs wrote one of the best novels about journalism, *The Street of Adventure*, in 1909. Having served as one of the five official British war correspondents, for which he was later knighted, he added a sober preface to the 1919 edition of his book: 'Those young newspaper men of whom I write in this book regarded the work as a peep-show of which they were critics and onlookers; but when the War came they found they could no longer be aloof from life nor from its pageantry and drama with Press tickets for the "show" and a cynical amusement at the folly of human nature.'

Gibbs, like other journalists during the First World War, was subject to heavy government censorship – he was actually sent back to England on one occasion. Under the Defence of the Realm Act, there was strict control which forbade anything that might spread 'disaffection or alarm'. This may well have played a part in the lavish and lengthy coverage afforded to the Brides in the Bath case, for the sheer escapism it provided. Here the press had a gripping story of sudden deaths that they could recount in all their gory detail, without fear of being called unpatriotic or having to run it past a censor.

As would happen again in 1939, many of the young men who would have been working in newspapers at this time were already in uniform. Murders and robberies might seem small beer both to reporters and readers when compared to the mass slaughter taking place at Ypres or Loos. Yet the Brides in the Bath case acted, in a grim way, as light relief, and the reports of the case reflected that.

The press played its own major role in the tale. Before Smith had been accused of murder, there was a tantalising headline in the *News of the World* on 3 January 1915: 'Found Dead in Bath: Bride's Tragic Fate on Day After Wedding'. Smith had just been arrested for the minor offence of making a false entry in a marriage register in Bath and had been quoted as saying, once it emerged that two of his wives had drowned in their baths, after supposedly suffering a fit: 'Well, I admit the two deaths form a phenomenal coincidence but that is my hard luck.' Indeed it was George Joseph Smith's hard luck that the *News of the World* contained details of how his brides met their ends, that a reader of the paper in Blackpool should note the similarity to a death which had occurred there the previous year and that the police should be alerted. This was an early example of the press sailing close to the wind in terms of contempt of court.

It was, as the *News of the World* put it on 11 April 1915, an 'extraordinary story of alternating wedding and funeral bells' that would lead to Smith's execution on a sunny morning on 13 August. It was a case of six weddings and three funerals. Everyone wanted to see the Brides in the Bath show. 'At one time the peerage, the stage, the Church, besides the law, were represented in the crowd of well-dressed spectators, mostly women, who listened to the unfolding story.' They would have learned from Home Office pathologist Bernard Spilsbury that Smith had killed his victims by grabbing and lifting their legs and thus forcing their heads under water.

But the war was never far away and the reports reflected the patriotic tone of the time. As the summing-up speeches of the prosecution and defence unfolded, the *Daily Mail* reported on 1 July: 'once during [defence counsel] Mr Marshall Hall's speech in his behalf, a passage visualising the figure of British justice calm and patient amid all the clamour of the war seemed to tilt the balance of his [Smith's] strained nerves and bring a sudden gush of teardrops from his eyes.'

The Times, on 2 July, also made reference to the war: 'And so the jury and himself approached, as if this were a time of peace instead of one of the greatest world disturbances ever known in history.'

Only one verdict seemed likely to anyone who had followed the case in their daily paper.

'Guilty! The fatal word fell on the ears of a tense and densely crowded court at the Old Bailey and George Joseph Smith – the most amazing criminal of modern times – knew his fate,' was how the *News of the World* summed up the case on 4 July. As for Smith, 'The feel of the tightening noose upon his neck had stricken him with a rabbit's quivering terror. There was nothing left of the jaunty air of the easy deceiver of women, nor of the force and daring of the ruthless destroyer of life in the pallid and hollow-cheeked wretch who shrivelled into his chair in the dock.' And as for women finding him 'interesting', now the *Mail* reported that

'"Whatever can they have seen in him?" was the whispered comment of a woman spectator', on the day of judgment.

The paper reported that Smith left the court for prison in a horse-cab accompanied by two police officers. 'A number of youths pursued the cab until it turned the corner into Holborn,' a harbinger of the pursuit of prison vans by press photographers and angry members of the public to this day. Meanwhile, Edith Pegler, the wife to whom Smith always returned after his murders and marriages, having assured her he had been working as a travelling antiques dealer, decided to tell her story. An ad for the *Daily Sketch* promised: 'My Life with Smith. The woman to whom he always returned. Exclusive story, written by herself, with photographs and sketches drawn by Smith. Order your copy now. The demand will be enormous.'

The *News of the World* understandably made much of its role in the investigation; after all, its coverage of the 'phenomenal coincidence' had helped to nail Smith. It told how the Blackpool woman in whose home one of the murders had taken place had presciently shaken her fist at Smith as he departed after the death, called him 'Crippen' (after the doctor famously hanged in 1910 for murdering his wife), and told him: 'I shall see you again some day. I am sure to see your face in the *News of the World*.'

One of the most prolific and successful crime reporters of all time was also operating at this time. This was Edgar Wallace, who is commemorated by a plaque erected in Ludgate Circus, at the end of Fleet Street. 'He knew wealth and poverty,' it reads, 'yet had walked with Kings and kept his bearings. Of his talents he gave lavishly to authorship – but to Fleet Street he gave his heart.'

And it was while he was giving his heart and soul to the national press that Wallace learned the ability both to tell a tale and knock out copy at amazing speed, a skill that never left him. Before he worked as a crime reporter, he made a name for himself as a Reuters correspondent in South Africa, irritating Lord Kitchener with his coverage of the Boer War to such an extent (he published details of the peace treaty, given to him by an inside source, without permission) that Kitchener had him kicked out of the country. When the First World War started, Kitchener remembered Wallace and made sure he was kept away from the front line.

War reporting's loss was crime's gain; Wallace went on to cover many murder trials and hangings, and went on to use his real-life experiences as a reporter for his later more profitable career as a novelist. Writing swiftly and concisely had prepared him for turning out a great deal of snappy crime fiction, and by the time of his death he had written more than 170 books, not to mention dozens of screenplays. 'It always amuses me when reviewers speak of the improbabilities in my books,' he wrote in the *Daily Mail* in 1927. 'I have invented nothing half as wildly improbable as the things that are happening every day under your eyes and duly recorded in the newspaper press.'

By the time of the Second World War, censorship and calls to patriotism were more nuanced but crime coverage often focussed on the 'bandits of the Blitz', engaged in post-bombing looting, black marketeering and thefts of rationing books. 'Hang A Looter And Stop This Filthy Crime!' exhorted the *Daily Mirror*, in November 1940, when Sheffield Assizes set aside two days to deal only with looters. The paper urged prosecutions of the 'ghouls who rob even bodies lying in the ruins of little homes'. The BBC was also critical of the activities of the 'spivs and drones', as the crime rate increased by 57 per cent from 1939 to 1945.

When the Café de Paris, which had a supposedly secure underground ballroom, suffered a direct hit in 1941, thirty people were killed and the press reported approvingly how many of the young women had torn up their evening dresses to make bandages for the wounded. Receiving rather less coverage was the fact that rescuers were shocked to find looters among them, yanking brooches and rings from the dead bodies of the revellers.

Normal service continued in Soho. On 1 May 1941 Harry 'Little Hubby' Distelman, the doorman of the Old Cue Club in Soho, was stabbed to death. Antonio 'Babe' Mancini, the manager of a rival club who was charged with the murder, claimed that he had acted in self-defence.

The *Daily Express* reported: 'This is a crime Hitler did not commit . . . It was just a good old-fashioned Soho crime' and added that 'Soho, well hit by the raids, chatted more over Hubby Distelman's death than of the night they hit the hospital on the corner. For they knew that Hubby was just the victim of an internal war between gangs that have run through Soho even in the Blitz.'

Prostitution flourished and the 'Piccadilly commandos', as they were nicknamed, plied their trade in Soho, catering to the thousands of soldiers about to depart for the front. On this subject the press were less judgmental than in peacetime. The *Sketch*, in its feature on 'cabarets of Wartime London', focused on the singer and impersonator Florence Desmond, who was to give the country one of the naughtiest songs of the war – 'I've Got the Deepest Shelter in Town'.

Although there was official pressure not to damage wartime morale by highlighting criminal activities, some stories could not be ignored. Ivor Novello, the composer of the famous First World War song 'Keep the Home Fires Burning', was sentenced to eight weeks – reduced to four – in 1944 for the fairly minor misuse of petrol coupons offered to him by a female fan. This case of the star and the 'stage-struck woman' was, of course, widely reported. 'Oh, the publicity it will mean,' Novello told the arresting officer. 'I don't mind myself but I detest causing a stain on the theatrical profession.'

Some of the most horrific crimes reported related very much to the war. In February 1942, Gordon Cummins, a young airman who liked to tell people he came from an aristocratic background, murdered at least four women, using the blitz to his advantage. He became known in the press as 'the Blackout Killer' or – because of the sexual mutilation of some of his victims – 'the Blackout Ripper'. Trials were swift in wartime – everyone had more important things to do – and Cummins was tried, convicted and sentenced in a single day.

The following day, under the headline 'Murderer with Three-way Mind Posed as Titled', Montague Lacey of the *Daily Express* told his readers that Cummins had three different personalities: 'Number 1 was his normal life in the RAF. "A very intellectual type of airman," said his commanding offi-cer. No. 2 was the vain young man known to his friends as "the Duke" or "the Count" who posed as the Honourable Gordon Cummins, acquired affected speech and boasted of his conquests of women. Number 3 was the murderer.' He was dispatched on 25 June by a hangman whose work now also involved disposing of spies and traitors.

Professional criminals, many of whom dodged the war by pretend-ing to be mad or unfit for service, carried on as before. Perhaps the most powerful of them, Billy Hill, got a Fleet Street crime man, Duncan Webb, to ghost his memoirs only a decade after the end of hostilities, in which he boasted about how well he had done from the black market. 'I don't pretend to be a King and Country man but I must say I did put my name down to serve and until they came to get me I was making the most out of a situation,' said Hill, in *Boss of Britain's Underworld.* 'Some day some-one should write a treatise on Britain's wartime black market. It was the most fantastic side of civilian life in wartime.' Hill made a packet out of the war and profited from the fact that, just as the police were too busy to take much notice of him, so too were the press.

From 1945 onwards, crime reporters had to come to terms with the fact that they were writing for a readership that was all too familiar with slaughter and hellishness, from reports of Belsen to Hiroshima, not to mention their own personal experiences of warfare at home and abroad. George Orwell noted the change of attitude. In his famous essay 'Decline of the English Murder', written in 1946, he referred to the perfect pre-war Sunday afternoon, with the wife asleep in an armchair and the children out on a walk – 'You put your feet up on the sofa, settle your spectacles on your nose, and open the *News of the World.*' He suggested that what the reader enjoyed was a report of the 'perfect' murder, one in which pas-sion and planning played a part, such as those carried out by Dr Crippen or George Joseph Smith. In the essay, he looked at the extensive press coverage of the so-called Cleft Chin Murder of 1944, in which a US army deserter, Karl Hulten, accompanied by teenage Welsh waitress Elizabeth Jones, carried out the motiveless killing of a taxi driver who had a cleft chin. Orwell reflected on its pointlessness. He wondered if the killing had attracted headlines because it proved a distraction from doodlebugs and the Battle of France, and whether a nation brutalised by war was no longer interested in the kinds of murder that had strong emotions behind them but only in those carried out mindlessly.

While the conventional conflicts were being waged, the world was soon to be informed of another rather more ambiguous one, first hinted at in the wake of the First World War victory celebrations – a war on drugs.

8

Dope and Dopes

Reporting on Drugs from the High Priestess of Unholy Rites to Mr Nice

N o aspect of crime has been covered in the press more hysterically and inaccurately than drugs. It merits particular scrutiny because it has been so spectacularly misunderstood and misreported. While journalists knew exactly what murder, robbery, kidnap and rape involved and could thus examine methods and motives, drugs often remained a mystery. In particular, the role of the 'other' – the foreigner, the bohemian, the addict – played a major part in the coverage until the end of the twentieth century.

Drugs first entered the national discourse in a major way towards the end of the First World War. Until then, they had enjoyed an ambiguous status. During the war, *The Times* even carried advertisements for the Mayfair chemists Savory & Moore, for sheets impregnated with cocaine and morphine which were promoted as 'a useful present for friends at the front' where they were known to the troops as 'fear-banishers'. But by the end of the war and in the wake of the passage of the 1920 Dangerous Drugs Act, the first signs of what would become nearly a century of often fanciful and frequently invented reporting on drugs had already started.

'You will find the dope fiend in Chelsea, in Mayfair and Maida Vale,' the *Daily Express* warned its readers in 1918. 'An obscure traffic is pursued in certain doubtful teashops. The sale of certain beauty products is only a mask for the illicit traffic of certain drugs.' The story unfolds: 'A young and attractive girl deeply interested in social conditions and political economy made the acquaintance of another woman through a mutual friend. Within months she had become a confirmed haunter of a certain notorious cafe. She had lost her looks and health. Before she closed her miserable existence a bare nine months later she had introduced at least four other decent girls to her practice of vice; and for the last two months of her existence she was acting as a decoy for a notorious gambling hell.' The *Daily Mail* warned its readers: 'Men do not as a rule take to drugs unless there is a hereditary influence, but women are more temperamentally attracted.'

One of the reasons for the outlandish coverage was the great ignorance of the subject. As with many other crimes, before and since, the chief danger often seemed to lie in the influence of the sinister foreigner. Initially, the menace arrived most spectacularly in the form of the 'Yellow Peril'. The Chinese opium supplier was made flesh in the shape of a man known in the press as 'the Brilliant Chang' (his real name was Chan Nan) who had come to England as a marine contractor and had opened one of the capital's earliest Chinese restaurants, in Regent Street. There, according to a report by a 'special commissioner' of the *World Pictorial News*, he 'dispensed Chinese delicacies and the drugs and vices of the Orient'. His 'obsession' with white women led to him demanding, the paper claimed, that he be paid in kind. When the women acquiesced to his demands, 'the flame of evil passion burned more brightly within and he hugged himself with unholy glee.' Some women were made of sterner stuff and retained 'sufficient decency and pride of race' to turn down Chang, who could be identified, according to the reporter, by his 'lips thin and cruel, tightly drawn across even yellow teeth'.

The *News of the World* gave the full treatment to the coroner's inquest into Billie Carleton, the twenty-two-year-old show-girl who died of a cocaine overdose in 1919 just after returning from the Victory Ball at the Albert Hall: 'the coroner's inquiry has revealed a state of things almost unbelievable . . . In the West End of London, in the quiet seclusion of luxury flats the "most disgusting" orgies take place. Men and women, the former in pyjamas, the latter in chiffon nightdresses, recline in a circle of soft cushions, and pass from hand to hand and mouth to mouth the opium pipe.' Mrs Lo Ping You, 'the Scottish wife of a Chinaman of Limehouse Causeway, described as "high priestess of these unholy rites" was jailed for five years.'

There was no telling how this fiendish traffic might spread. In 1922, the *Empire News* warned that 'mothers would be well advised to keep their daughters as far away as they can from Chinese laundries and other places where the yellow men congregate.' The *Daily Express* took its readers to a 'dancing den' where the clientele were 'the same old sickening crowd of under-sized aliens, blue about the chin and greasy, the same predominating type of girl, young, thin, underdressed, perpetually seized of hysterical laughter, ogling, foolish'. Then enter the dealer: 'He was not the Chink of popular fiction, a cringing yellow man hiding his clasped hands in the wide sleeves of his embroidered gown.' He greets the room with 'that fixed Oriental smile which seems devoid of warmth and humanity . . . who are these smiling yellow men?' In 1920, the *Daily Express* ran an exposé entitled, 'The Yellow Peril in London – Vast Syndicate of Vice with its Criminal Master'.

After Chang was arrested in 1924, he was told during his trial by the Recorder of London that 'It is you and men like you who are corrupting the womanhood of this country.' The *Daily Express* celebrated his demise: 'The yellow king of the "dope runners" has been caught at last in the web of British justice.' He had, it was suggested, used only women as his runners, one even transporting the drugs from Paris in her bloomers. Arthur Tietjen of the *Daily Mail* wrote: 'Chang possesses a strangely macabre – some said hypnotic – power to persuade women to sniff cocaine. It may well have been that he did so as a member of the yellow race to degrade white women.' Deported, Chang was last heard of, according to the *Daily Telegraph*'s report, in reassuringly pathetic circumstances in Shanghai: 'A strange Nemesis overtook him. He went blind and ended his days not in luxury and rich silks but as a sightless worker in a little kitchen garden.'

The other notorious dealer of the period was Eddie Manning, a Jamaican who supposedly had a silver-topped cane packed with drugs. Once again, race became a predominant aspect of the coverage. The *News of the World* hailed his arrest in 1923 with the headline 'Evil Negro Caught'. After being picked up once more for possession of goods stolen from Lady Diana Cooper's car, he was described by the arresting officer as 'the worst man in London'. He died in Parkhurst prison hospital in 1931.

There was never a shortage of outlandish tales on the subject and in the interwar years they tended to the exotic. The *News of the World* reported how 'Sapper', the pen name used by H. C. McNeile, the creator of gentleman adventurer Bulldog Drummond, had inspired the creation of a 'black gang' consisting of 'young men of energy'. They were apparently 'disgusted by the degenerate parasites of the West End against whom the police were powerless' and had pounced on 'dope peddlers and other crooks' and taken them to a garage off the Great West Road, where they were supposedly flogged with dog-whips until they agreed to mend their ways. The paper also reported on the broken engagement of a young officer whose fiancée had become addicted to marijuana: 'she has been going to these cigarette orgies. It will be years before she is well.' *The Times* was anxious to make sure its readers knew the risks posed by drug users: 'Most cocainomaniacs carry revolvers to protect themselves from imaginary enemies.' In his excellent and entertaining book, *Dope Girls: the Birth of the British Drug Underground*, Marek Kohn analyses and uncovers much of the wonderfully purple prose of the 1920s and 30s and catalogues the ways in which drugs were described in the most exotic of terms.

In response to this fearmongering, Edgar Wallace was moved to write an article to readers of the *Daily Mail* in February 1928 explaining: 'Why We Have No Gangsters'. Clearly not including the Glasgow razor gangs in his thesis, he wrote that, 'The existence of gang warfare in any country depends not so much on the methods employed to deal with it as upon its cause; and the cause is inevitably dope. Our own criminals do not dope; that ghastly practice is left to a comparatively few degenerate weaklings.'

The drugs panic in the press eased and the outbreak of the Second World War meant that everyone had clearer threats to civilisation to concern them. By the end of the forties, the *Telegraph*'s Stanley Firmin suggested that Scotland Yard had subsequently solved the drugs problem. 'A force of detectives was given the job of rooting out the dope traffickers and putting an end to their nefarious activities once and for all,' he wrote in 1950. 'Today dope trafficking has practically ceased to exist. Now and again one comes across the case of a foreign seaman smuggling in cocaine or opium.'

But even as Firmin was writing the obituary of the drugs menace, his competitors in the tabloid press were alerting their readers to a fresh threat, this time brought to British shores supposedly from the west rather than the east.

'Coloured men who peddle reefers can meet susceptible teenagers at jazz clubs,' Chapman Pincher informed *Daily Express* readers. 'Reefers and rhythm seem to be directly connected with the minute electric "waves" continually generated by the brain surface. When the rhythm of the music synchronises with the rhythm of the brainwaves, the jazz fan experiences an almost compulsive urge to move their bodies in sympathy. Dope may help the brain "tune in" to the rhythm more sharply, thereby heightening the ecstasy of the dance.'

Arthur Tietjen, who had handled press communications at the Nuremberg and Belsen trials, was the crime correspondent of the *Daily Mail*. Writing in 1952 in his book *Soho: London's Vicious Circle*, Tietjen clearly found the world of drugs fascinating. He describes hearing, through the basement grille in the pavement, the sound of the blues, and how, 'A little group of West African negroes in light grey fedoras and bright blue suits talked together in their strange clipped tongue, white teeth shining in the darkness. With them was a portly blonde, balanced unsteadily on her high-heeled platform shoes. Perhaps they were peddling reefers, or merely discussing the benefits of National relief or the Queen's visit to Nigeria. It is part of the spicy charm of Soho that its denizens can be just as bad or as good as one's imagination decrees.' This was perhaps the key to much of the reporting on drugs at the time: reporters felt that their imaginations could be allowed free rein.

The Times in 1957 developed this theme, informing its readers that 'white girls who become friendly with West Indians are from time to time enticed to hemp smoking . . . this is an aspect of the hemp problem – the possibility of its spreading among irresponsible white people – that causes greatest concern to the authorities.' The paper suggested that the main reason for 'the coloured man' to smoke hemp was to stimulate sexual desire. Indeed, the corruption of white British womanhood by the Chinese and West Indians through drugs was a theme in the British press from the twenties through to the seventies.

But the complacent attitude shared by the police and the mainstream press was already starting to change. John Weeks, who covered crime for the *Daily Telegraph* at the time, recalled that on his first day on the paper in 1964 he was introduced at Scotland Yard to a detective sergeant, 'Benny' Lynch, then thought to be the only person in the drug squad. 'He said to me, "Are you the new boy? Come with me."' Weeks was taken to his office and shown a large brown suitcase full of drugs. 'He said, "This is heroin, this is cocaine, cannabis oil, cannabis resin. You are going to come across a lot of this in the future."'

Even when drugs became a key part of the counter-culture in the sixties and seventies, there was little in the way of accurate coverage in the national press. If one wanted to find out the true price, potency, risks, availability and provenance of drugs then being consumed – mainly cannabis from Morocco, Lebanon and Afghanistan – one had to turn to the so-called underground press, such as the *International Times* whose journalists, unlike most of those in the national press at the time, had not only seen the drugs being consumed but consumed them regularly themselves.

Newspapers printed as gospel the estimates of a drugs seizure's worth given to them by either Customs and Excise or the police. This sloppiness suited both the law enforcement agencies and the reporter covering the story, in that it made the bust that much more significant and newsworthy.

In early 1967, the *News of the World* produced a series of articles entitled 'Pop Stars and Drugs: Facts that Will Shock You'. This led to police raids on the homes of Keith Richards and Brian Jones and the arrest at different times of Richards, Jones and Mick Jagger, the last of whom was convicted of possession of four amphetamine tablets and sentenced to three months' imprisonment. William Rees-Mogg, then editor of *The Times*, wrote a brave editorial in his paper, taking its headline from Alexander Pope: 'Who Breaks a Butterfly on a Wheel?'

Rees-Mogg pointed out that Jagger had been charged with being in possession of four tablets containing amphetamine sulphate and methyl amphetamine hydrochloride which had been bought, quite legally, in Italy, and were not regarded as highly dangerous drugs. He hinted that the real reason for a jail sentence rather than probation was that people felt that Jagger had 'got what was coming to him' because they resented the anarchic aspects of the Rolling Stones and their music and suspected them of 'decadence, a word used by Miss Monica Furlong in the *Daily Mail*'. The editorial in *The Times* seemed to have the desired effect on the establishment: Jagger's sentence was reduced on appeal and the press could claim to have played its part, both in fuelling and in calming the panic.

It was not until 1968 that an organisation emerged to challenge some of the nonsense being written. Release, founded by Caroline Coon and Rufus Harris, and based in the heart of doper country in west London, was created to give advice to those being arrested at the time. They were able, if reporters were so inclined as to ask, to give context to some of the more ridiculous claims. One of their early researchers and legal advisers, Don Aitken, became recognised as an expert on the actual monetary value of many of the drugs, and gave evidence in many trials, explaining that the actual value of the drugs was a fraction of that claimed by the prosecution. Aitken would patiently tell reporters how much a seizure would actually have made when sold in the streets, and gradually a clearer picture of the drugs market emerged.

Since then, such organisations have grown in number. Transform, the Institute for the Study of Drug Dependency, the Standing Conference on

Drug Abuse, the Legalise Cannabis Campaign, all arrived on the scene, some proving more resilient than others. It meant that reporters could contact a body other than one connected to law enforcement to check rumours or claims. Former senior police officers appear regularly in the media now calling for the decriminalisation of drugs and are accorded a polite hearing.

The dealer, usually foreign and swarthy, remained a sinister figure, at least in the world of the mainstream press, throughout the sixties and most of the seventies. So when a bright and charming young Welshman called Howard Marks, a graduate of Balliol college, Oxford, and a bunch of his savvy and well-educated compadres appeared at the Old Bailey in 1981, there was some puzzlement even if, at that stage, it could not have been predicted how influential the case would be in changing the perception of the drug dealer in the media. 'Eggheads Ran £20 million Drug Ring' was how the *Sun* described the case while the *Mail* reported that 'an Oxford graduate was the mastermind in a brainy gang'.

When the police first caught up with him, Marks went on the run, so the initial trial in which he should have been involved, in 1974, started without him. Little did the reporters know that he would one day become a best-selling author and be writing regularly for the press himself. The *Daily Mirror* wondered where he was and described him as an MI6 agent who had been kidnapped, beaten up and persuaded to become an IRA sympathiser. The *Daily Mail* suggested that the police were exploring the possibility that he had been executed by the IRA. Marks's lawyer, the genial Bernie Simons, alerted the press to say that Marks had been in touch with him and was not being held against his will, but this made little difference to the coverage.

In April 1975, the *Daily Mirror* ran a front-page picture of Marks in a glasses-and-moustache disguise under the headline, 'The Face of a Fugitive'. By now he was said to have 'worked for three separate bosses: the Mafia, the IRA and British secret service'. It asserted that Marks had turned up in Padua, Italy where the Mafia had agreed to protect him in exchange for his silence. The *Daily Mirror* also splashed with 'THE

INFORMER', suggesting that the Mafia had taken Marks in, in order to dissuade him from informing on their drug dealing during the Old Bailey trial.

When his eventual trial started, years later, the role of the press became crucial to his defence – that he had been secretly working for Mexican and British intelligence and carrying on the cannabis smuggling activities to keep his cover story intact. 'Lord Hutchinson [his defence counsel] managed to get all the newspapers read by an enthralled and sympathetic jury,' Marks wrote in *Mr Nice*, his memoir, which noted how press coverage inadvertently helped him by linking him to the secret service and the IRA. Amazingly, he was acquitted.

Neil Darbyshire covered the trial for the *Evening Standard*. 'It was a fantastic case. A more guilty man you couldn't possibly imagine yet he was acquitted and – it sounds sexist – but there were seven women on the jury and they were all charmed by him.' He got two years for having false passports but had already served the time on remand and so he was released, and moved to Mallorca.

But the tale was not over. The United States drugs enforcement administration (DEA) became interested in Marks, their Madrid-based agent, Craig Lovato, having read about him in David Leigh's book *High Time*. The DEA became obsessed with a desire to catch him. They launched Operation Eclectic, working with the Spanish and British police, and persuaded one of his contacts in Manila, the late and louche Lord Tony Moynihan, to set him up. Marks and his wife, Judy, were arrested. While in custody in Mallorca, he was interviewed by the press: 'I spent three hours being rudely interrogated by the *Daily Mirror*, gently questioned by *Paris-Match* and heavily sympathised with by *El Pais*. The *Paris-Match* lady said that in France I was already a hero.'

This led to a *Mirror* splash: 'Behind Bars – Drug King of the World' in which he supposedly spoke exclusively to the *Mirror* from a hell-hole of a Spanish jail that smelled of stale sweat. Inside the paper, friends of Marks's attested to his normality, with a local expat restaurateur explaining that his favourite meal there was a couple of Welsh rarebits and a piece of cod. In the *Daily Mirror* on 26 July 1988, it was claimed that 'English toff's power rivalled Mafia barons', which was a bit hard as Marks was neither English nor, as a grammar school boy and son of a merchant sailor and a teacher, a toff. He supposedly had a ruthless organisation matching anything operated by the Mafia or the feared Colombians. To the *Daily Express* he was now 'the epitome of the cheeky chappie, the mischievous boyo from the Valleys'.

According to the DEA, Marks was 'the Marco Polo of drug trafficking' and the *Express* and the *Mirror* suggested that he ran a £200 million cannabis empire using 'undersea hollows and hideaways marked by oceanographic buoys'. One of these hideaways had supposedly been found to contain a 'huge hashish supermarket' with 15 tons of Lebanese hash, fast boats and machine guns. No suggestion was too outlandish. He also supposedly owned a fleet of freighters and finance houses.

In West Palm Beach, on 13 July 1990, Marks pleaded guilty to racketeering and conspiracy to racketeer and was eventually jailed for twenty years. During his time inside, the *Daily Telegraph* made reference to the suggestion that he had salted away £50 million and he wrote a letter to the editor: 'It was such a wonderful and much needed Christmas surprise to read in your columns that I am the owner of £50 million concealed in the Caribbean and/or Eastern bloc bank accounts. I was totally unaware I had this loot. All they say about the damaging effects of cannabis on the memory must be true.'

Marks then offered to transfer all the money to wherever the *Telegraph* wanted in exchange for them settling his fine, paying his wife's mortgage and his children's school fees and keeping his family from starving. The letter was published but the offer not taken up. The *Mail on Sunday* suggested that he had lived with the American president Bill Clinton in his Oxford days, although he had no recollection of him: 'I never met anyone who smoked joints without inhaling.'

I went to interview him when he was serving his sentence in Terre Haute federal penitentiary in Indiana. 'Ah, you've come to see Marco Polo?' chuckled the prison officers who had read the press reports of his case; guards are not immune to a prisoner's media reputation. After his release in 1995, he was approached by the publicist, Max Clifford – himself later to end up in jail for sexual offences – who brokered a £10,000 fee from the *News of the World* for his story. He has often been in the media since, writing for the *Guardian*, the *Observer* and the *Oldie*, promoting his fiction and non-fiction works and his popular one-man shows. In the 1997 general election campaign, he was approached by the *Sunday Times* who wanted him to give £2,000 to the Labour Party so that they could write a story that Labour was accepting backing from a convicted drug dealer.

There have also been plenty of other 'eggheads' in the dock in the wake of Operation Julie. This was the name given to the busting of the largest LSD manufacturing outfit in Britain which led to raids involving more than 800 police officers in March 1977. It was a further example of the addictive quality of drugs stories for the press, producing a mixture of fascination and puzzlement. One of the accused, Leaf Fielding, in his later account of the bust, *To Live Outside the Law*, recalls being told by a policeman: 'You're all famous now. The BBC extended the news by fifteen minutes last night for you lot. Operation Julie – that's what they're calling it.'

John May, writing at the time in *NME*, quoted one of the defence lawyers as saying that 'never in the history of British crime has the police public relations been so effective and so exaggerated. It has been accepted blindly and blithely by all concerned.' As he put it: 'The police offered the press their version of an exciting story, and they took it hook, line and sinker.'

The press certainly tripped out on the case. The *Mirror* went for a fanciful suggestion that the accused had been planning to put acid in the water supplies 'to blow a million minds simultaneously by pouring LSD into the reservoirs serving Birmingham'. The *Guardian* suggested that 'the flower of British post-war education were in the dock' and described them as a mixture of 'evangelists, middle-aged Americans and get-rich-quick merchants, many of them Cambridge-educated'. Their story, it was said, 'sounded like the history of enterprising businessmen, too busy making their venture succeed to worry about a few social casualties'. In the *Evening Standard* an article headlined 'Exploding The Myth of Pop Festivals' suggested that the idea that free pop festivals were innocent happenings had been finally exposed. It went on to claim that open-air festivals were financed from LSD profits to attract hardcore drug takers and enough 'innocent fans' to cover up the drug-dealing.

Nonsense about drugs continued in the media long after the generation who had only 'experimented' with drugs had taken on senior positions in the newspaper industry, parliament and the police. Hypocrisy ruled. One tabloid reporter in the 1980s was himself a heroin addict, partly financing his habit by ratting on and exposing in the press those with whom his addiction brought him into contact.

When I worked at *Time Out* magazine in the 1970s, we were curious about the decision by Rizla, the cigarette-paper manufacturers, to produce longer rolling papers – very popular with people making joints – and asked them why they were doing so. They explained that they were for long-distance lorry-drivers so that their roll-ups would last longer when they were at the wheel. When we ran a jokey story about this, a member of the advertising department came through to the newsroom to announce that Rizla were planning to withdraw their advertising.

Drugs continued to be a main source of stories and sometimes it was not even necessary for a real person to be involved. The former *News of the World* reporter Graham Johnson recounts in his very entertaining memoir, *Hack*, how one of his journalistic coups was the exposé of a far-right fanatic, Mark Nodder, who sold ecstasy tablets to finance his support for the neo-fascist group Combat 18. The story was that 'Britain's most evil racist thug has found a new way to discriminate against blacks – through the killer drug he peddles to raise cash for his Nazi-style hate campaign.' The story was illustrated with a slightly indistinct photo of the evil thug and concluded with the reassuring information that 'our dossier has been passed to Scotland Yard'. The only problem was that not only was there no dossier but no Nodder either. He was an invention and the blurred photo was of one of Johnson's obliging friends who had had his hair dyed blond for the occasion and was wearing sunglasses. Another *NoW* spoof of the time, also fictitious, was that 'guerilla gardeners' were using Princess Diana's Kensington garden to grow weed – 'Dopes Grow Cannabis in Di's Back Garden'. This sort of invention was much more widespread than it is today; information is much more readily available now, particularly on the internet, and so the risk of getting caught out is much higher.

By the turn of the century, most stories involving drugs had to involve a 'celebrity', who would either be the victim of a sting or an unreliable 'friend'. An example of the former came in 2013 in the *Sun on Sunday*'s story, 'Tulisa's Cocaine Deal Shame', about the singer and talent show judge, Tulisa Contostavlos. It led to a historic court case. Contostavlos claimed successfully that she had been entrapped by Mazher Mahmood, the reporter known as the 'fake sheikh' because of the disguise he had often used in stings for the now defunct *News of the World*. The case against Contostavlos collapsed in dramatic fashion at Southwark Crown Court in 2014 and the trial judge, Alistair McCreath, described the reporter as 'someone who appears to have gone to considerable lengths to get Ms Contostavlos to agree to involve herself in criminal conduct'.

Times have certainly tempered drugs coverage. In 2012, a couple in their sixties, Michael Foster and Susan Cooper, were jailed at Lincoln Crown Court for selling large quantities of marijuana which they had grown on their farm. It transpired during their trial that they had given away much of their profits to a hospital and a school in an impoverished part of Kenya. They were treated by the media as fairly harmless eccentrics, the sort of people you would be happy to have as neighbours, and far from the dangerous creatures of a century earlier who preyed on the weaknesses of young white women. However, they were still sentenced to three years, and had an appeal turned down.

The official position of most newspapers remains anti-legalisation although many now carry articles calling for, at least, decriminalisation of cannabis, sometimes penned by former police officers or lawyers.

Some attitudes remain. Richard Peppiatt, the former *Daily Star* reporter, is quoted in the book *Narcomania* as saying: 'If a scientist announces their research has found ecstasy to be safer than alcohol, my job as a tabloid reporter is to portray this man as a quack.' While drugs were providing a new source of material, murder remained an enduring topic and by the middle of the twentieth century the previously anonymous reporters were to find themselves in the spotlight.

9

Fleet Street's Murder Gang

Skid Marks That End in a Pool of Blood

'**N**o two crime reporters look alike, talk alike, or even work alike, yet the odd thing is that anybody who has met one even on a most casual or social occasion would probably guess the man's profession,' wrote Hilde Marchant in *Picture Post* in May 1947. Entitled 'Fleet Street's Murder Gang' and illustrated with photographs by the great Bert Hardy, it was a major feature in the booming and campaigning magazine and over four pages it painted a flatteringly romantic picture of crime reporters. It was a historic moment in that, for the first time, it gave a public face and identity to the men – and they were all men – whose daily crime stories were now feeding a ravenous and growing reading public. It helped to create the image of the crime reporter as tough and relentless in pursuit of stories.

Many of the reporters had returned to Fleet Street after service in the armed forces in the Second World War and so were not too thrown by the odd torso in a suitcase or a razor slashing in Soho. Marchant, who worked for both the *Daily Express* and *Daily Mirror*, was no slouch herself. She made her name first through covering the Spanish Civil War and then from her Second World War coverage of the Blitz, about which she wrote with great courage and elan. She was also reporting trials from the Old Bailey during that period and her own experience of the war and the courts may well have given her a rapport with the 'murder gang' – the first time they acquired the name.

By chance, there was what was to prove a major murder story on which Marchant could witness the gang at work and describe how they responded. She reported that many of the reporters had been having a drink and a couple of cold sausages in the Red Lion near Scotland Yard when news came through of the shooting of Alec de Antiques, a motorcyclist who had tried to stop a jewel thief in Charlotte Street, London's West End. One of the reporters who was in the Yard press room ran into the pub to alert his colleagues and soon they were on their way. Elsewhere in Fleet Street, after a tip-off, other crime reporters had 'grabbed their hats, stuffed copy paper in their pockets, borrowed somebody's pencil and some small change for a taxi and were on the scene of the crime almost as quickly as their colleagues from the Yard'. Marchant successfully portrays the camaraderie of the job, creating the image of crime reporters as members of a team who could be both rivals and pals.

Amongst the gang was Reg Foster of the *News Chronicle*, later to become a heroic figure in Fleet Street because of his refusal to disclose a source. Other members were Bill Jones of the *Daily Herald*, Len Hunter of the *Daily Express*, Syd Brock and Arthur Tietjen of the *Daily Mail*, Norman Rae of the *News of the World*, 'Jeep' Whittall of the *Daily Mirror*, 'Tich' Leach of the *Exchange Telegraph* and Bill Ashenden of the *Daily Graphic*.

The photos played their part in the creation of the image of the Crime Man and the reporters could not have hoped for a finer person to immortalise them than Bert Hardy. A working-class boy who had left school at 14, he had been hired by *Picture Post*'s editor, Tom Hopkinson, and had already made his reputation by his coverage of the Blitz in London. His moody black-and-white photos of the reporters add to the aura: Whittall is seen in profile in a picture captioned 'Night Watch on the Underworld' suggesting that he is waiting to see 'one of the boys', while 'Tich' Leach grabs a sandwich, which was described as the crime reporter's staple diet. Syd Brock is pictured on a doorstep and described as The Man Who Works Alone – 'he prefers a lone wolf role'.

Marchant suggests that the crime men mostly work in twos, one supplying the necessary colour – 'skid-marks that end in a pool of blood'

– while the other does the nuts and bolts. She reckons that they sometimes have to listen to hours of waffle to get their nugget of truth and 'they have in fact to surrender themselves entirely to the crime on hand, never thinking of food, sleep, comfort or even a clean collar while they follow every line of enquiry'. She is also impressed by the fact that they never swear in front of a woman – 'even one of a shady profession' – because it is against their professional code. And Marchant also captures the atmosphere of the rural murder investigation, when the crime reporters would decamp to some unsuspecting hotel and cause havoc with their bar bills and late-night phone calls.

One crime reporter's technique, she noted, was to pretend to be naive and a bit slow which made his sources want to help him, while another had such a reassuring West Country accent and rural manner that one murderer even told him where he had hidden the body. Interestingly, she notes the culture change that was already underway at that time, as a result of the intervention of the new Commissioner, Sir Harold Scott: 'Until recently the police regarded crime reporters as second only in villainy to the criminal himself but years of proving their value and discretion has changed the attitude of Scotland Yard.'

Obtaining confessions of guilty murderers was as much a part of the trade as it had ever been, the more so because of an increasingly competitive newspaper business. One of the gang, Norman Rae, who had served in the First World War in the fearsome 51st Highland Division and trained as a reporter under the Officers' Resettlement Scheme, had already established his credentials. Rae was, in the words of Neil Root, author of *Frenzy!*, a 'no-nonsense gruff Scot'. And the cases of three famous killers – Dr Buck Ruxton in the 1930s, John Haigh in the 1940s and John Reginald Christie in the 1950s – highlighted the way that members of the 'gang' operated.

The hunt for Dr Ruxton began when, in 1935, parts of bodies, including three female breasts, were found in parcels near Moffat in Scotland. Rae was a canny operator and celebrated as such in the book *150 Years of True Crime*, which covered his and his fellow *News of the World* crime reporters' tales, and he noted that around one of the wrappers was a Morecambe edition of the *Sunday Graphic*. So he slipped away from Moffat claiming that he had personal issues to address and left the story with John Howie Milligan, the northern reporter of the paper (and also, coincidentally, the author of Harry Lauder's famous song, 'Roamin' in the Gloamin'). In Morecambe, Rae picked up a story about a doctor whose wife and maid had disappeared, contacted Dr Ruxton and interviewed him, still protesting his innocence.

The story ran in that Sunday's paper as 'The Ravine Murders Riddle'. Rae also talked to a number of Ruxton's patients and found that he had given them different versions of where his wife had gone. The police followed Rae's lead and, when Ruxton was finally arrested, he was with John Milligan who wrote about the encounter: 'He paced up and down the library floor, nervously fingered an oriental knife, ran trembling fingers through tousled hair, and occasionally thumped his forehead with the palm of his hand. Now and again he stopped, swung round and almost screamed: "I did not kill my Belle."' Ruxton was tried, convicted and executed.

In May 1936, as a crowd gathered outside Strangeways prison waiting for the black flag to be raised to signal Ruxton's end, someone sidled up to Rae and gave him a letter that Ruxton had asked him to deliver after his death. This became what the paper described as 'one of the journalistic sensations of the present century'. It was only five lines long but it was a full confession: 'I killed Mrs Ruxton in a fit of temper because I thought she had been with a man, I was mad at the time. Mary Rogerson (the maid) was present at the time. I had to kill her.' Ruxton had instructed his friend 'in the impossible event of a verdict of guilty and if – God forbid – I am to die, I want you to hand this envelope unopened to the editor of the *News of the World*. But remember – it has not to be opened until I am dead.'

In 1949, the big murder story was of John George Haigh, the 'vampire killer' who murdered at least six people, then dissolved their bodies in an acid bath and stole their property. Gerald Byrne, the crime reporter for the *Empire News*, wrote a book about Haigh in which he suggests that, before he was arrested, 'crime reporters and police alike' knew that he was 'the man in the case', as they routinely shared information, an indication of how closely the police and the press then worked. 'The law of libel prevented me from openly accusing Haigh but if you read Haigh's name in place of "a man" it becomes quite clear that the crime reporter's art was nailing the right man,' wrote Byrne. 'There was a wealth of detail in that story which I telephoned in evening dress from a function at the Connaught Rooms.'

Byrne also spells out the wrangle over murderers selling their stories to the press: Haigh intended that the sale of his story to the *News of the World* should benefit his mother but Byrne informs us that it was doubtful that she would ever have benefited as there were many relatives of his victims who would have contested it. The great thing about making a deal with a condemned man, of course, was that if the payment failed to go through after his execution, there was not much he could do about it. Byrne said it was clear even before Haigh's execution that his story had been sold to the highest bidder and once again Rae of the *News of the World* was the man in the confessional, curious to find out whether Haigh really was a 'vampire'. Haigh told him: 'I first acquired the taste in childhood when my hand was smacked with a hairbrush. The sharp bristles drew blood. I licked it off and found it an agreeable sensation.'

Haigh was, in fact, quite chatty to the press as they circled round him before his arrest, as a temporary member of the murder gang, Donald Zec, was to discover. Zec, later to become better known as a show-business writer for the *Daily Mirror*, was working as a crime reporter for the paper at the time and was sent to interview Haigh while he was a suspect but before his arrest. Zec was aware of the story through Percy Hoskins, the revered crime correspondent of the *Daily Express*. Hoskins often drank champagne in El Vino's with senior detectives, 'whose confidential nose-tapping unmistakably signalled "the Met",' as Zec wrote in his memoir, *Put the Knife in Gently*. 'The received wisdom was that Hoskins learned about murders and other serious crimes almost as swiftly as the detectives themselves. Watching Hoskins was therefore the crime reporter's first imperative. For Hoskins to leave his Bollinger and exit the bar in mid-anecdote was significant.'

On one occasion, both Hoskins and Zec were in pursuit of a tale about the disappearance of an elderly widow called Olive Durand-Deacon, who, it would later transpire, had been lured by Haigh to his workshop in Crawley, where he killed her and dissolved her body in acid. Haigh agreed to meet Zec at the Onslow Court Hotel, invited him to his room and offered him a cup of tea with the words 'shall I be mum?' He gave Zec a flattering framed portrait of himself which duly made the front pages when he was finally arrested.

Norman Rae also had another encounter with one of the century's most famous killers. 'John Reginald Halliday Christie, the bald bigot who half-gassed his girls and then strangled them and kept their corpses in a cupboard, was on the run,' he wrote in March 1953. He described how Christie had rung him up at 11.20 on a Saturday night which would have been perfect for a Sunday paper scoop as no rival would have had enough time to catch up. Christie asked if he recognised his voice and then told him that he was being hunted like a dog and was cold and hungry. He said that if Rae got him a meal and a smoke he could have a story. The deal was that Rae would not alert the police and they duly arranged to meet near the Wood Green town hall clock in north London. It was the dream interview for any reporter and Rae pictured himself calmly interviewing Christie over bacon, eggs, chips and beans and then calling Scotland Yard and saying, 'By the way, if you're looking for Christie, I'll bring him along.'

Alas for Rae, a couple of uniformed coppers happened to be in the area. Christie spotted them, panicked and fled. Two days later he was arrested on a towpath in Putney, south London. When Christie was eventually tried, convicted and hanged in July 1953, just after the Coronation, the paper ran a comprehensive 'Casebook of John Christie', headlined 'He Started Just Like Any Other Innocent Babe.'

Innocent babes were soon in short supply for the murder gang. The climate of crime was changing and, with it, the style of reporting which was now being influenced from the other side of the Atlantic. When Tommy 'Scarface' Smithson was shot dead in 1956, the *Daily Express*'s 'crime bureau' assigned to the story consisted of no fewer than nine reporters. 'With Smithson's death, 1929 Chicago has come to 1956 London,' they reported. There was more: 'now it is guns instead of knives and knuckle-dusters. Now it is death instead of the warning slash of a cut-throat razor.' Smithson worked for the 'Heavy Mob – the elegant gang leaders in £45 suits, handmade shoes, flashing signet rings, with their guards of hatchet-faced henchmen'. The *Mirror* reported that 'a gang of crepe-soled killers climbed quietly up a flight of stairs in a London lodging house. . . in a room at the top of the stairs a young man was shot – murdered Chicago-style.' The *Daily Telegraph* splashed on the story, quoting the police as saying it was 'gang war with the lid off'.

Times were changing for reporters. And newspapers would no longer have the monopoly on reporting on crime.

10

'Mr Murder'

The Man Who Brought Gore to the Airwaves and Screen

Edgar Lustgarten could claim with some justification to be the man who took crime reporting from the printed page to the airwaves and the screen. By the twenty-first century, coverage of crime had been a staple of television for decades but in the 1950s it was still very much the preserve of the printed press and regarded as a rather vulgar subject for the airwaves. Lustgarten was to change that perception.

A debonair barrister and actor manqué turned presenter, his radio programmes at their peak were listened to by six million people and his black-and-white B-movie reconstructions of famous Scotland Yard cases were as much a part of going to the cinema in the post-war years as a choc ice and a Player's Navy Cut in the back stalls. His languid style and purple prose led to many imitators and he also wrote prolifically, both fiction and non-fiction. He represented, too, an era of uncritical deference towards the police. And his own life was touched by its very own bizarre mystery not long before his death.

Born in Manchester in 1907, the only son to a Latvian Jewish barrister father, Edgar Marcus Lustgarten attended Manchester Grammar School and went to St John's College, Oxford where he became the president of the Union in 1930, no mean feat for a young Jewish student at a time when anti-semitism was rife. Fellow student Quintin Hogg, later Lord Hailsham, recalled him as urbane and witty. He followed his father in becoming a barrister on the Manchester circuit in the thirties and his legal background would prove useful and add to his air of theatrical self-confidence.

Turned down for active military service in the Second World War on health grounds, he worked instead, from 1940, on counter-propaganda at the BBC under the name of Brent Wood, a way of disguising his Jewish name. One of his tasks was to mock the Nazi radio propagandist, William Joyce or 'Lord Haw-Haw'.

He wrote two crime novels, *A Case to Answer* (1947), filmed in 1951 as *The Long Dark Hall* with Rex Harrison and Lilli Palmer, and *Blondie Iscariot* (1948), before getting his breakthrough in 1952 with the BBC radio programme *Prisoner at the Bar*. This brought well-known trials to the airwaves for the first time and became a great success, with listening figures that shot up from two to six million within a month. Suddenly the 'forty-five-year-old poker-faced ex-barrister', as he was described at the time, was a household name. While detective fiction was already well established, for the first time it became clear that the British had a vast appetite for true crime.

Lustgarten's fame spread. In 1955, *Time* magazine described him as 'equipped with a sharp legally trained mind and novelist's eye' and a 'top writer in the true crime field.' Other accolades followed, not least an invitation from Roy Plomley to appear in 1957 on the BBC's *Desert Island Discs* radio show. He chose as his luxury a woman's evening gown. He was nicknamed 'Mr Murder'.

At that time, most cinemas showed both a main feature and a shorter film and it was the latter slot that Lustgarten was to fill with his *Scotland Yard Files*. Made by Anglo-Amalgamated and shot at their Merton Park studios in south Wimbledon, the films provide a glorious snapshot of that era of policing and reporting. 'Good morning, super,' one policeman greets his senior officer. In those days, crime news on a screen, either through the BBC on television or Pathé News in cinemas, was treated with greater respect than the daily press. Lustgarten's role, as almost an official police spokesman, was that of the all-knowing crime expert. His much-lampooned Scotland Yard series seems almost like pastiche today.

It was introduced thus: 'London – the greatest city in the world and home of the oldest democracy. A city whose worldwide reputation for honesty and integrity is firmly based on a thousand years of the rule of law, enforced and safeguarded by a police force whose headquarters is as well-known as London itself – Scotland Yard.'

The format was for Lustgarten to talk straight to camera from behind a desk, although he might, on occasion, rise to pour himself a sherry from a decanter. Many of the films, based on actual cases but with names changed, involved a murder, always solved by the Yard's detectives, who had to go to some dark and dangerous places, such as Soho, 'a haunt of some of the city's less desirable characters'. Sometimes he addressed the viewer directly: 'Have you ever murdered anyone? Perhaps you'd rather not say.' The tone was reassuring – Scotland Yard always get their man or woman because 'the murderer always overlooks something'.

But Lustgarten was already out of tune with the times. In one television spoof, Stanley Baxter, imitating Lustgarten, solemnly recounted a case in which many had died from the same cause: 'deadly boredom'. The Lustgarten character claims that his films must have caused the deaths, and vows 'when the doors of Wormwood Scrubs open again, I shall be back to claim further victims with grainy film, pedestrian plots and sluggish direction. Goodnight.' Robbie Coltrane's satire, as 'Edgar Dustcarten', was more savage, portraying him as having a lascivious fascination with the details of murders such as the Limbless Limbo Dancer of Leytonstone and mocking the link with Scotland Yard – 'so called because it is neither in Scotland nor is it a yard'. Indeed, his languid, mannered style now seems comically dated but he was the first person to popularise the detailed reporting of true crime, first on the radio and then on screen.

The journalist and union organiser Peta Van den Bergh knew Lustgarten as a teenager because he worked with her father, the broadcaster Tony Van den Bergh. 'He was very charming, very kind, slightly shy,' she said. 'I used to see him with my father in the Marie Lloyd club (near the BBC) and he was part of a very interesting crew that included Louis MacNeice and lots of other writers. He was, as they all were at that time in the BBC, a heavy drinker, hard-living and hard-working and he had this thing for prostitutes – I remember seeing him once with this very beautiful woman in an expensive mink coat and someone saying "she's actually a tart". It was for all of them a very exciting time because so much of what they were doing was new.'

In 1965, he appeared on the BBC's *Any Questions* and expounded his views on crime and punishment: 'I think the way to deal with crimes of violence is to adopt not kindly treatment, not psychiatric treatment, not investigations into the minds of those that do it, but to treat them with the severity that they used to be treated with and which very often stamped it out.' This was greeted with applause, as was his rider: 'If I may just add, I would say quite unrepentantly . . . I would bring back the whip, I would bring back the birch.'

By the time of his interview with Peter Gillman in the *Sunday Times* in 1975, his views had become even stricter: 'I'm in favour of capital punishment. Secondly, I'm in favour of corporal punishment. Thirdly, I'm in favour of much heavier sentences . . . I am quite convinced that the country is degenerate . . . The degeneracy of Rome I only read about in Gibbon. I've got a front row seat this time – although in a masochistic way I enjoy it.' Gillman later recalled being 'troubled by his moral certainty . . . Everything was black and white, there were no shades or nuances, and he admitted to no doubts about anything. The fact that he dismissed all the notorious capital cases where there were major doubts absolutely reeks of a personal and intellectual arrogance. If there was something murky in his background then that moral absolutism served as a protection against it.'

But despite his support for capital punishment, one case that troubled him was that of Edith Thompson, whom he described as 'the only person in England in this century known to me who has been wrongly hanged'. He was not alone in this view. Thompson had been convicted with her young lover, Freddy Bywaters, of the murder of her husband, Percy, who was stabbed to death by Bywaters in Ilford in 1922. The press played their own part in this case, not least in giving her the tortuous title of 'the Messalina of Ilford', a reference to the promiscuous wife of the Emperor Claudius. Part of the evidence against Thompson was the inclusion in letters to her lover of cuttings from the *Daily Sketch*, *Sunday Pictorial*, *Daily Mail* and *Daily Mirror* describing different methods of killing, from putting ground glass in chocolates to using potassium and cyanide for poisoning. But the evidence against her was slim and there was a feeling that she was being hanged as much for her adultery as for the murder.

Lustgarten's coverage of famous trials was to play its part many years later in a remarkable tale told by film critic Derek Malcolm in his memoir *Family Secrets*. As a schoolboy, Malcolm discovered a copy of Lustgarten's book *The Judges and the Judged* in his father's house in Bexhill-on-Sea with an entire chapter ripped out. The curious young Derek got hold of another copy of the book and found that the missing pages concerned his own father, a lieutenant and First World War hero, who had returned from service overseas to discover that his wife was having an affair with a Russian who called himself a count but was, in fact, plain Anton Baumberg. Lieutenant Malcolm, with some assistance from Scotland Yard, traced the bounder to his lodgings in Paddington and arrived there with a horse-whip and a gun, telling the housemaid who opened the door that he was 'Inspector Quinn of Scotland Yard'. There was an altercation and Malcolm shot Baumberg dead before giving himself up to the police.

Here is how Lustgarten described the case when it reached the Old Bailey: 'Everyone wanted the prisoner to get off. The privileged and breathless company in court, gripping their precious seats from a subconscious fear of losing them; the unlucky and disappointed throng outside, unable to tear themselves away, the unseen multitude . . . devouring each edition of the papers, and then waiting in mingled hope and apprehension for the next one, all devoutly wished Lieutenant Malcolm to go free.' The trial was over in two days and the jury reached their verdict in half an hour. He was found not guilty of either murder or manslaughter. Derek Malcolm described Lustgarten's coverage of the case as 'in the manner of a bad Victorian melodrama'. Indeed, much of Lustgarten's writing was in spectacularly florid prose, a style that would often be adopted by crime writers in the future.

Of the hundreds of cases Lustgarten covered, one had a particular resonance towards the end of his life. In his *Famous Trials* series, in which he would act out the main characters, there is an episode on George Joseph Smith, the Brides in the Bath murderer. Describing how Smith laid his traps, Lustgarten pronounced in classic clipped verbless style: 'Seaside promenade. Country beauty spot. A church. A genteel boarding house. Anywhere that attracted a proportion of young or middle-aged ladies that were unattached and susceptible to gentlemen with smooth manners and bow-ties.' He described how Smith flattered his targets by professing his love for them and proposing marriage. 'He fixes it. He knows the ropes. He fixes the appointment with the registrar. He fixes the legal side. He fixes the honeymoon, with great concern for hygiene. No bath. No good unless I can install one. Finally the doting husband visits her in the bath and finds her lying under the water. Dead.'

Nearly sixty years after the original Brides in the Bath case, a woman was in fact found dead in Lustgarten's own bath. She was a young woman known as Gabrielle Gilbert who it appears he was having a relationship with. She became besotted with him and gradually moved in to his flat. In a fascinating BBC profile on Lustgarten, one of a series called *Radio Lives* broadcast in 1992, the tale unfolded. His loyal Swiss au pair, Trudy, who had looked after him and his wife since 1953, told how she had moved out of the Lustgarten home after Gabrielle's arrival and that he had clearly found Gabrielle a problem and wanted out of the relationship. He would ring Trudy to tell her that he couldn't stand Gabrielle any more and did not know how he had got into the situation.

Trudy told *Radio Lives* that she had been rung by Lustgarten in the middle of the night to tell her that he had come home and found Gabrielle dead in the bath. Trudy sped from her home in Wimbledon to the West

End to find the flat swarming with policemen and Lustgarten behaving irrationally, irritated at the time the police were taking. Lustgarten was prancing around and saying, 'I wish they would get on with it, I want go to bed.' He even suggested to Trudy that she should sleep in Gabrielle's bed, an idea that appalled her. Asked by presenter Jonathan Goodman if she thought it was suicide – after all, this was a case of a woman found dead in the bath of a man who had reported in great detail on how another man had disposed of women in baths – Trudy replied: 'Of course it was suicide.' She said that barbiturates and alcohol had been found in her blood.

The late Peter Underwood, the writer on paranormal affairs with whom Lustgarten shared an interest in notorious murder cases, has written that 'it was all something of a mystery but after her death Lustgarten was never the same and he rarely spoke of her or what had happened. Soon he came down in the world and his flat became dark and murky; his mind was elsewhere.' He embarked on a chaste affair by letter with another woman, to whom he confided that he was lonely and impotent, and who later told the *Daily Mail* that 'he wanted to be virile so that we could be lovers in the true sense of the word.'

On 15 December 1978, he walked from his flat to the Marylebone public library and collapsed, while reading the *Spectator*, and died of a heart attack. He left £8000, some of it to the Lockwood Home of Rest for Donkeys. But while Lustgarten brought murder and mayhem to British radios and screens, his newspaper colleagues in the business of crime were in their pomp.

11
The Sultans of the Newsroom
From the Vice Man to the Prince of Darkness

What is often described as the golden age of crime reporting ran from the end of the Second World War to the abolition of capital punishment in 1965. Newspapers were in their heyday. Circulations were enormous: no fewer that 31 million Sunday newspapers were bought each week in Britain in 1950, an extraordinary average of two per household, compared to 9.9 million sixty years later. The *News of the World*, which specialised in crime, sold eight million copies, its rival, the *Sunday People*, more than five million.

Expenses were generous. Television news was in its infancy. Murders were, compared to the twenty-first century, limited in number, allowing for detailed analysis. The crime reporters of the era included in their number no shortage of characters, some of them already drawn to the public's attention as members of the Murder Gang in *Picture Post*. Smart newspaper editors realised that a high-profile crime man would do wonders for circulation and duly promoted them, so that they were often better known than the villains and detectives whose activities they covered. The editor of the *People*, Sam Campbell, spotted the potential of one young reporter, Duncan 'Tommy' Webb, who had started as an office boy on the *Evening Standard* and soon became the best-known crime reporter of the era.

In his 1955 memoir, *Dead Line for Crime*, Webb spells out his credo: 'It is not easy to obtain facts relating to crime. There is competition in being the first to obtain them. The police want them first. Rival newspapers want them first. The criminal world does not want anyone to have facts about crime. Its very success and existence depends entirely on secrecy, in the concealment of facts.'

Webb was unusual amongst his contemporaries in that he had a wide network of underworld contacts. He lists his main sources as 'informers, tip-off men, Nosy Parkers, traitors of their friends', police officers and members of the public. He makes it clear to his readers that he understands the underworld lingo and goes on to explain that 'the underworld chaps' spoke to him because they trusted him and knew he could not be bought or sold: 'When I walk through Soho, or similar parts of other cities than London, the tea-leaves, the screwsmen, con men, members of the whizz-mob, racecourse gangsters, protectionists, extortionists – and the Heavy Mob, stay on the same pavement. They know what I want.'

He gives his readers intricate details of the 1952 Eastcastle Street post office van robbery, which was as famous in its day as the Great Train Robbery was a decade later. It was masterminded by Billy Hill, whose autobiography Webb later ghosted; Hill was never charged with it. It says a lot about the level of trust that Webb enjoyed in the underworld, that Hill told him intricate details of the robbery that the police would have loved to have had. Webb does not – quite – name Hill as the organiser, just referring to him in his book as 'Bill'. He later relates how said 'Bill' had given him a stack of toys to take to 'some children in whom I am interested'. This gesture, suggested Webb, went to show that crooks were not all bad. 'There's goodness in them somewhere. Sometimes it takes a Big Mailbag Robbery to find it.' Webb thus repaid Hill's trust by portraying him as a big-hearted man, just as future reporters wanting access to the Kray twins would write glowingly of their charitable works.

Vice was now a major source of interest for Sunday newspapers, mixing, as it did, prurience and salaciousness. And Webb was a key figure in exposing the Soho vice rings run by the Messina brothers in the forties and fifties. The Messinas had come to England from Malta – they were known as 'the Epsom Salts' (rhyming slang for 'Malts') – in the 1930s and gradually established a network of brothels, bringing in prostitutes from mainland Europe. For a while, they seemed untouchable: neither the police nor reporters were investigating them – until Webb started looking into them and brought them to public attention.

It was an investigation fraught with dangers and threats. Webb recounted that he had gone to Soho for a meeting with a contact who did not show up and how a speeding car had driven up behind him and 'some inexplicable instinct impelled me to throw myself into the doorway of the shop as I heard the screeching of brakes.' He was trying to read the car's registration number when 'a street-walker came up to me. With a sneer on her lips she said "That was meant for you, deary," and walked away. As though I did not know!'

On another occasion, also in Soho, his car was stolen and as he looked around he was pointed to where it had been moved, a bomb site used as a car park. As he got in he was told not to start the car as there was a knife close to his throat and it might just slip. The voice – 'distinctly a Maltese or Cypriot' – delivered a warning not to carry on with his investigation. 'I uttered one word. It is an old-fashioned basic English word usually applied to an important function in life, and generally used by men when exasperated.'

His editor, Sam Campbell, backed his investigation, even risking the libel laws by publishing pictures of the Messina brothers, under the headline 'ARREST THESE FOUR MEN! They are the emperors of a vice empire in the heart of London'. The exposure of the Messinas, which none of Webb's contemporaries had attempted, was certainly a journalistic coup. Scotland Yard set up a special task force and the Messinas decamped to France, their empire at an end.

It was not the only occasion in his career that Webb faced threats and violence, and he didn't always come out unscathed. On one occasion in 1954, he had his arm broken by Hill's main rival, Jack Spot, whom he had been denigrating in *The People*. Spot was duly convicted of grievous bodily harm and fined £50.

Although he was the lover of Cynthia Hume, who had been married to the notorious murderer Donald Hume, Webb lived alone and supposedly had eight locks on the door of his flat. Underworld figures used to tease him that when Hume was about to be released from jail that he would be coming after him, although, in fact, Hume was more interested in selling his story to a rival paper. Webb was a legendary figure in Fleet Street, and in 1955 *Time* magazine called him 'the greatest crime reporter of our time'.

Another journalist and former editor, the late Bob Edwards, also worked at the *People* at that time, and remembers Webb's approach to investigations, whose 'style was to present "dossiers" – favourite word for the *People* at the time – to the (unimpressed) Home Office'. He also recalled, in his autobiography *Goodbye Fleet Street*, his own encounters with Webb. Edwards once faced the possibility of being charged with contempt of court for offering £1,000 to persuade an alleged phoney spiritualist to plead guilty in a court case. When two Yard detectives arrived at the *People* office, Webb intervened from behind his bullet-proof protected glass desk and told Edwards to leave the matter to him. Two days later Webb told Edwards to go to their local pub, The Enterprise, and watch the proceedings from a distance. 'To my intense shock he carefully handed over a roll of pound notes to one of the detectives so that I would witness the transaction. Nothing was heard of the complaint against me.' A classic example of the mutually beneficial relationship crime reporters could build with the police in those days.

But Webb did not enjoy universal approval. 'They hyped him up at the *People*, with tales of his bullet-proof office and so on but he was much disparaged by several people I knew on the grounds that he was, in fact, living a fantasy all the time,' said Roy Greenslade, the former *Mirror* editor and media commentator who was a young reporter in the East End in the 1960s. 'He used to speak out of the side of his mouth in the patois of the gangs. But he did get stories, he did expose the Maltese gangs.'

Webb's legman for a while was a young Australian, Murray Sayle, who later became a distinguished foreign correspondent. Sayle wrote a novel, *The Crooked Sixpence*, published in 1960, which essentially spilled the beans on Webb's modus operandi. The book included a louche character called

Michael Macedon based on a friend of Sayle's called Michael Alexander, a hard-up toff who thought he could make some easy money by threatening to sue for libel when the book came out. Alexander's ploy misfired and the publishers spinelessly pulped the book. It did not appear again until 2008, after Alexander's death, when Revel Barker republished it with a front page recommendation from Philip Knightley: 'The best book about journalism – ever.'

Webb is disguised in the book as Norman Knight, 'the best crime man in Fleet Street', who gives an Australian ingenue James O'Toole (Sayle) a master-class on reporting on vice. 'The secret of this game is never open your fly,' he tells him helpfully. 'Not on the job that is.' In one prescient episode, Knight/Webb tells his quarry: 'We're fighting vice and rats like you who run it.' To which his victim replies: 'What do you mean, fighting vice? You're selling it, same as me. Don't give me any of that high-and-mighty talk.'

Soho was indeed the honeypot for the crime desk's worker bees, made synonymous with vice and the forbidden. The *Daily Mail*'s crime man, Arthur Tietjen, in his own memoir on Soho, *London's Vicious Circle*, described the regular processing of the area's prostitutes through Bow Street Magistrates' Court, covered routinely by reporters, known as 'the 10.30 a.m. Follies' in which 'every morning appear the dozen or so midnight beauties, whom the street lamps treat gently. But the brisk morning light in the court is harsh and, in spite of their paint and powder and their smart clothes, these women look tawdry and brash.' But he noted that there was no longer a typical prostitute, some of them being 'intelligent women of charm and breeding who have turned to this form of livelihood for the money it earns them'. These *belles de jour* supposedly lived in luxury and holidayed on the Riviera. He described the booming trade of the blackmail of gay men at a time when homosexuality was still illegal and how 'young perverts' were enlisted and trained by a 'modern Fagin' at a blackmail school and then planted in hotels in the West End, where they would seduce their prey, claim it had been a terrible aberration and that they would have to tell their brother. The victim was then squeezed for money. 'The mental torture for the victim – though few will hold a brief for his conduct – then begins. Manacled to the rack he awaits the turn of the wheels.'

Unlike Webb, Tietjen was not one who sought the favour of criminals and was scathing about the fashion for them – like Billy Hill – to pen their memoirs. 'They dropped their razors and picked up their pens to be the first to rush into print and proclaim themselves Gangster, King of Soho,' was how he saw it, appalled that criminals gave long interviews to reporters 'telling how they rose to "power"'. In contrast, he was very supportive of Scotland Yard. 'In my opinion, they are the public's finest bargain in this inflationary era.'

One of the more reflective crime reporters of the time was Harry Procter, who had been inspired by a novel, *The Street of Adventure* by Philip Gibbs, to embark on a career as a journalist when still a teenage errand boy in Leeds. He started as a junior reporter on the *Armley and Wortley News* where his story on the dodgy dealings of a local charity led to advertisers withdrawing their support from the paper. 'I never dreamed then that later on I was to become one of Britain's best-known experts on newspaper exposures and that my name would be feared by every scoundrel and confidence trickster in the land,' he later wrote in his heavy-hearted autobiography, *The Street of Disillusion*.

While Webb made much of the way he was trusted by criminals, Procter recounted in his memoirs how close the press and police could be. When he was investigating the murder of a young Canadian woman in a lonely Kent lane, he contacted the chief constable, Sir Percy Sillitoe, saying he had come across some information that the police might be interested in. Sillitoe introduced him to the head of the investigation, Superintendent Frank Smeed, and they worked on several murder cases thereafter: 'always as good friends, always as a helpful team'. Procter wrote in *Lilliput* magazine, the mildly risqué forerunner of *Playboy*, *Penthouse* and the rest, that, 'When I can't sleep, I don't count sheep, I count the murderers in my life.'

Procter knew Neville Heath, notorious later for his horrific murders of two young women, and first met him in a club off Fleet Street because

'Colonel Heath' had agreed to fly a friend to Copenhagen and Procter had been asked to check his credentials. They got on well and had another drink that evening in the Nag's Head pub in Knightsbridge when Heath received a phone call from his future victim, Marjorie Gardner, to make a date for the following day. The next day Heath killed her in a flat near where Procter lived in Notting Hill. At first it was suggested that Gardner had died as a result of a botched abortion, but Procter met a policeman friend in the Sun in Splendour pub and was told of the whip-marks on her back and the fact that her ankles had been tied up. Because the rest of the press was still claiming that it was an abortion, his news-desk, to Procter's fury, would not run the story; then, as now, cautious news-desks could be wary if their own reporter had a story that differed wildly from every other paper's.

On the run, Heath called Procter, then working at the *Daily Mail*, and asked him to meet him in Surrey with £50. Procter tipped off the Yard and hurried to the meeting place but local police thought that Procter, also quite a handsome man, was Heath and arrested him.

Sean O'Connor, in *Handsome Brute*, his book about Heath, noted that the policeman who cornered Heath, Detective Inspector Reg Spooner, wrote tellingly to his wife: 'The job has done me quite a bit of good and I am getting congratulations from high and low. The press say it is one of the best stories for years.'

Procter also met the acid bath murderer, John George Haigh, just before he was arrested and when he was under suspicion. Haigh told him that the police were 'imbeciles' who had nothing on him. Procter claimed that he responded 'you're a dead pigeon already, Mr Haigh'. Procter believed that crime reporters often knew as much as the police. 'Any good CID man knows it is folly to ignore the Press,' he wrote. 'The crime reporter investigates dozens of murders every year, the CID man in charge perhaps only one.' But he became disillusioned by the increasingly salacious stories he was required to write for the *Sunday Pictorial* and was under pressure from his wife to work for a different kind of newspaper. The breaking-point came he had to cover the suspicious death of the three-year-old Clark twins in a houseboat fire in Benfleet in 1956 and attend their funeral. He decided he had had enough and, with failing health, quit. He died of cancer aged just forty-seven.

Writing many years later on the Gentleman Ranters website, Procter's daughter, Val Lewis, explained that he had been diagnosed as bipolar and the original title of his memoir was to have been *With These Dirty Hands*: 'He was sickened by some of the things he was asked to do by his newspaper. He felt he had sold his soul to the Fleet Street devil.'

But Procter was unusual in his disdain for the job. For most of the Sultans, it was a world of booze and tobacco and camaraderie and cheerfully creative expenses. The crime reporter on the *Daily Telegraph* then was Stanley Firmin, whose memoirs, like Webb's and unlike Procter's, were not plagued by self-doubt. *The Crime Man*, published in 1950, opens thus: 'The voice on the phone was low, clear and direct. It was the voice of my news editor asking the same question I had heard a thousand times after giving my paper the first few brief sentences that meant a new sensational murder case had "broken". "Well, Firmin," said the voice, "What's behind it?" – a question that was being asked by every news editor in Fleet Street of his crime man. A question to which the crime man had to have an answer.'

With crime being such a big seller, the pressure from news-desks on their reporters to come up with ever greater stories and details on crime was now intense and was eventually acknowledged by the police. When Sir Harold Scott became Commissioner of the Metropolitan Police in 1945, he realised that a close relationship with the press was essential not only for assistance in solving crimes by asking, through reporters, for the assistance of the public but also for the image of the Yard. He changed the set-up of the press bureau and had it staffed by police who would feed information to journalists, who in turn formed their own organisation, the Crime Reporters' Association (CRA), the same year. The previous press operation, set up in 1919 by Sir Nevil Macready, had been staffed by civil servants and provided only the most basic of information. Percy Hoskins, the chief crime reporter for the *Daily Express* in the 1950s and president of the CRA, described the new body as 'a group of professional journalists who are to Scotland Yard what the lobby journalists are to the House of Commons – an elite body who can be trusted with confidential information to mutual advantage'.

Firmin describes the benefits of that mutual advantage and also the sacrifices the Crime Man must make and recounts how at any time of the day or night there were always up to a dozen crime reporters in the press room at Scotland Yard. 'These are the aces of the game, the men who have chosen to give up all ideas of a social life and home ties and devote all their time to crime hunting.' Any writer who spent an evening in their company, he suggested, would come away with enough material for a dozen novels.

By this time, Firmin had been a crime reporter for more than twenty-five years and claimed to be telling the story of the crime reporter for the first time. He had no doubt that he was talking about an elite band of journalists who knew more about the psychology of murderers and criminals than the average copper. He lets his reader know that the 'crime man' was on call for twenty-four hours a day seven days a week and he spells out the intimate details of what this dedication involves: 'the crime man sleeps with the telephone at his bedside. The bell may – and often does – ring and bring its summons in the middle of the night. The crime man's wife – and most of them are married men – soon gets resigned to that, and to seeing her husband, awaked after a couple of hours sleep, leaving the house on a trip into the country that might last weeks.'

Firmin seemed to have had good luck with helpful quotes from his subjects. He reports on one murderer, Abraham Goldenberg, who was being held in a rural police station but allowed to exercise in a place from which Firmin was able to grab a photo of him for his paper. Goldenberg happily posed for the shots and told him helpfully: 'Now mind you send me a copy of the best one – I want to hang it in Hell.'

Dirty tricks were sometimes employed. Firmin admits to a sly admiration for a colleague who pulled off a remarkable stunt during a murder inquiry near the Blackwall Tunnel in London. He bought a cheap handkerchief, pricked his finger, soaked some of his blood onto the hankie and left it in the tunnel where a passer-by would find it and hand it to the police. Then he was able to run a story about 'the clue of the bloodstained handkerchief'. Firmin wrote that such conduct was indefensible, but felt that the story demonstrated 'the quality of initiative and enterprise that the present-day crime men have, so to speak, inherited'.

Another of the larger-than-life crime men of the time was Percy Hoskins, the 17-stone *Daily Express* crime man, who died in 1989 aged eighty-four. Hoskins achieved his greatest fame through his defence of Dr John Bodkin Adams, whose career had many similarities to that of Dr Harold Shipman – convicted in 2000 of the murder of fifteen of his patients, but widely believed to have killed more than 250. Adams, who was based in Eastbourne, was the beneficiary of 132 wills which allowed him to indulge an extravagant lifestyle of Rolls-Royces and antiques. He was widely suspected of killing off his patients for their inheritances. He was arrested in 1956, tried at the Old Bailey the following year and acquitted.

Hoskins believed that Adams was innocent and went out on a limb to support him. After the verdict, the *Express*'s owner, Lord Beaverbrook, called Hoskins to tell him that 'two men were acquitted,' meaning that Hoskins had been vindicated. Adams then spent two weeks holed up in a hotel with Hoskins for an *Express* exclusive. It has been suggested that Hoskins may have been partly motivated in his support for Adams by his dislike of the investigating detective, Herbert 'Bert' Hannam, known as 'The Count' at Scotland Yard, not least for his snappy dress sense. When Adams died in 1983, he left Hoskins £1,000 of his £400,000 fortune, which the latter, somewhat embarrassed, gave to charity.

Hoskins wrote a book on the case, using Beaverbrook's supportive words as its title. When Scotland Yard went through the Adams file many years later, they found that he was suspected of killing 163 of his patients. Hoskins went on to present a forerunner of *Crimewatch*, called *It's Your Money They're After*, in cooperation with Scotland Yard. He enjoyed the support of Beaverbrook in other ways: he had a grace and favour residence at 55 Park Lane, where he entertained senior police officers some of whom, so rumour had it, came to the house to relax with their secretaries.

Another of the Sultans was Tom Tullett, a legendary figure who worked for the *Sunday Express*, *Sunday Pictorial* and *Daily Mirror* after serving with distinction in the war. Born in 1915, the son of a policeman, he had an early career in the CID at Scotland Yard, during which he received seven commendations.

Roy Greenslade recalled of an occasion in the early 1960s when he himself was a young reporter: 'I remember covering a case in Dagenham, a young girl had been murdered by her neighbour. I went down to the local nick and, like other local paper reporters, wasn't allowed in, but in strode Tom Tullett, accompanied by two cops, and he just simply walked past the rest of the press. I heard my colleagues whisper, "That's Tom Tullett, that's the man." This was an era in which the football reporters were more important than the players, and crime reporters were treated like that, too.'

Tullett, like many of his colleagues, wrote a number of books with or about the police, including *Portrait of a Bad Man*, *Strictly Murder* and *No Answer From Foxtrot Eleven*, about the shooting dead of three officers by Harry Roberts and others in west London in 1966. He was also involved in what must be one of the most gruesomely remarkable events in the life of any crime reporter.

On 11 September 1961, Tullettt was in the *Mirror*'s office and was due to give a talk at an official lunch arranged by his boss, Hugh Cudlipp. He received a call from reception telling him that a young man wanted to see him urgently. The man was Edwin Sims who told Tullett that the previous day he had strangled two sixteen-year-olds, Lilian Edmeades and Malcolm Johnson, in the marshes near Gravesend in Kent. To prove this, he produced their wristwatches and a parcel. Inside the parcel were the female victim's breasts. Tullett immediately called the police and Sims was arrested, convicted of manslaughter on the grounds of diminished responsibility and jailed for twenty-one years. The story entered *Mirror* folklore; sometimes it is told with a hand or even a head in the parcel.

His daughter, Susie Tullett, recalled that her father, who died in 1991, had very friendly relationships with many senior detectives and as a child she referred to her father's closest friend, the legendary Detective Superintendent John Gosling, as 'Uncle John'; Tullett appears alongside Gosling on the cover of the latter's memoir, *The Ghost Squad*. Of her father she said: 'He was very fair, and very honest. I always loved the fact that he left the police force because he said he couldn't bear to go on arresting women who stole to feed their families.' He covered many murder cases, she said, but was vehemently opposed to the death penalty although he admitted it was a powerful deterrent. 'Tom was an institution,' said journalist Phil Mellor, who worked as a young reporter with Tullett. 'In those halcyon days you could talk to the police and they all knew Tom.' He recalled Tullett's rapport with the police: 'you would go into the Stab (the White Hart, the *Mirror*'s local, nicknamed the Stab in the Back) and see him with a lot of big gentlemen, all coppers.'

Many of the Sultans had individual detectives with whom they were particularly close. The *Telegraph*'s Tom Sandrock, who died in 2004 aged eighty-three, covered the hanging of Ruth Ellis, the Great Train Robbery and the disappearance of the Labour MP John Stonehouse. He had a particular rapport with Detective Superintendent Reg Spooner of the Flying Squad, who would brief his officers in a corner of the St Stephen's dive bar, off Whitehall, and would then tell Sandrock which stories he could print. As his obituary in his old paper recalled, if Sandrock was drinking with detectives when they received a tip-off, he would sometimes be enrolled as a supernumerary driver to take them to the scene of the crime. He was criticised by some as being something of a PR man for the police, but, said the *Telegraph*, 'He remained adamant that the entire force was not corrupt, and was highly critical of the tendency to glamorise crooks.'

Drinking was a common theme among the crime reporters, and one who was a regular of El Vino was Bill Driscoll, sometimes known as Derek Driscoll. In many ways he was the template for the Lunchtime O'Booze character in *Private Eye*, the magnificently unprincipled and drunken Fleet Street hack caricature. His CV included most of Fleet Street's papers but it is clear that he did not always take his calling as a crime reporter quite seriously enough. He was sacked for beginning one story about a Leicestershire murder: 'they called him the gold-haired Adonis of the Market Harborough smart set.'

When capital punishment was abolished and there was less call for crime reporters, he moved into gossip. With money troubles he moved to Addis Ababa and became William O'Driscoll, getting an Ethiopian friend to return all missives from the Inland Revenue, 'due to decease of addressee on the envelope'.

He was an all-round colourful character, who created an exotic back-story for himself in which he claimed to be of Prussian origin and to have fought on both sides in the German-Russian war, as well as being the first mate on a rice ship in the South China Sea. The truth, which only emerged after his death at the age of sixty-seven in 1992, was more prosaic, as his obituary in the *Daily Telegraph* made clear. His father was not a professor of logic at Heidelberg but a Fleet Street printer, although his war history proved difficult to clarify, whether he had been Ribbentrop's jailer before Nuremberg, fought in the Ardennes or simply been discharged on psychological grounds.

One of the few still practising the trade in the eighties and known by everyone, from fellow reporters to judges, as the 'Prince of Darkness', was Jimmy Nicholson. There are various stories as to how he came by his name. The version he told himself was that, while reporting on covens in the Isle of Man, he was given a black cape which became his trademark outfit. At the Balcombe Street siege in London in1975, at which IRA men had taken hostages, a senior police officer spotted him and remarked that 'That devil Nicholson is here.' Someone suggested that perhaps he was not the devil but the Prince of Darkness. The name stuck. Another version, told by colleagues, suggests that the name was given to him during the slightly earlier Spaghetti House siege – in which black militant robbers held restaurant staff hostage for six days – when a colleague spotted him holding his cape as if about to fly from a hotel balcony and pronounced: 'Fuck me – it's the Prince of Darkness.'

'I suppose I helped to create the bloody monster,' Nicholson said later of the name. 'It's become a bit of burden.' Even judges referred to him as 'prince'. He tried to alter the image once, arriving dressed entirely in white for the 1976 murder trial of Donald Neilson, the so-called Black Panther, but the name had firmly stuck.

Famous for addressing senior police officers with a cheery 'Hello, big noise' and for having 'covered every siege since Troy' and 'been on more doorsteps than a milk bottle', Jimmy Nicholson was, as he might himself have said, a legend in his own lunchtime, a larger-than-life character who epitomised the larky side of that lost era of Fleet Street crime reporting and the days of Fleet Street's heavy drinking and smoking. His curriculum vitae included almost every tabloid of the present and recent past, and he continued working well into his eighties, slipping cheerily onto the press benches at the Old Bailey as a jury came back with a verdict, or holding forth in the basement press room.

From Batley in Yorkshire, his first reporting task was to cover funerals for the *Batley News* and he credited the experience of dealing with the bereaved as good training for his later life as a crime correspondent. His first big crime case was in the north; a Salvationist called Louisa Merrifield, who poisoned her landlady and was hanged for it by Albert Pierrepoint, Britain's official hangman for many years, and with whom Nicholson became friendly. Eight years of covering 'fish and chip murders' in Blackpool ended and Fleet Street beckoned when he came up with an exclusive about George Formby's will, who had left everything to his young fiancée and nothing to his family. Nicholson's first big national story was on James Hanratty, executed for the 'A6 Murder' in 1962 and the subject of a number of books questioning his guilt. For the *Daily Sketch*, Nicholson reported on the Moors Murders; the murderer Ian Brady complained about his coverage to the then Press Council, but did not pursue the matter, instead sending Nicholson a 'wish you were here' Christmas card from Parkhurst prison.

He was an expert 'buy-up' man, persuading people to tell their story for a fabled cheque, often knowing full well that his paper would not come through with the promised cash. 'I used to lie, I'm afraid,' he confessed later. 'Got to meet fire with fire.' The practice of offering large payments, which are then rarely paid, to victims of crime or relatives of criminals, continues to this day. Money was also available for those acquitted of a high-profile crime: in 1990, after the boxer Terry Marsh was cleared of the attempted murder of boxing promoter Frank Warren, bidding for his story took place in a Greek restaurant in Stratford, east London, with a joint *Sun/News of the World* offer of an estimated £140,000 defeating the *Mirror/People* competition. Nicholson defended the practice of knocking on the doors of the bereaved: 'After a horrific murder, people want to talk to you. If they're guilty, I've had people rehearse their story to me before they speak to the police. You go in and say, "James Nicholson, crime reporter. I'd like to talk to you." In a lot of circumstances, you have to put your foot in the door.'

Nicholson was actually given his break in Fleet Street by another crime reporter, George Hollingbery, who had met him on the Moors Murders case in the 1960s and been impressed by his tenacity and lack of deference towards authority. Hollingbery, who was born in 1929 and worked for the *Evening News* and then the *Sun*, decided that the crime beat was for him when he saw the *News* crime reporter setting off to cover an out-of-town murder. 'I thought – that's for me!' It was Hollingbery who designed the Crime Reporters' Association tie – crossed quill pen and handcuffs.

As in the past, executions had to be covered even if no longer observed in the flesh. 'You would go down to the prison and there would be almost riots,' Hollinbery goes on. 'There was this anti-hanging woman, Mrs Van der Elst, who would be there with a big hat and all the prisoners would have these aluminium plates and would bang them against the bars, shouting and screaming. There were mounted police outside. It was a big story, that would be the splash of the day.' Mrs Van der Elst was an eccentric who devoted much of her life to campaigning against the death penalty – and providing copy for crime reporters, for whom she was a sort of early Lord Longford, well-meaning but daft. A millionairess, through a shaving cream fortune, she would arrive by Rolls-Royce outside a prison's gates on the day of a hanging and address the crowds with a loudhailer.

Many crime reporters of this era noted what a difference the abolition of the death penalty had on their trade. A former editor of the *Evening News*, Lou Kirby, once told me that one of the reasons for the decline of sales of the London evening papers in the 1970s was that reports of murder trials could no longer conclude with a judge solemnly donning his black cap and telling a defendant that he was about to be taken from that place and hanged by the neck until he was dead.

Away from London on murder tales, Hollingbery often found himself having to help out colleagues who were the worse for wear. 'I have slept in a bath when the hotel or pub didn't have enough beds and put over stories knowing a chap was blind drunk in his room. I would shake and shake him and if I couldn't wake him up, having put my story over, I then would say to the copy-taker for the opposition: "I'm putting this over for so-and-so because he's suddenly been called out." We all did it.'

Indeed they did. Revel Barker records in his memoir, *The Last Pub in Fleet Street*, a tale about the late *Mirror* journalist, Bill Marshall, who had been covering a murder in Manchester and drinking so heavily with a colleague from the *Mail* that he passed out. The *Mail* reporter, Sean Bryson, having filed his own report, very decently rang over a story on Marshall's behalf. The next morning he was confronted by an agitated Marshall brandishing a copy of the *Mirror* open at the story about the murder under his own by-line. The ungrateful Marshall told his saviour: 'See this, arsehole? Don't ever tell me I can't write a story when I'm pissed!'

Hollingbery described his technique for covering major trials. 'I would talk to witnesses outside the courtroom. If it was a woman, I would give her a lovely warm smile and say, "It's so kind of you to talk to us". Then I would begin asking questions very slowly and, if I noticed she was getting worried, I would change the subject and gradually get what I wanted. We used to wait for the jury to come back in the Magpie and Stump (sometimes known as Courtroom Number 10, the pub across the road from the Old Bailey). The guv'nor used to allow us to use the upstairs bar and by the time the jury came back we were all blind drunk so we would go flying across the road. Sometimes the judge was already there and would look very crossly at us.'

The more leisurely coverage of trials in those days, when it was only necessary to file for a newspaper deadline, gave reporters a chance to tap detectives, lawyers or relatives of the accused in the lunch hours and adjournments to glean background details. That all changed with the arrival of the internet and twenty-four-hour news coverage.

Hollingbery recalled one of his contemporaries, Peter Earle, a wonderfully colourful reporter, being asked by a woman how she could be sure he was from the *News of the World*, to which he replied 'Madam, I'm admitting it!' One of Earle's big stories was the Richardson gang torture case in which Charlie Richardson was jailed in 1967 for twenty-five years, the highest sentence ever passed for grievous bodily harm. He and his associates were convicted of torturing people who crossed them or owed them money. Earle's paper described him as 'the reporter who helped bring them to justice'.

Earle recounted at the end of the Old Bailey trial: 'Charlie Richardson has a chest like a barrel and eyes that are strangely yellow, almost like a cat's . . . he turned those yellow eyes on me, and glared. For Charlie Richardson hates me.' He claimed that Richardson had put a £1,000 bounty on his head to silence him and that he had then phoned Richardson to taunt him with the words 'I didn't think you'd do it yourself, Charlie.' He suggested that, after the *News of the World* reported the price on his head, the police came round and asked them to 'lay off' Richardson because he was getting in the way of the investigation on the grounds that 'if the gangsters dare threaten a crime reporter of the biggest newspaper in the world, what chance had the police of expecting ordinary people to come forward.' Earle wrote that he had persuaded some of his underworld contacts to give evidence against Richardson.

A temporary member of the Sultans' club was Victor Davis, who later specialised in show business. He wrote in the *British Journalism Review* in 2004 that 'of my varied jobs in Fleet Street, crime proved the most exhilarating. I loved it so. The car chases, the thick-ear gangsters with their own sub-Runyon language, the dopey tarts, the joy in being one jump ahead of the opposition, the outrageous confidence tricks, wickedly giving witnesses the impression they were talking to a welfare worker, a lawyer, probation officer or the like, to get at the heart of the story.' While he loved the louche company, he realised early on that he lacked one vital qualification for a life as a full-time crime reporter – the ability to drink vast quantities of alcohol and still be able to file his copy. He recalled arriving at murder scenes to find all the big names already there – Hoskins, Tietjen, Foster and others – because they, unlike Davis, knew the senior investigating officers well. However, he reckoned that this actually gave him advantages in that the 'big names' were obliged to stick to the line handed down by their very senior contacts while he could create mischief.

And it was true that the relationship between crime reporter and police officer in this period was extremely close. Peter Burden, who died in 2015, was the crime correspondent for the *Daily Mail* for more than twenty-five years, and explained in his memoir, *How I Changed Fleet Street*, that detectives trusted crime reporters implicitly and were entertained accordingly. 'They knew the sources of their stories (relayed over beers, purchased by reporters) would never be disclosed,' he wrote. 'I decided that, while the official information was vital, this pub scenario was not the life for me.' Instead he took senior officers to upmarket restaurants like Manzi's in the West End. Burden became the first – and almost certainly the last – crime correspondent to be awarded the OBE for services to crime journalism and crime prevention. He had a major role in helping the police introduce media blackouts during kidnaps so that kidnappers would not know that the police were already onto them.

In the sign-off to his memoirs, Stanley Firmin pondered that crime would always be with us but was consoled by the fact that Britain had the finest police force in the world, 'and there are the crime men and their newspapers, always at the service of the public in the ceaseless fight against those who prefer to break the laws rather than tread the ways of honest men'. But not long after Firmin's book was published, one of his own crime reporter colleagues would be charged with breaking the law and would fight the charge by arguing, in effect, that he was treading the path of an honest man.

12

Silent Men and Scapegoats

Looking at the Dock from the Other Side

Although the jailing of W. T. Stead of the *Pall Mall Gazette* in 1885 for his actions in exposing child prostitution had caused a national uproar, journalists would continue to fall foul of the law over the way they reported on crime in subsequent centuries. The reasons for their arrests varied greatly but all raised ethical issues.

Sylvester Bolam, editor of the *Daily Mirror*, was jailed for three months in 1949 and his paper fined £10,000 for contempt of court because of coverage of the arrest of John George Haigh, the acid bath murderer. Crime reporters had already been heavily tipped off by the police that Haigh was the murderer but, with a trial in the offing, had to be wary of identifying him too obviously. The *Daily Mirror*, competing heavily against the *Daily Express* and their man with the inside track, Percy Hoskins, went just too far. Under the headline 'The Vampire Confesses', their story clearly implicated Haigh. There were objections from the police as soon as the first editions appeared and the story was watered down but not enough to avoid a criminal charge.

Bolam had to appear in front of the famously fierce Lord Chief Justice, Lord Goddard, who described the publication as 'scandalous and wicked' and added the story had been run 'not as an error of judgment, but as a matter of policy, pandering to sensationalism for the purpose of increasing the circulation of this paper'. Soon afterwards, Bolam was on his way to Brixton prison in a taxi, sentenced to three months in jail.

As Roy Greenslade recounts in his book *Press Gang*, 'the reference to sensationalism bit hard, because Bolam had famously lauded the concept months before in a description of the genre which had never been bettered. In a *Mirror* leader, he wrote: "We believe in the sensational presentation of news and views, as a necessary and valuable public service . . . Sensationalism does not mean distorting the truth. It means the vivid and dramatic presentation of events so as to give them a forceful impact on the mind of the reader."' Bolam's jailing led to no outcry about threats to the freedom of the press, probably because people thought that he had indeed overstepped the mark. He died not long after, aged only forty-eight.

A much more controversial case was that of the so-called 'Silent Men'. In 1963, Reg Foster, the crime reporter of the *Daily Sketch*, and Brendan Mulholland of the *Daily Mail*, were jailed for contempt of court. They had refused to reveal their sources for stories they had written about the sexual peccadillos of John Vassall, who had been convicted the previous year of being a Soviet spy.

Vassall, who was gay when homosexuality was still illegal in Britain, worked as a clerk at the British embassy in Moscow in the 1950s and was targeted by Soviet agents. He was photographed having sex with a number of men, after being plied with plum brandy, and blackmailed into agreeing to supply information when he continued his work as an Admiralty clerical officer back in London. He was eventually caught, charged with espionage, pleaded guilty and sentenced to eighteen years.

His case received wide press coverage at the time and was deeply embarrassing to the government. After Vassall's conviction, Foster and Mulholland wrote that he was known to buy women's clothes and was called 'Aunty' by colleagues. The *Sketch* wanted to know, 'Why did the spy-catchers fail to notice Vassall who sometimes wore women's clothes on West End trips?'

In the *Sketch*, which folded in 1971, Foster, along with Peter Burden and Desmond Clough, also went into detail about Vassall. Mention was made of his ability to avoid games at his Monmouth public school (fees £201 a year) by having a record number of colds and sprains. His former headmaster recalled him as 'colourless and rather effeminate'. The conclusion was that 'by day, Vassall was still the office toady, by night the big shot from Whitehall who liked to spend the evening in the West End haunt of perverts'.

In an article entitled 'Epitaph for a Spy', in the *Mail* on 23 October 1962, Mulholland and fellow reporters Alfred Draper and Gilbert Lewthwaite, described Vassall as a 'fawning mediocrity', who had 'flunked a moral leadership course in Belgium'. The article spelled out the strange life of a £15-a-week Admiralty clerk who could afford a £10-a-week Dolphin Square flat, which supposedly had a Persian carpet, Queen Anne tallboy and antique writing desk. They quoted a 'girl typist' at the Admiralty who reckoned that no clerk on his wage could possibly live the way he did by honest means. The article suggested he had nineteen Savile Row suits and nearly a hundred ties, ordered his sherry from Bond Street and dined regularly at Simpson's on the Strand.

In the wake of the scandal, an inquiry, chaired by Lord Radcliffe, was set up into the affair by Prime Minister Harold Macmillan, whose government had been badly damaged by the case. The inquiry asked Foster to tell them who had informed him that Vassall bought women's clothes in the West End. Foster clenched his fists and delivered an impassioned speech to Lord Radcliffe: 'My lord, with the greatest respect – and I mean that – you ask me to do something which is beyond my conception of ethics and principles. To tell you who gave me that information would mean committing an act of treachery on my part. It would be unfair to myself and untrue to myself.' He continued: 'I have been in journalism for forty years. From the first I was taught always to respect sources of information. I have always done that. In that time most of us have been involved in two world wars. I lost a number of close Fleet Street colleagues in places like Singapore, the Middle East and Europe and I would feel guilty of the greatest possible treachery to them if I were to assist . . . in this matter.' Mulholland also refused to divulge his sources. They were jailed for contempt, Foster for three months and Mulholland for six. A third reporter, Desmond Clough, also of the *Sketch*, faced prison too, but was cleared when an admiralty press officer came forward and identified himself as his source.

The jailed pair, who became known in the press as 'The Silent Men', enjoyed great support right across Fleet Street and from the National Union of Journalists. The jailing raised the issue of how far a journalist should be prepared to go to keep his or her word, and was widely portrayed as a threat to free speech. Both men emerged from prison, reputations enhanced, to resume their careers.

There the case rested until three books published more than forty years later reopened it. *An English Affair: Sex, Class and Power in the Age of Profumo* by the historian Richard Davenport-Hines was published in 2013 and challenged the received wisdom. 'They went to prison masquerading as martyrs in the sacred cause of press freedom,' wrote Davenport-Hines of Mulholland and Foster, 'but the truth is that they did not want to admit that they were liars who had invented their stories.' The reference to Mulholland provoked an angry response from the *Daily Mail*, which ran an article headlined: 'Sex, lies and the smearing of a brave man: why is a historian blackening the name of this *Mail* reporter who went to jail rather than betray a source?' It quoted a friend and former colleague of Mulholland, Graham Lord, who was adamant that he had not invented his story.

Another book, *When Reporters Cross the Line* by Stewart Purvis and Jeff Hulbert, re-examined the case in greater detail, noting that there were 'whispers in Fleet Street' at the time that the stories were invented. Purvis and Hulbert wrote that veteran Fleet Street crime reporter Rodney Hallworth, who later worked with Brendan Mulholland at a news agency in Devon, came to the view that the men had made up at least some of the facts. And in *The Remarkable Lives of Bill Deedes*, published in 2009, Stephen Robinson took the same view, writing that 'Fleet Street puffed itself into a scandalised offence at this encroachment of the freedom of the press although most journalists privately thought that their overheated accounts of sex parties were largely, if not entirely, fictitious'. But Alfred Draper, of the *Daily Express*, who knew both men, backed their version of events. 'The public in general believed the press had got its comeuppance for fabricating stories,' he wrote in *Scoops and Swindles*. 'I personally knew Brendan's and Reg's source of information for much of what they had written and if they had taken the easy way out and named him there would have been a far greater scandal.'

When Foster, by all accounts a charming and entertaining character, died in 1999, at the age of ninety-five, there were many affectionate tributes. Matthew Engel, in an addendum to the *Guardian* obituary, quoted Foster's recollections of old Fleet Street thus: 'Someone might find a bloodstained garter in a ditch,' reminisced Foster, 'marvellous story, but no relevance at all to the investigation . . . There was a certain amount of freedom of expression. I think I'd better leave it like that.' Engel continued: 'This was the background that produced his reporting of the Vassall case, when he may have had a genuine scoop, or may just have used his freedom of expression. I think we had better leave it like that.' Roy Greenslade also spoke to Foster not long before his death and says that he remained adamant that the story was true. 'Reg did stick to his guns,' said Greenslade. 'He was, by the time I met him, rather infirm but he regarded the jailing as the high point of his journalistic career. He had done something principled.' And the former *Daily Telegraph* crime correspondent John Weeks said of him, 'He was a very straight fellow. I heard that his main informant, rather than have him sent to prison, said "I will tell them it's me" but Reg said no. He did have a source and he protected him and gallantly went to prison.'

Other journalists fell foul of the law in other ways. In the mid-seventies, the hierarchy at the Met were unhappy about officers either selling or passing over police photos or information about arrests. In May 1976, John Ponder, chief crime correspondent of the *Evening Standard*, found himself in the dock. He was charged with dishonestly handling police photos and inducing an officer to commit a breach of discipline after he had received pictures of three men charged with murder.

The circumstances were that he had received photos of the three men accused of the murder of 'Ginger' Marks, a minor crook killed in 1965 and whose body was either set in concrete or buried in a 'civilian' coffin by a bent undertaker, depending on which version you wanted to believe. Ponder had been given photos of the three men by a police officer and had passed them on to a larger-than-life Fleet Street news agency man, Tommy Bryant, who specialised in crime tales and had himself been charged with and acquitted of a similar offence less than a year earlier. Bryant was something of a Scotland Yard bogeyman; he and John Elgar of *Lambeth News* would listen to the police radio, which was not illegal, and would be first on the scenes of crime, chatting to the detectives, much to the chagrin of the Yard hierarchy.

Ponder refused to reveal his source, but became depressed during the long period between his arrest and trial, and shot himself in the thigh, not fatally, but causing permanent damage. He was found not guilty and said afterwards: 'I believe I was a scapegoat and I was used to stop the long-accepted system of police officers and journalists sharing confidential relationships.' Ponder, sacked by the *Standard*, suggested that his prosecution was part of a police strategy to control all information and 'a move towards what I find abhorrent – a police state'.

Other members of the fourth estate who found themselves in the dock in the 1970s tended to work for publications outside the mainstream – *International Times*, *Oz*, *Nasty Tales*, *Gay News* and *Time Out* – and certainly did not receive the fulsome support of Fleet Street that was offered to Foster and Mulholland. The crimes that they were accused of were a reflection of the mores of the time and most of the trials would not take place today: *IT* was prosecuted for running contact ads for gay men; *Oz* for conspiracy to corrupt public morals by publishing a scatological 'Skoolkids' issue; *Nasty Tales* for obscenity, for running cheerfully explicit cartoons; *Gay News* for blasphemy, for publishing a poem about Christ on the cross; and *Time Out* under the Official Secrets Act, in the wake of its revelations about the existence and activities of GCHQ.

Perhaps not coincidentally, most of those publications had been highly critical of the police for different reasons. One of the journalists prosecuted and acquitted against the odds, Mick Farren of *Nasty Tales*, told the

Old Bailey jury that 'it seemed from where we were in the underground press that being raided by the police was almost a fact of life, like rain.' The *Oz* case was of particular, if tangential, interest for crime reporters: writing about it for the *Spectator* in its 31 July 1971 edition, Tony Palmer suggested that those covering the trial included 'regular crime reporters [who] coughed and spluttered their beer-sodden way through a summer's day'. This drew an angry riposte from the Crime Reporters' Association and four of those who covered the trial sued the magazine for libel and won 'substantial damages' for what their barrister described as an 'an extremely unattractive attack'.

Journalists who have refused to divulge their sources since the Foster–Mulholland case, have tended not to go to prison, although in 1972 the BBC reporter Bernard Falk was held for four days in the cells in Crumlin Road jail in Belfast for refusing to identify an IRA man in the dock as the source of his story. In 1988, the *Independent* journalist Jeremy Warner was fined £20,000 in a case brought under the 1986 Financial Services Act for refusing to divulge his sources in a story about purported insider trading by civil servants. 'Parliament in a democratic free society lays down what is the law and what must be done,' the judge, Sir Nicolas Browne-Wilkinson, told Warner. 'Journalists are no more entitled to say they do not comply with it than anybody else.' Asked by the judge if he thought journalists were 'above the law', Warner – who later moved to the *Daily Telegraph* and whose stance received wide support – responded that while they were not above the law, reporters 'feel they must adopt the principle of confidentiality throughout their dealings with people and must suffer the consequences if, as a result, they are brought into conflict with the courts'. The judge sensibly decided that he was not going to risk 'the creation of a martyr' by jailing Warner and imposed a £20,000 fine instead.

Judges have considerable powers to deal with members of the press whom they feel are not respecting the trial process. A famous photo was illicitly taken of Dr Crippen and Le Neve in the dock when they appeared in Bow Street Magistrates' Court in 1910. Such photos were taken with a camera hidden under a hat and the sound of the shutter obscured by a loud cough. In order to combat any spread of the practice, the 1925 Criminal Justice Act was introduced, banning photography or the sketching of a judge, juror or a witness. At the time, the maximum penalty was a £50 fine but anyone taking a photo nowadays could expect to be prosecuted for contempt of court and could face jail; in 2011, teenager Paul Thompson was jailed for two months at Luton Crown Court for taking a photo with his BlackBerry from the public gallery.

The ban on photography means that our view of trials comes courtesy of court artists, whose work often appears on television and in the press during major trials. They are not allowed to draw in court but must make notes and then retreat to the press room to make their illustration. Julia Quenzler, the queen of the court artists, whose work appears frequently as part of the BBC's coverage of trials, said that rules forbidding any actual sketching in court are still strictly enforced. A self-taught artist whose career began drawing portraits in Beverly Hills night-clubs and covering trials for CBS news, Quenzler recalled covering a horrific double murder trial in San Diego during which the defendant turned to her and asked: 'Are you getting my best side?'

So if the cases of Foster, Mulholland and Ponder had shone a light on reporters and their sources, what about their relationships with criminals?

13
Getting Away With Murder
Reporters and Criminals

Three intriguing ethical issues have arisen historically from the relationship between reporters and criminals: should money ever be paid to those convicted of a crime; should a reporter ever betray a criminal source to the police; and should a criminal's nationality, race or religion ever be a significant part of a report?

In 1910, Dr Hawley Harvey Crippen was hanged for the murder of his wife but, apart from being famous as the first person to be arrested as a result of wireless communication, he also played a part in the history of crime reporting. The captain of the SS *Montrose* recognised his fugitive passenger, who was en route to Canada with his lover Ethel Le Neve, disguised as a boy, because he had seen his picture in the *Daily Mail*. And while Crippen was awaiting execution, his slippery lawyer, Arthur Newton, offered his 'confession' to the *Evening Times* for £1,000. More than a century later, the issue of whether money should be paid for such stories continues.

The *Evening Times* ran the story despite concerns about the authenticity of the confession and Edgar Wallace, who was then on its staff, wrongly claimed to have 'unimpeachable authority' that it was genuine. Sales doubled but, when no proof emerged (and it never did), rival papers mocked the confession as false and the *Evening Times* folded not long afterwards. The magazine *John Bull*, then edited by Horatio Bottomley MP, who put up money for Crippen's defence and was a friend of Newton, ran a letter that was supposedly the confession from the condemned doctor but that also was a fake. And Ethel Le Neve, who was acquitted of being an accessory, had her own dealings with the press after the trial: the *Daily Chronicle* bought her story and it was serialised in their sister publication *Lloyd's Weekly Newspaper*, for whom she posed in the boy's clothes she had worn as her disguise in the flight to Canada. Her story was ghosted by Philip Gibbs, author of the Fleet Street novel *The Street of Adventure*.

Nearly half a century later, in 1953, crime reporter Harry Procter was at the high-spending *Sunday Pictorial* where one of his roles was as a 'buy-up' specialist, persuading people to sell their stories or family photos for money. In his sights was John Reginald Christie, who was about to be hanged for the murder of seven women. In order to secure Christie's story, the paper agreed to pay for his defence, a not uncommon way at the time for crime reporters to gain the inside story. There was competition. The *Sunday Dispatch*'s reporter, James Reid, also told Christie that his paper would pay for his defence in exchange for his exclusive story, but Procter had already done the deal. One can only imagine the furore in the twenty-first century if newspapers were fighting each other for the privilege of hiring a top team of barristers to defend a clearly guilty serial killer of women.

Procter's involvement in the case had started in 1949 when he first met Christie, the landlord of 10 Rillington Place, in Notting Hill, west London. He had gone to the house in the wake of what seemed like a routine murder case, that of Beryl Evans, who had lodged there with her husband, Timothy, and their baby daughter, Geraldine. According to the police, Timothy Evans had already confessed and was clearly guilty. As a witness, Christie put on a convincing show of the shocked and distressed landlord, even weeping as he gave evidence. Perhaps understandably, the jury and press believed the word of the ingratiating landlord and former special constable with the War Reserve Police against that of the semi-literate Welshman. Evans was hanged at Pentonville prison in March 1950. Three years later another of Christie's lodgers stumbled across the bodies of three women in a papered-over cupboard and a fresh investigation was launched, leading to the discovery of the other four bodies. This time Christie admitted the killings but pleaded insanity as a defence. He was convicted and hanged from the same scaffold as Evans had been. The case became a cause célèbre as a miscarriage of justice.

Not long after this Christie controversy, on 1 June 1958, the *Sunday Pictorial* – 'the newspaper for the young in heart', as its masthead proclaimed – had what was, by any standards, quite a front page exclusive. 'I KILLED SETTY . . . AND GOT AWAY WITH MURDER' was the headline, beneath which was a signed statement: 'I, Donald Hume, do hereby confess to the *Sunday Pictorial* that on the night of 4 October 1949, I murdered Stanley Setty in my flat in Finchley Road, London. I stabbed him to death with a dagger while we were fighting.'

Inside there was the full story and confession, complete with a photograph of Hume holding a dagger 'like the one I used to kill Stanley Setty'. The prose was on the puce side of purple: 'I was wielding the dagger just like our Stone Age ancestors did 20,000 years ago. It seemed to come naturally to me . . . I watched the life drain out of him like water down a drain. This man who kicked my dog.'

Donald Hume was a strange character who had been brought up in children's homes, joined the RAF but had been invalided out and had become a post-war smuggler and small-time crook. He fell out with a bent car-dealer from London called Stanley Setty, whom he accused of kicking his dog, Tony, after it had scratched a repainted vehicle. He stabbed Setty to death with a SS dagger in his own flat and then dismembered the body. He also stole the money that Setty had on him and paid in some of the notes to his own bank to cover an overdraft.

A qualified pilot, Hume made two trips from Elstree airport to deposit parts of the body at sea. The second trip, however, in which he dumped the torso from which he had not removed the arms and hands, was unsuccessful and it was washed up in the marshes in Tillingham, in Essex, and spotted by a man shooting wildfowl. The police identified Setty through his fingerprints.

Hume was traced via the bloodstained banknotes and charged with murder. He concocted an elaborate defence in which he claimed that three gangsters called 'Mac, Greeny and the Boy' had asked him to dump the parcels which he had thought were printing plates used for forging petrol coupons and had paid him with £100 (hence the notes he had deposited in his bank). The first jury could not agree but a second acquitted him. He then pleaded guilty to being an accessory and was jailed for twelve years of which he served eight.

It was when he emerged from jail that he sold his tale to the *Sunday Pictorial*, who paid him £2,000 for a series of interviews with their reporter Victor Sims, which took place in a hotel in Westcliff-on-Sea. The *Pictorial* obligingly agreed to wait until he had left the country before they published the story. As his money ran out, he carried out bank robberies abroad, finally killing a taxi-driver as he tried to escape after a bungled job in Zurich. Jailed for life, he served sixteen years and returned to Britain where he was held in Broadmoor and finally died in 1998.

As *Time* magazine reported it: 'Hume is getting an estimated £3,600 from the *Pic*, with nothing to fear from British justice in all probability.' The magazine pointed out that Hume could not be tried again for murder and if he was tried for perjury, he only needed to say that the story was a lie committed for money. The *Daily Sketch* headline was: 'Arrest this man' while the *Star* opined that 'It is bad for a nation when a man can get away with murder and show a profit.'

The disapproval shown by rival papers certainly included a measure of sour grapes and hypocrisy. Hume had initially been in discussions to sell a confession to Duncan Webb of the *Sunday People*. While Hume was still in Dartmoor prison, Webb had kept in touch, even sending him a new suit for his release, and had worked with the prison authorities to smuggle him out at night without being spotted by rival papers and spirit him off in a car. In an intriguing letter to the *Spectator* in May 1962, Webb's colleague John Deane Potter, who was also in the car, suggested that they had offered £10,000 for a confession but Hume had been unhappy with the way the paper treated him back in London and thus took the tale elsewhere.

Not that the idea of criminals selling their tales was regarded as too unusual. In the *League of Gentleman*, the 1960 film about disgruntled ex-servicemen carrying out a heist, as the police close in on the robbers one tells another: 'Give them their money's worth at the trial and then flog your memoirs to the Sunday papers.'

But the days of criminals selling confessions are past – officially, at least. Under the 2009 Coroners and Justice Act, criminals are now forbidden from profiting from their crimes by writing about them, although it does not take too much imagination to find a way round this when the occasion arises. There was already a rule prohibiting criminals from benefiting from their crimes under item 16 of the Editors' Code of Practice of the now-disbanded Press Complaints Commission. This stated that no payment either directly or indirectly should be made to anyone seeking 'to exploit a particular crime or glorify or glamorise crime in general'. There was a limited public-interest defence but an editor was obliged to demonstrate what it was. However, the notion of 'glamorising crime in general' was so vague as to be more or less meaningless.

In the same year as Setty's paid confession, came another tale of crime reporters' dealings with criminals which raised a different ethical question and one that would have resonance for the next half century: what duty do reporters have to criminals to whom they have given their word?

Walter 'Angel Face' Probyn can claim to have been the greatest escaper since the eighteenth-century days of Jack Sheppard. In 1958, he absconded from Maidstone prison while serving a sentence for an office break-in and was written about in the press as a dangerous man. While on the run, he decided to put the record straight and contacted a reporter at the *Mirror*. They agreed to meet. 'I was a bit naive,' he told me years later in his flat in Hoxton, east London. 'I agreed to meet him in order to talk. I said, I think, that I was prepared to give myself up but not in that sort of atmosphere.' But as they met, Probyn was grabbed from behind in an arm-lock by a plain-clothes detective.

The front page of the *Mirror* for 11 October 1958 shows Probyn's startled face and the headline 'CAUGHT! Police Trap Angel Face.' The

Mirror's crime bureau informed their readers: 'In this exclusive *Mirror* picture, Angel Face is about to be handcuffed after being bundled into a police car by detectives. Last night, twenty-seven-year-old Probyn was in a cell at Stoke Newington police station.' The *Mirror*'s tale suggested that the police had 'set their trap' for Probyn and hid in shop doorways until 'a lone figure silhouetted in the street lights' came into view. The story said that, earlier in the day, a woman had delivered a letter from Probyn to the *Mirror* and had then 'vanished into busy Fetter Lane'. The letter was quoted: 'I am writing to you hoping you will try to be fair with me.' He explained that the only reason he would not give himself up was because of his children about whose custody he was concerned. 'Give me a break. I'm just a guy with a heart full of sorrow. Don't make me something I'm not. I know my history. I was just a boy then. Give me a chance to live it down.'

The former Metropolitan Police Deputy Assistant Commissioner Ian Forbes recalled the incident in his memoirs, *Squad Man*. 'Probyn had made an arrangement to meet a friendly newspaper man and was expecting him any time. Instead, however, he was being watched by detectives hiding in shop doorways and behind walls.' Forbes described him, mirroring the tabloid style of the time, as 'Britain's public enemy number one and the Houdini of the underworld . . . gunman, burglar, receiver of stolen property, cop-hater and jailbreaker extraordinary'. Probyn, who many years later featured in the film *McVicar*, played by Adam Faith, was better known for his escapes than his crime career and was to spend many more years in prison, but the experience changed his view of the press. 'It destroyed my perspective of reporters,' he said. The *Mirror*'s story made no mention of the fact that they had set him up. While those who turned Probyn in might argue that he was a threat to society and the press had a duty to inform on him, doing so was a betrayal which was damaging to journalists in general. If it is not a matter of life or death, sources should always be protected even if they are on the run.

Not unnaturally, most professional criminals remain wary of dealing with the press although there have been many occasions when it has suited them financially. Perhaps the person with greatest experience of this would have been train robber Ronnie Biggs. His first experience was in 1970 when a young Rupert Murdoch was settling in as the owner of the *Sun* and the *News of the World*. From Australia came news that another of his papers, the *Melbourne Daily Mirror*, had been contacted by a lawyer, supposedly acting for Biggs, who had by then been on the run for five years since hopping over the wall at Wandsworth prison. Biggs, now under an assumed name and desperate for cash, wanted to sell his story, using the money to set up a 'trust fund' for his three children.

To prove that the story was genuine, Biggs appended a fingerprint and signature to each page of the manuscript. But how to check that the dabs were genuine? Metropolitan Police files released to the National Archives in 2012 showed that the police were contacted and invited to a meeting with the paper's editor, Larry Lamb, who had 'in his possession a document regarding a crime of importance and wished to hand a copy to the assistant crime commissioner'. Lamb handed the documents over to Commander Wally Virgo and asked if the Yard would oblige by authenticating them.

Virgo was obviously anxious for some assistance from the press and 'made it clear to the editor that it was his bounden duty to pass any information he might receive notifying the whereabouts of Biggs to police'. But, amazingly enough, the Yard cooperated and confirmed that the fingerprint was genuine. Publication went ahead, prompting outrage from Down Under. A furious commissioner of police in New South Wales, Norman Allan, rang Scotland Yard and expressed amazement that the Met had cooperated. The publication caused anger in Britain, too. Arthur Lewis, the Labour MP for West Ham North, asked then home secretary James Callaghan, whether he had 'considered the information . . . showing that a newspaper has paid either Ronald Biggs or his agents money in relation to the mail bag robbery, whether he will take action against the newspaper concerned for aiding and abetting a convicted criminal'. Nothing happened and, coincidentally, Virgo soon turned out to be almost as active a villain as Biggs. He had been receiving £2,000 a month

– plus a Christmas bonus – in bribes from the Soho pornographer Jimmy Humphreys, who kept a meticulous note of such payments. Virgo was arrested, charged, jailed for twelve years, cleared on appeal and died not long after.

Having had his cover blown in Australia, Biggs escaped to Brazil where he was to have even more spectacular dealings with the British media. It was in Rio de Janeiro that the *Daily Express* tracked him down in 1974. By this time, some of his fellow robbers were approaching the end of their sentences so Biggs contemplated selling his story to the press, giving himself up and returning to serve his time. He asked a middleman to see if he could find someone in Fleet Street prepared to do a deal. The middleman duly made contact with a young and relatively inexperienced *Express* reporter, Colin Mackenzie, who realised that he had a scoop on his hands. But the *Express*'s editor, Ian McColl, was adamant that Scotland Yard should be involved and that his reporters should cooperate with the police to have Biggs arrested in Rio and brought home without any money being paid. Unaware of what was afoot, Biggs met Mackenzie in Rio only to discover that the Yard, in the shape of the Detective Chief Superintendent Jack Slipper, was part of the deal. There followed the famous saga of Biggs wriggling out of extradition by virtue of fathering a Brazilian child, Michael, and poor old Slipper having to return home empty-handed.

In his book, *Odd Man Out*, Biggs says that he had asked the *Express* for £50,000 for their scoop and that £35,000 had been agreed. He admitted that he had been wary about dealing with the paper because they had been partly responsible for the capture of another train robber, Jimmy White. Anthony Delano, in *Slip-up*, his entertaining account of the whole saga, quotes Biggs as telling the middleman: 'Don't go near the *Daily Express*. They're a treacherous lot of bastards there. They did a hatchet job on Charlie Wilson [another train robber who escaped and was recaptured].'

But the *Express* got their scoop, printing an extra 800,000 copies to take their print run over four million. 'Train Robber Biggs Captured in Rio,' was the splash, along with the smug subhead: 'our men are there'.

As with Probyn, the ethical question again was: what duty, if any, does a newspaper owe to a criminal to whom they have given their word? Delano suggests in his book that Biggs should have been able to trust the *Express* not to rat on him to the police: 'It was not a very highly polished moral argument but it had been applied to many a workaday journalistic situation down the years and was fairly generally accepted, even by most policemen.'

Mackenzie supposedly told Biggs, apologetically: 'It wasn't us, Ronnie, it was those bastards in London.' Biggs accepted that the dirty had been done back in England. 'You're two nice guys,' he told Mackenzie and the photographer, Bill Lovelace, 'but you work for a shitty organ.' McColl had no regrets: 'The simple fact is that I outwitted Mr Colin Mackenzie and Mr Biggs. I am proud of the fact that we got the story and did not have to pay a penny for it,' he said a couple of years later. Mackenzie left the *Express* a year after his scoop and eventually became the *Daily Mail*'s senior racing correspondent and a horse-owner himself. In 2009, he told the UK *Press Gazette* on the eve of his horse, Fleet Street, running in the Grand National, that winning that race would compare with his scoop: 'Finding Biggs gave me a huge adrenalin rush. But those days are long gone.'

Biggs stayed on in Brazil and by 1975 was charging $2,000 for interviews to make ends meet, although he would cheerfully offer a quote over the telephone for free. Attitudes in the press and the police had softened and in 1993 the *Sunday Express* paid for Slipper to fly out to Rio for a reunion with Biggs. He survived another attempt to hoist him back to England when a bunch of bounty-hunting chancers kidnapped him and took him to Barbados but by 2001, following a series of strokes, he was ready again to return home. This time the *Sun* stepped in with an offer to bring him back at his own speed and without stitching him up. The paper's crime editor, Mike Sullivan, played a leading part after Michael Biggs – Biggs's Brazilian-born son and the reason he was able to stay legally in Brazil – had come into the *Sun* office. 'We took some money over with us to show we were serious and we had about eight people on the ground: it became known as the Gravy Train Robbery in reporting circles!' Biggs flew to

Britain with the *Sun* and was immediately sent back to prison. 'The rest of the money was paid over in London once the job was done and poor Biggsy was banged up in chokey. I had to take a very large brown envelope to Michael and felt like doing a runner to Brazil myself. Tragically, Mike gave all the money over to lawyers campaigning for his father's release.'

The *Sun* had their splash – 'Biggs On Way Back' – on which he commented later that 'it was in this issue that my famous wish to walk into a pub in Margate and buy a pint of bitter came out as well as my apparent craving for a curry. As the *Sun* had a monopoly on the news and access to me, the story and quotes were printed verbatim in most of the other papers. It did not seem to matter that I had not touched booze or solid food for months.'

A *Sun* poll suggested that 57 per cent of the readers thought he should go free and 43 per cent that he should 'rot behind bars'. He was finally released from prison in 2009 after suffering a series of strokes. The Press Complaints Commission looked into what role the *Sun* had played in Biggs's return and accepted that the payments made to the middleman in the deal – some of which were passed on to Biggs – 'secured the return to justice of a notorious criminal'.

The *Sunday Mirror* ran a story on his return headlined 'Biggs Will Be Dead In a Month'. Well, technically it was a month – he was dead in the month of December but it was twelve years later. At his funeral at Golders Green crematorium in north London in 2014, in a tearful eulogy, Biggs's loyal son Michael said that he knew that 'the *Mail* will be slagging him off tomorrow'. Biggs's friend and ghost writer Chris Pickard told the congregation that 'Ron hardly ever called the press, the press always called him,' which was certainly true.

While the press could be accused of using criminals, the opposite could also happen and no criminals were more concerned about their image in the media than the Kray twins during their active years in the 1960s. One of the Krays' more controversial relationships tells us much both in terms of the way the twins manipulated the press and the symbiotic relationship that developed between them and the media.

Lord Boothby, the Tory peer and television personality, was attracted to rough trade at a time when homosexuality was still illegal. He also liked to hang out with the Krays, whose acolytes knew him as 'the Queen Mother'. He and Ron dined together at the House of Lords and afterwards went for a drink at White's Club in St James's. It was here that Ron – possibly apocryphally – when asked what he would like to drink, said: 'I've always wanted to try one of those prawn cocktails.'

In the early 1960s, Norman Lucas, chief crime reporter of the *Sunday Mirror*, who had impeccable police connections and helped officers with their memoirs, was told about the police investigation into the Krays. This centred around their brief contacts with the American Mafia and the fact that it had turned up a relationship involving a peer in a homosexual vice ring. On 12 July 1964 the paper ran a story headlined, 'PEER AND A GANGSTER. YARD INQUIRY.' Two days later, *The Times* ran a piece in which the Commissioner of the Metropolitan Police, Sir Joseph Simpson, said that he had 'asked senior officers for some enlightenment on newspaper reports [about] allegations of a homosexual relationship between a peer and a man with a criminal record . . . the relationship that exists between gangsters, a peer and a number of clergymen . . . blackmail is alleged. None of these statements is true and beyond this fact it is not my intention to make any report to the Home Secretary.'

Two days later the *Daily Mirror* responded with a story about 'the Picture We Dare Not Print' – Ronnie and Boothby – but still did not name the latter. In Germany, free from the fear of the strict British libel laws, *Stern* named Boothby in a tale headlined 'Lord Bobby in trouble'. Boothby was not mentioned in the British press although the suggestion was that he was a household name, something that applied to few peers at the time; in fact, Viscount Montgomery wondered if he should take legal action as he did not think any other peer was as well known as himself. While the story would have been damaging to the government it also embraced the Labour Party through the Labour MP Tom Driberg, who also enjoyed a bit of low-life risk-taking. For this reason, as John Pearson recounts in his book *Notorious*, both political parties were concerned. The heavy-hitting lawyer Arnold Goodman was employed to suppress the story.

Boothby duly wrote an unblushingly dishonest letter to *The Times* on 1 August in which he described the story as 'a tissue of atrocious lies'. He concluded: 'This sort of thing makes a mockery of any decent kind of life, public or private, in what is still supposed to be a civilised country.' He then sued the *Sunday Mirror*. When he pocketed £50,000 in damages – an amazing sum in those days for a libel in which his name had not even been mentioned – even the *New Statesman* congratulated him. 'Boothby has demonstrated, for all the world to see, that the right way to tackle a news-paper smear is to hit back hard and openly. Not all have the courage.' The end result was that the unfortunate editor of the *Sunday Mirror*, Reg Payne, was dispatched to edit the downmarket magazine *Tit-Bits*. Boothby passed £5,000 of his winnings on to Ron Kray with the tacit understanding that he would remain silent about their relationship. The twins then featured in a *Sunday Times* piece by Lew Chester and Cal McCrystal and, because the libel laws prohibited them from calling them gangsters, they were referred to as 'two famous sporting twins', a jocular phrase then adopted by the rest of the media. Their colleague Francis Wyndham asked for an inter-view with the Krays and described their company as a chance to 'enter the atmosphere (laconic, lavish, dangerous) of an early Bogart movie'.

Behind bars, both twins were more than receptive to press inquiries. Ron was cordial and talkative when I visited him in Broadmoor in the 1980s despite there being no money in it for him. Conscious of his image, he was as immaculately dressed as always – pastel blue suit, blue and white shirt and tie, monogrammed handkerchief, cufflinks, gold bracelet, diamond ring; he was fitted for a new suit every year by a tailor who went to Broadmoor to take his gradually expanding measurements. He drank non-alcoholic Barbican lager and chain-smoked John Player Specials and talked about where he would go if ever released – 'Morocco, for the boys.' He added, 'Don't print I'm mad.'

Reggie was a prolific writer of letters to journalists and was also happy to be visited, usually in advance of a project or a book he was about to launch, telling me when I saw him about his plans for an exercise book for people confined to small spaces. Reg also kept reporters informed of any books he was writing himself. In a slim volume of his writings from prison, *Thoughts*, published in 1991, he wrote that 'my eventual aim is to be recognised, first as a man and eventually as an author, poet and philosopher'.

One of the Krays' key links with the outside world and the media was Maureen Flanagan, a very personable former model and actress who had appeared on television in both *Monty Python* and *Benny Hill*. She knew the twins because she had been their mother, Violet's, hairdresser and was their surrogate little sister. After Violet died in 1982, Flanagan visited them faithfully, dealing with Ronnie's demands from inside Broadmoor, which included smoked salmon from Harrods and bagels from Brick Lane, plus gifts for the young prisoners who took his fancy. One of her roles was to ring the *Daily Mirror* from a phone booth outside Broadmoor after a visit with tit-bits about Ron. The paper would pay anything from £50 to hundreds of pounds for a story, depending on how big it was, and Flanagan would pass the money to their big brother, Charlie, who would share it with the twins; Flanagan would get a 'finder's fee'. Broadmoor was a secure hospital rather than a prison, and the canteen could be used by inmates to order in expensive items from the outside world, which were put on tick. At one stage, Ron's canteen bill stood at £7,000. His largesse was one of the reasons that the Krays needed to capitalise on their name and amongst the handy earners was the selling of media rights to his two weddings. In 1985, he wed Elaine Mildener, who had been writing to him in Broadmoor – as did many women – and had visited him with Flanagan. Ron had been told that the *Sun* would be the best payers for an exclusive and a fee of £20,000 was agreed (although only £10,000 was paid). This gave the paper access to the wedding in the Broadmoor chapel. When Ronnie and Kate Howard were planning to wed at the end of 1989, the chance for a 'brief interview' with Howard, plus wedding photos and guest list, were offered to the press with 'all offers for this exclusive to be in by 10 October and in excess of £25,000'. The new bride, 'bubbly blonde Kate', soon became a Fleet Street regular.

No tale about the Krays was too implausible. When Nelson Mandela was released in 1990, the *Sun* put the event in context with a story headlined: 'If Mandela can get out, so can Reggie!' and reported that 'former gangland boss Ronnie Kray reckons the release of Nelson Mandela could herald freedom for his twin, Reggie'. Although one of the newspapers most critical of criminals, the *Sun* remains the most popular behind bars.

Those connected with the Krays were also aware of the press's fascination. Chris Lambrianou, who was jailed for fifteen years for his role in the aftermath of the murder of Jack 'the Hat' McVitie, recalled how, when he played tennis in prison in a Robbers v Gangsters doubles match and had a mild confrontation with the train robber Bruce Reynolds, the story about it was in the papers the following day and Lambrianou was sure that prison officers had been paid for the tale. When he emerged from jail having become a born-again Christian, he was approached by both the *Daily Mail* and the *News of the World*, who offered him £50,000 for his story.

Not infrequently, prisoners call the press from jail to air grievances, not always with the happiest results. When a group of prisoners broke into the assistant governor's office in Durham jail in the 1970s, one of them, Dennis Stafford, serving time for the so-called 'one-armed bandit' murder, rang the *Daily Mirror*'s Manchester office. He announced, 'This is Dennis Stafford and I am calling you from the governor's office in Durham jail.' As journalist Revel Barker recalled in his memoir, the *Mirror* man who picked up the phone on the night newsdesk responded: 'And this is Henry VIII and I'm speaking to you from the throne room.'

Money has always been available for criminals' families and partners. When Brian Reader, later to come to prominence as a member of the 2015 Hatton Garden 'Dad's Army' gang, was arrested in connection with the death of undercover police officer John Fordham in 1983, his wife, Lyn, was offered £1,000 for a photo of him drinking champagne. When Valerio Viccei was jailed over the 1987 Knightsbridge safe-deposit robbery, his former girlfriend popped up in the *News of the World* thus: 'sultry Pamela Seamark lay naked on her lover's bed and felt her skin crawl as she looked down at the £4 million plum-sized diamond nestling in her navel' and so on.

Erwin James, who served twenty years of a life sentence for two murders and was released in 2004, said that 'generally among prisoners journalists are seen as sources of hope or sources of strife. Prisoners who claim innocence often depend on journalists for the oxygen they need to keep hope alive that they will have their cases overturned . . . Some journalists are universally respected – when Paul Foot visited Nottingham he got a standing ovation from the 150 or so prisoners congregated in the main prison television room before he even said a word. And some are universally loathed – like Mazher Mahmood [the *News of the World* and *Sun* reporter famous for his 'fake sheikh' exposés].'

James observed that prisoners sometimes cynically use the press as an earner: 'a couple of chaps in Nottingham prison sold a story to the *People* about how they had fashioned keys out of a couple of old Perspex rulers and then smuggled out the dodgy "keys", a total nonsense story but it brought them a few quid.'

Quite a few prisoners aspire to a career in writing. 'After I had my first article published in the *Independent* in 1994,' Erwin James goes on, 'the Prison Service supported my application for funding to undertake a journalism course – I completed the course, but when a few years later I got the chance to write my column for the *Guardian* I asked the Governor of the jail I was in and he said "Not a chance!" I said to him, "But you helped me do the journalism course . . ." He said, "We didn't expect you to do any real journalism." He said he was afraid that if I started writing for a national newspaper the *Daily Mail* might write a headline along the lines of, "Has the World Gone Mad!"'

Noel 'Razor' Smith, now the author of two intriguing volumes of memoirs and a guide to prison slang, kick-started his writing career by interviewing Jonathan Aitken in Belmarsh prison for *Punch* magazine when they were in neighbouring cells.

Eric Allison, who spent sixteen years in jail for various theft offences before going straight and becoming the prisons correspondent of the

Guardian, had personal experience of the press's methods. In the 1990s he was caught by a *News of the World* sting in which he was arrested handing over a stash of blank passports to their reporter who had posed as a member of a London crime family. The subsequent story was headlined 'We smash plot to supply IRA killers with fake passports'.

When Allison stood trial, the prosecution admitted 'there is no terrorist element in this case, it is a straightforward criminal enterprise'. But the *News of the World* had not finished with him. When he was appointed by the *Guardian* to his new job in 2003, they ran a story which read: 'a crook who was jailed after the *News of the World* exposed his role in a plot to supply passports for terrorists has been handed a job as a columnist by lefties' bible, the *Guardian* . . . Now he is cashing in on his past, by writing for the newspaper as part of his campaign to give inmates a cushy time behind bars.' Who would have thought that, a decade later, a former *News of the World* editor, Andy Coulson, would be behind bars himself?

However damagingly criminals may be portrayed in the press, it has been rare for any to sue for libel. But in 2013, David Hunt, who claimed to be an East End businessman, sued the *Sunday Times* whose reporter, Michael Gillard, had suggested in an article in 2010 that he ran a major criminal network and was regarded as untouchable by the Metropolitan Police. The article, published under the headline 'Underworld kings cash in on taxpayer land fund', was in part based on leaked Serious and Organised Crime Agency (SOCA) and other police documents. The paper contacted the Met prior to the trial to say they would be using the documents in its defence but would redact the names of informants, officers and other sensitive material. The Met sought an order banning their use and launched an unsuccessful hunt for the leaker.

A spectacular five-week trial ended in victory for the paper in July 2013. The trial judge, Mr Justice Simon, said that he accepted that Hunt was the head of 'an organised crime network implicated in extreme violence and fraud'. Gillard duly won the Investigation and Journalist of the Year prizes at the British Journalism Awards for his story – but was unable to accept it in person, on police advice, in case of reprisals.

In a leader after the victory, the *Sunday Times* wrote that 'when the libel trial began, the bodyguards protecting our witnesses withdrew after one day. Another renowned security firm refused to step into the breach. Such is the fear that Mr Hunt's name engenders.' One of the witnesses, Peter Wilson, who worked for the *Sunday Mirror* and approached Hunt in 1992 in connection with a crime story, told the court: 'he grabbed me by the lapels. He whacked me with his head straight into my orbit, shook me round like a rag doll, swore at me and dropped me, and he was off. I got into the car hardly knowing which day it was. I haven't exaggerated a word of this. I'll never forget it.' The libel laws, so often used to suppress information, had come full circle in that Hunt was now better known than he ever had been – and not in the way he would wish.

If the payment of criminals and the protection of sources were key ethical issues for crime reporting, so too was the issue of race, nationality and religion and newspapers have often over the centuries highlighted those factors for dubious reasons. In 1911, wanted posters offered a £500 reward for information that might lead to a team of ruthless criminals: 'Peter Piatkok, a native of Russia, an Anarchist . . . complexion sallow; Joe Levi . . . foreign appearance, speaking fairly good English, thickish lips, erect carriage . . . A woman aged 26–27, fairly full breasts, sallow complexion, face somewhat drawn . . . Foreign appearance.' The quarry being hunted were Latvian anarchists engaged in a struggle with the tsar of Russia and in need of funds, to which end they had already carried out a deadly robbery in Tottenham, prompting the *Times* headline: 'Alien Robbers Run Amok'. They were tracked down to 100 Sidney Street, in Stepney, east London. Famously, the then home secretary Winston Churchill arrived on the scene in his top hat and called in the Scots Guards from the Tower of London, directing the operation himself. When the house caught fire during the siege, he prevented the fire brigade from extinguishing it: 'I thought it better to let the house burn down rather than spend good British lives in rescuing those ferocious rascals.' The press called for tighter restrictions on immigration from eastern Europe, just as they would in 2014 when a Latvian man, Arnis Zalkalns, who had already confessed to murdering his wife, was allowed into the country to murder a west London schoolgirl.

Since Churchill's 'ferocious rascals' perished in the flames, newly arrived immigrants from all over the world have been blamed in the press for importing professional crime and violence into Britain. The pattern has been that, within most waves of immigration, there is a small criminal group. They benefit from the fact that the police don't speak their language, know their records or have their fingerprints. Some of their compatriots, to whom they are an embarrassment, will eventually join the police, which means, a generation or so later, they can no longer act with impunity. In chronological order, from the start of the last century – Russians/Jews/Latvians (robbery, firearms), Chinese (opium in the 1920s), Italians (protection rackets, robbery, gaming in the 1930s), Maltese (vice in the 1940s and 1950s), Chinese again (heroin in the 1960s), Pakistanis (heroin in the 1970s), West Indians (marijuana, gangs, gun crime in the 1970s), Turks (heroin in the 1980s), Colombians (cocaine in the 1990s), Nigerians (fraud in the 2000s) have all been associated in the public mind with the breaking of a new crime wave on the shores of Britain. From the 1960s onwards, West Indian and Asian communities in Britain became familiar with being labelled as criminal in the wake of arrests of any of their members. The absence, until recently, of black or Asian crime reporters undoubtedly played a part in this.

By the start of the millennium, the fingers were pointed at eastern Europe, with Russians and Albanians to the fore. In 2014, the *Sunday People* ran a story headlined 'Poles top foreign inmate list as Britain's overcrowded jails groan under pressure'. The story reported that 'nearly one in ten of the 11,000 foreign prisoners – 989 lags are from Poland'. It went on to explain that 'The next worst offenders are Ireland, Jamaica and Romania followed by Pakistan, Lithuania and Nigeria.'

But while journalists have had an ambiguous relationship with criminals of all races, which has included both paying and betraying them, there has also been another, less obvious connection between the two professions. Both newspaper and magazines have, inadvertently, acted as guidebooks for the research-minded villain.

One of the most prolific high-end burglars of the last century was the late George 'Taters' Chatham whose first conviction was in 1931. He was a gambling addict who, if he was losing money in a card game, would ask for a brief adjournment so that he could go out and steal some jewellery in Mayfair and return to continue playing. He told me that he was a regular reader of *Tatler* and *Country Life*, which he said were 'like Exchange & Mart' for him. And he said he chuckled when, after he had carried out a solo burglary of a painting, using only a screwdriver and some wire, he would read in *The Times* or the *Daily Telegraph* that it was the work of an 'international crime gang'. He said that he had once stolen the fur coat belonging to the then Lady Rothermere, whose family owned the *Mail* newspapers, but had returned it at the request of one of Associated Newspapers' editors.

After another cat burglar, Peter Scott, died in 2012 a loyal friend who cleared out his flat passed on some of his papers. What caught the eye was a battered folder labelled 'Possible Victims File'. Here were pages and pages from the gossip columns of the *Daily Express* and the *Daily Mail*. Items about a gift of expensive jewellery or news of plans for a lavish party merited an entry in the file. The late Ross Benson, the *Express*'s diarist, would doubtless have been intrigued to know that his story from October 1995, headed 'Aga's bid to halt auction', was squirrelled away. The reference to the Aga Khan's ex-wife's 'fifty-item collection . . . valued at more than £10 million' was clearly what caught the eye of Scott. The late gossip columnist Nigel Dempster was also the unintentional source of helpful ideas for Scott's plundering. His tales about Lady Renouf, the ex-wife of millionaire racehorse-owner Robert Sangster, were clipped. A later cutting from the *Evening Standard* records: 'Ex-Sangster Wife Robbed of £300,000 treasures'. According to the report, jewellery and antique furniture were stolen from her cottage near Newmarket. Underneath this report, Scott wrote 'mission accomplished'.

Over the years, Scott stole tens of millions of pounds' worth of jewellery and artworks, was the author of *Gentleman Thief*, and the subject of *He Who Rides a Tiger*, the 1965 Charles Crichton film, starring Tom

Bell and Judi Dench. In *Gentleman Thief*, Scott wrote: 'I have an inbuilt suspicion that I was sent by God to put back some of the wealth that the outrageously rich had taken from the rest of us.' The book did well, its sales boosted in the immediate wake of publication by some friends from the criminal fraternity who had access to credit cards that they used to buy copies all over London and thus persuade the publishers they had a bestseller on their hands.

He lived the last of his eighty-two years on a tough estate near King's Cross, just up the road from the *Guardian* offices and I used to meet him for lunch or a drink every so often. Once, after a gap of a few months, he looked suddenly very ill, and I remarked on the fact. 'I'm not ill, Duncan, I'm dying!' he said. 'Write a nice obituary.' He was anxious to be remembered in the press and in 1994 he wrote to the *Daily Telegraph* to say that he would consider it 'a massive disappointment if I were not to get a mention in your illustrious obituary column'. He explained that he derived much pleasure from reading accounts of the exploits of war heroes, adding: 'I would like to think I would have fronted the Hun with the same enthusiasm as I did the fleshpots in Mayfair.'

Back in the seventies, in Highgate, I met a robber called John Moriarty, who told me that he bought *The Times* on a daily basis because of their death notices. If you knew the time of a funeral, he said, the chances were that the house of the deceased would be empty at that time and thus available for a break-in.

There is doubtless a dissertation to be written on criminals' favourite newspapers. Thanks to Sean O'Connor's book *Handsome Brute* we now know that the psychopathic murderer Neville Heath wanted the *Daily Mail* to publish his pre-execution apologia. From Brixton prison, Heath asked for copies of the *Tatler*, *Life*, *Esquire* and the *Illustrated London News* and wrote to his mother suggesting that she contact the *Mail*. 'I want £500 and legal aid,' he instructed her. In the end, the *Sunday Pictorial* carried his account over three weekends after the trial. But if reporters had sometimes ambiguous relations with criminals, what about their relations with the other team?

14

Mind How You Go

Cops and Hacks

I n his last address as president to the Superintendents' Association conference in Bristol before his elevation to the House of Lords in 1998, Brian Mackenzie – shortly to become Baron Mackenzie of Framwellgate – told a story about a gravestone bearing the legend 'Here lies a journalist and an honest man' to which the response had been 'I didn't know you could put two bodies in the same grave!' Much laughter.

Around the same time, the Police Federation's magazine, *Police*, ran a cartoon which portrayed the press as machine-gun-wielding chaps firing wildly from a balcony at two unarmed constables. Simultaneously, in the magazine *Policing Today* Elizabeth Neville, at that time the chairwoman of the media advisory group for the Association of Chief Police Officers (ACPO), concluded an article by saying that 'the public has little right to know much about individuals. It has developed an expectation – fed by a prurient press – and I should like to see that curtailed.'

These were the early signs that relations between the police and the media were starting to cool, although it was not until 2011 and the Leveson Inquiry into the culture of the media and the arrests of scores of journalists in connection with the phone hacking scandal that the chill reached freezing point.

How had it come to this?

We can go back all the way to 1877, when the press was transfixed by the so-called Trial of the Detectives. According to *The Times* of 27 October, the trial 'continues to excite great public interest both in and outside the court and hundreds of people continue to throng the Old Bailey from day to day in the vain hope of gaining admission or gleaning some information as to the progress of the trial and its probable result'.

The trial had arisen out of a police investigation into two con-men who had fooled gullible wealthy people into thinking that they had a fail-safe betting method. The investigation was hampered by tip-offs to the pair from within Scotland Yard which eventually led to the arrests of the officers. At the end of a forty-eight-day trial, three detectives and a solicitor were convicted and jailed and one detective was acquitted.

The *Daily Telegraph*, in the early years of its commitment to covering trials in great detail, reported on its conclusion: 'everyone who possessed a curious mind or whose strange idiosyncrasy was to watch this long mental agony of five of their fellow-creatures – unfortunate, however guilty; miserable, however innocent – had made himself or herself familiar with the features, the nervousness, the stolidity or the anxiety, as the case might be, of the four police officers and the solicitor.' The *Telegraph* even described the scene, familiar in some aspects to court reporters of the present day, when the jury has retired to consider its verdict and the judge has also left the court: 'the long pent up silence gives way to what looks like heartless animation.'

Baying crowds greeted the arrival of the police defendants with ridicule when they appeared at Bow Street magistrates' court for the committal hearings. The relish with which the press reported this fall from grace was an indication that relations between press and police were not at their sunniest. The weather has chopped and changed ever since.

As the popular press grew and the appetite for crime stories became insatiable, a symbiotic relationship was established: the press needed the police for inside information on major crimes and the police needed the press to reach the public when they needed their help in, say, the hunt for a killer. There were, of course, exceptions to this arrangement: W. T. Stead's haughty ridicule of the Met Commissioner's failings in the Jack the Ripper investigation were not untypical of the press's attitude in the twentieth century to what would sometimes be portrayed as a bumbling organisation. But gradually a pattern emerged. By the 1920s and thereafter, the police and the press largely saw their interests in common.

Edgar Wallace, for instance, was supportive of the police in his time at the *Daily Mail*. 'A new terror has been added to the life of the wrongdoer in London by the Flying Squads, controlled by Scotland Yard,' he wrote in April 1928. 'It is the unexpectedness of the Flying Squad, the devastating shock of its appearance from nowhere that has got on the nerves of the criminal world.' He praised them in a lecture to London University students, noting that 'the success of Scotland Yard, staffed by officers who have had none of the advantages of a public-school education, is amazing'.

Wallace, as a working-class boy made good, was all too conscious of the snobbery of the period but not every reporter was so sympathetic and there was regular coverage of police malpractice. Thus, when Lord Byng, the Met Police Commissioner between 1928 and 1931, felt that the press were making too much of police disciplinary cases, he said as much to a gathering of the Newspaper Proprietors' Association. As Rob Mawby noted in his book *Policing Images*, this led directly to a two-year moratorium on such tales.

The crime reporters of this era were well regarded by the police, not least because many of them shared the same class background and were fairly gentle in their coverage of any misbehaviour. In his 1948 memoir *The Flying Squad*, former detective George 'Jack' Frost writes of them: 'My experience is that these journalists come from every walk of life and are usually not the weedy individuals so often depicted in Hollywood films, or as eccentric as depicted by Edgar Wallace in *The Squeaker*.' Reporters, wrote Frost, did not try to outwit the police by carrying on their own investigations. 'They are part of the nation's news-gathering team which always seems to obtain help from the Yard, an enviable position of trust which would not have been obtained if these crime reporters had constantly tried to outwit Scotland Yard's own CID network.'

The relationship between police and press came under the spotlight in connection with the murder in 1959 of Kelso Cochrane, a West Indian carpenter ambushed by a white gang in Notting Hill for which no one has ever been convicted. Mark Olden, in his book on the case, *Murder in Notting Hill*, reveals how the *Sunday Express* was onto the case and able to be on sale with news of the murder just over three hours after it had happened. 'A coloured man was stabbed to death in a street brawl in Notting Hill early today,' read the scoop. How did they know?

A few days later, a letter from the *Express* arrived at Harrow Road police station with a £10 cheque and an invoice that read: 'description of contribution: Harrow Road murder tip etc.' An inquiry was ordered under two senior detectives and the two journalists responsible for the story, Frank Draper and John Ponder – later to face charges of contempt over his refusal to identify a police source – were interviewed. Papers in the National Archives show that Draper's explanation – that an East End crook had tipped him off – was regarded as completely implausible and Draper was described by the police as 'the sort of man who would tell any story if it suited his purpose'. He told the police that an anonymous caller had tipped him off and 'said three white youths had stabbed a darkie named Cochrane'.

Ponder, the detectives felt, was 'the most indiscreet man in Fleet Street'. Ponder's explanation was that 'someone rang up and I made the rest up myself . . . Can't we square this up somehow? I don't want to be put up against the police.' What happened then was that the police, especially the man in charge of the investigation, Detective Superintendent Ian Forbes-Leith, who had close links to Ponder, found themselves under investigation when they should properly have been concentrating on the murder inquiry. Did the links between press and police lead to a murderer getting away?

The case also raised the issue of the press routinely paying the police for information. Had this been standard practice since the formation of the police, or were the police just happy to chat over a lunch or a beer?

Rupert Murdoch, the owner of the *News of the World*, the *Sun*, *The Times* and the *Sunday Times*, suggested to his own staff that bribing the police had been going on for a hundred years. Clandestinely recorded in March 2013, at a staff meeting after the hacking balloon went up, he suggested that, 'I would have thought 100 per cent – but at least 90 per cent – of payments were made at the instigation of cops saying "I've got a good story here. It's worth 500 quid" and you would say, "No, it's not" or "we'll check it out" or whatever and they'd say "well, we'll try the *Mirror*" . . . It was the culture of Fleet Street.'

Indeed it was. Peter Burden, the former *Daily Mail* crime correspondent, recalled that the director of a major newspaper organisation once asked for his advice when delivering a speech to an international conference on press/police relationships. He noted that the director, in his speech, recalled how, as a young reporter himself, he had regularly paid police station sergeants for information and for the home addresses of famous people caught up in investigations. 'I told him that he was making public that in his early days he regularly bribed policemen – a criminal offence,' recalled Burden in his memoirs. 'He immediately deleted the paragraphs and I received a bonus cheque. And the famous newspaper man's reputation remained intact.'

In 1962, the Royal Commission on the police, which examined corruption in the ranks, also looked at relations with the media and found links between the two. 'The defaulting policeman, like the defaulting parson or school teacher "is news", and stories of the prosecution and conviction of policemen are frequently given prominence in the press,' it concluded. 'We do not think that the reputation of the police service stands or falls by the occasional sensational reporting of the allegations against a particular policeman. Sensible people realise that there are black sheep in most families.' This was very much the establishment line and one that most newspapers were happy to follow.

Alcohol was, in the post-war years and up to the 1990s, the essential lubricant in the relationship between police and press. Roy Greenslade recalled his days as a young reporter in east London the 1960s. 'The whole culture of both police and journalist was booze – there was even a snooker table in the nick. One night I got drunk and they gave me a cell for the night. There was no animosity at all between us.' He became friendly with a young constable, one of the first graduate officers, who told Greenslade that a colleague he mentioned was bent. 'I said "are they all bent?" and he said "every one but me". I named a lovely, avuncular officer known for his charity work and he said, "he will let a villain off, if the villain pays him – and he may give some of that money to charity."'

Greenslade also became very friendly with a police sergeant called Fred Pye, who was close to the local Labour MP Tom Driberg. 'I used to babysit for him and his wife and he said one night, "Do you want to come up to Soho?" I was nineteen, of course I did.' They went to a jazz club below a brothel and, as the underground stopped running early in those days, Pye said that Greenslade could stay at Driberg's flat in Wimpole Street for the night. 'I spent all night on the couch fighting him off. Then Fred said the next day, "How did you get on?" and I said I had a lot of trouble. I realised that he was a procurer for Tom and procured prisoners for him, including a boy who had gone AWOL from the army: Fred let Tom into the cell from which he didn't emerge and then Tom helped the boy with his case.' Pye later married the singer Kathy Kirby and became a journalist himself.

'The corruption I found in Fred all turned out to be true but there was never any question of writing about it,' said Greenslade. 'First of all, I could never prove it and, secondly, you were locked into a culture where your job was to turn over villains not the police. The idea that the police were any more corrupt than the occasional cuff over the ear did not form part of the culture. You depended so much on them. Your stories were on the effects of crime and the only way you got them was by being friendly with the police. Now I teach journalism and see it in the round: what you most want are stories and you were not going to piss off your sources.'

In the sixties, the police cooperated happily with the press on what was to become a regular feature, the Celebrity Bust. The arrests of Mick Jagger and Keith Richards in 1967 led the way, followed as they were by arrests of another Rolling Stone, Brian Jones, and Marianne Faithfull. Such arrests have led to many accusations, some justified, that the police have tipped off the press when a big name is about to be arrested, leading to photos of the event, known in the United States as 'the perp walk', whereby an alleged perpetrator of a crime, often handcuffed, is taken by the police into court or police station in a way that allows the media to photograph or film it. It has been described by the American journalist, Nat Harris, as 'the crime reporter's red carpet'. Smart British defence lawyers used to tell clients in such situations to smile pleasantly; the same lawyers always ensured that, if their client was appearing in court in Britain during the run-up to Remembrance Sunday, he or she would be wearing a poppy.

As we have noted, the close relationship between police and press carried with it other risks. As John Junor, the former editor of the *Sunday Express*, once noted, the greatest corruptor of journalists was not money or power but friendship and for much of this period the standard press line was that Britain had the finest police in the world. There was a logic to this: if the police thought that a reporter was aiming to expose or denigrate their colleagues, cooperation would swiftly end and the tip-offs and inside information, on which crime reporters relied, would soon cease.

So when the detective branch of Scotland Yard was at its most corrupt in the 1960s and early 1970s, most of the scandal either passed by the crime reporters or they decided not to bother investigating or reporting it. The corruption involved the widespread taking of bribes. One former bank-robber, Bobby King, who was very active in the 1960s and 1970s, said that it was a relief when the police appeared on his doorstep after a robbery he had carried out because he could pay them off and know that nothing more would happen. Then on 29 November 1969, *The Times* published an article by two non-specialist reporters, Julian Mounter and Garry Lloyd, which exposed widespread police corruption, under the headline 'London Policemen in Bribe Allegations'. They quoted one officer assuring a small-time crook, in a taped conversation, that he could sort anything out for him because 'I'm in a little firm in a firm.' This 'firm within a firm' became shorthand for the network of corrupt officers which was gradually exposed over the next few years.

One of the most spectacular exposés of bent coppers came on 27 February 1972 with the *Sunday People* headline over the story: 'Police Chief and the Porn King'. Smart work by their reporters had traced Commander Ken Drury to Cyprus where he was being entertained by the man who ran pornography in Soho, Jimmy Humphreys, and his wife Rusty. It was a great scoop to which the *News of the World* clearly felt obliged to respond by talking to Drury, who gave them the bogus information that he was there to hunt the train robber Ronnie Biggs, and Humphreys was helping him.

It was this level of corruption that led to the introduction of the out-of-town Commissioner for the Met in 1972, Sir Robert Mark. He famously said that it was his ambition to arrest more criminals than he employed and his cleansing of the Augean stables lead to the early departure of 478 officers, a rate six times higher than under his predecessor. Some fifty appeared in court, and the wholesale, institutionalised corruption of the 1960s and 1970s within the CID was ended.

The high point came in February 1976 when twelve senior detectives were arrested on corruption charges. Reporters and photographers were on hand in large numbers to record the arrests, which led to a question being asked in the House of Commons by Robin Corbett MP of the Home Secretary, Roy Jenkins, as to whether he would order an inquiry into who within the Met had tipped off the press. Jenkins had no intention of ordering an inquiry and managed to dodge the question neatly by replying, 'The Commissioner assures me that no information about these arrests was given to the press by the Metropolitan Police Press Bureau until after the arrests had been made.' The photos of the shamed thief-takers were memorable. Jenkins may have known that at this time some reporters referred to the press bureau as the 'suppress bureau'.

In the wake of the scandal, Sir Robert saw the building of relations with the media as one of his main tasks, and decades after he left the post he is remembered as one of the most open of Commissioners in terms of relations with the media. His memorandum issued to the Met on 24 May 1973 acknowledged that the effectiveness of the police was dependent on the cooperation and goodwill of the public but noted that, 'Relations with the media are not as good as they could be . . . the police have made unnecessary difficulties for themselves by tending to withhold information which would safely be made public.' He urged that the police should supply the media with information 'within officers' knowledge at as low a level as possible' – that is to say that a detective constable on a minor case should be able to talk directly to a reporter. And he also acknowledged that, 'The new approach to dealings with the news media will of course involve risks, disappointments and anxieties; but officers who speak in good faith may be assured of my support even if they make errors of judgment when deciding what information to disclose.' Mark was widely applauded in the press for his stance and his stock remained high, as evidenced by many glowing obituaries when he died in 2010.

Steve Chibnall in his book *Law-and-Order News*, an analysis of crime reporting in the British press published in 1977, found that most of the crime reporters he interviewed felt they had a duty to be supportive of the police. He quotes a number of them anonymously to that effect: 'If I've got to come down on one side or the other, either the goodies or baddies, then obviously I'd come down on the side of the goodies, in the interests of law and order.' Another added: 'We do not make it our business to criticise the police – there are plenty of other people in Fleet Street who do that sort of thing.' Chibnall reached the conclusion that 'rather like the golfer, the crime reporter tries to keep to the fairway, avoiding the sand traps of police deviance'.

The police can sometimes understandably make use of the press when trying to crack a case. In 1991, Oxford student Rachel McLean went missing. The police were suspicious of her boyfriend, a New Zealander student called John Tanner, but there was no body and no evidence of foul play. Tanner had told the police that he had last seen Rachel at Oxford station with a long-haired stranger and he agreed to a press conference in Oxford at which he would make a televised appeal for Rachel to make contact. We were unofficially briefed by the police beforehand that they suspected Tanner of murder and we were told not to hold back in our questions; the police wanted to see how he would handle questions like 'Did you kill her, John?' which they were still reluctant to ask. Tanner was certainly unconvincing during the press conference, denying the murder and claiming 'In my heart of hearts, I know she is still alive.' A few days later, the police confronted him with fresh evidence that showed he was lying about his trip to the station. He confessed to strangling her in a fit of jealousy and hiding her body under the floorboards of the house. He was convicted, jailed for life and served twelve years.

The Tanner case was an example of how the police and press could cooperate, and this relationship continued, to a great extent, until the rupture in the wake of the Milly Dowler hacking scandal in 2011 and the subsequent police investigations. But from the police's point of view the relationship had always been double-edged. Jackie Malton has seen the media from both sides, first as a Flying Squad detective and then as the model for *Prime Suspect*'s Jane Tennison and as a script adviser to numerous television programmes, including ITV's long-running police serial, *The Bill*.

'The general view was that the press were not to be trusted,' she said. 'But there was also a recognition that you couldn't do the job without them. You needed them to appeal to the public.' She had both bad and good experiences. 'In 1991, when *Prime Suspect* came out, the *Daily Mail* pursued my sexuality as to whether I was gay, they were fishing around all the time. But you might have individual reporters who were honourable, certainly more honourable than they are today, they didn't "verbal you up" [attribute to you words you had not said]. Others would often refer to a "police source" when you would know that no one had spoken to them but we couldn't do anything about it. We had the information but they had the power.'

Sue Hill, a former detective chief superintendent in the Met's murder command with thirty-three years' service in the police, said that the basic attitude within the police towards the media when she first joined was 'suspicious'. Of occasions when the press and police had worked together very successfully, she recalled the rape and murder of a girl after which the killer had fled to Latvia. 'A crime correspondent tracked him down and alerted us to where he was rather than run a story on it and alert the man. His priority was getting this man arrested and that's how it worked out. In the end, they got their story and we got our man.'

John Grieve, the former deputy assistant commissioner at the Met who headed both the anti-terrorist and racial crimes units and joined the police in 1966, has also seen the changes in relationship between press and police in his time both in the police and in his subsequent academic work. He said that a major dilemma for the police was how much information should be released to the press. 'When I was in India,' he said, 'I spotted that outside the police station they put a list of people who had been taken into custody. So, on the one hand you have the idea that people should not disappear into a police station without people knowing you are there but, on the other hand, should you be advertising the fact that someone has been arrested when it's only an allegation?'

Of occasions when the media have played a major part in stories, he highlighted the case of the murder of Stephen Lawrence, the black teenager who was stabbed to death in south London in 1993. The police, frustrated by the failure to convict the killers, cooperated with the *Mail* to keep the case in the news. It is not uncommon for detectives to release fresh details of an unsolved case to a journalist in the hope that the suspects will read the subsequent story and then discuss it and incriminate themselves in bugged conversations. When it looked like no one would ever be convicted of the killing, the *Daily Mail* ran a famous front page, naming the suspects under a headline 'Murderers: the *Mail* accuses these men of killing. If we are wrong, let them sue us.' Although it would take many more years before two men were finally convicted of the murder in 2012, Grieve said that the *Mail*'s story, and the work of Mark Daly of the BBC, Simon Israel of *Channel 4 News* and *Guardian* reporters on the case had 'an enormous impact', both in ensuring that the story was kept alive and in helping to flush out the killers.

Grieve also cited the part the media played in the investigation of the Docklands bomb (which killed two people and caused £100 million worth of damage in 1996) with the publication of the need to track the trailer in which the bomb had been planted. 'Everybody ran it,' he said. 'The *Sun* appealed to their "army of truckers" – and ran it opposite page 3. We had something like 280 calls on the hotline and that took us to the bombers and to the trial.'

Regarding journalists going on police raids, Grieve suggested that, 'Embedded journalists go back to Dickens and the night inspector, so being embedded has a long history but is it mere voyeurism of the misery of other people or an important part of the democratic process?'

For many years, from the seventies until 2008, if you read in a newspaper that 'a police source' had confirmed details of a crime, an arrest or an explosion, that 'police source' might well have been Bob Cox, a genial Irishman who went to Scotland Yard's press bureau in 1973 from a job as a court reporter for a north London news agency. Not all press officers were regarded favourably by journalists but Cox managed to walk the tightrope between serving both the Met and the reporters, even getting a plaudit for his balancing act from the late campaigning journalist Paul Foot who wrote from the *Daily Mirror* to say that getting helpful responses from Cox to hostile questions was 'one of the few remaining pieces of evidence that we live in a civilised society'.

'Robert Mark introduced an open door policy emphasising "withhold what you must" rather than "only tell them what you must", and he encouraged openness,' said Cox, who retired as Chief Press Officer having turned down an offer in the past to be the *Evening Standard*'s crime correspondent. 'I was told by Malcolm Johnson [then head of press bureau] when I was recruited "Whatever you do, don't lie, because your credibility will go down the pan for ever."'

If senior police officers felt they were unfairly attacked in the press, they rarely went public. An exception to this rule, in 1986, was James Anderton, then the chief constable of Greater Manchester, who announced that AIDS sufferers were 'in a human cesspit of their own making', prompting a major media storm and calls for his sacking. The following year, he claimed in the *Sunday Times* that the media were not concerned with painting an accurate picture of him but wanted to portray him as 'a Bible-thumping, baton-swinging, autocratic, self-centred, right-wing dictator', despite the fact that he had preached at synagogues, mosques and black churches. He explained that his pronouncement on AIDS was 'a revelation to me from God'. He survived calls to resign and letters now available show that he enjoyed the support of the then Prime Minister, Margaret Thatcher, in his views.

And sometimes the police have felt let down by the press when they think they have done the right thing. We were told at a Police Superintendents' Association conference of the occasion when a male officer who had a sex change was allowed to keep her job. This was seen as a sign of a tolerant police service but the headline the next day was 'No Knobby Bobby Keeps His Jobby'.

The police have opened their doors to television cameras on many occasions, sometimes with striking results. In 1982, the documentary-maker Roger Graef was given access to Thames Valley Police for a three-part BBC series called *Police*. In the third programme, 'A Complaint of Rape', a woman victim was subjected to what was widely seen as dismissive questioning by detectives. The subsequent media reaction led to major changes in the way that police handled such cases.

In 2015, the Commissioner of the Metropolitan Police, Sir Bernard Hogan-Howe, granted access to the BBC for a five-part series, *The Met: Policing London*, narrated by the actor Lennie James. Sir Bernard justified his decision in an article in the *Guardian*, explaining that the Met received over a hundred requests a year from programme makers: 'often they are after the same thing – cops banging in doors, charging around with their blue lights on and a macho commentary. These can be entertaining and get enough viewers to encourage endless repeats but they are short on the informative side.' He wanted to avoid this type of coverage and was aware of the risk of allowing broader access to his officers. 'But I can hardly complain that the public are not given the opportunity to understand policing if we don't open up our doors.' The series was judged a public relations success for the police in that it both humanised them and explained their predicaments. It won plaudits from television reviewers across the political spectrum.

Few police officers cross the road and become reporters but there have been some. Brian Hilliard, a former officer with the Met's special patrol group, became the editor of the *Police Gazette*. In 1986, after a group of officers had beaten up a group of youths in Holloway, north London, but escaped prosecution, he wrote a memorable editorial under the headline 'A Conspiracy of Bastards', in which he attacked the Met officers who had shielded their colleagues from prosecution. 'The hard work of home beat officers, school visits, the hundreds of charities that benefit daily from the unselfish efforts of off-duty police, the bravery, heroism, the sheer day-to-day professionalism of the ordinary bobby on the beat, all lie hidden in the shadow of this shameful silence,' wrote Hilliard. 'Meanwhile, the bastards still walk round in the uniform they have disgraced. Someone knows them, but who will speak up?' Someone did. The article prompted a witness to step forward and the violent officers were jailed.

For many years the Police Federation, which was created in 1919 to support rank-and-file officers up to the rank of chief inspector, backed members who felt that they had been libelled in the press. They won ninety-five cases in a row, which became known as 'garage actions' because they were almost invariably settled before they ended up in court with the newspaper concerned, often a local paper, paying around £5,000 – supposedly the cost of a new garage – and legal costs, which might be around £20,000. Once a case went to court, the costs accelerated dramatically so almost every paper avoided that risk, even if they felt they had a reasonable case. There was also a feeling that juries were more sympathetic to police officers, who did a difficult, dangerous job, than to flash-Harry reporters. This attitude still holds true: an Ipsos MORI poll in 2013 indicated that 65 per cent of Britons surveyed trusted the police to tell the truth as opposed to 21 per cent for journalists.

When working for the *Guardian* in the early 1990s, I became aware of allegations of police corruption in Stoke Newington, north-east London. After talking to local lawyers, activists from the Hackney Community

Defence Association and people in prison, it became clear that a pattern of malpractice was emerging and we prepared to run a story in the *Guardian*. At this stage, we were contacted by the anti-corruption branch of the Metropolitan Police, who were already investigating the allegations but having trouble persuading people who had been at the sharp end of the corruption to talk to them. I was asked to go to Tintagel House, where the anti-corruption team was based, to talk to the detective in charge of the operation, who asked if we could persuade people that they were carrying out a fair investigation.

In due course the Met announced that eight officers had been transferred to eight different stations. We then ran a story to that effect with a detailed background of what was being investigated but without naming the officers or suggesting that they were involved in any of the allegations. In those days, anyone wanting to sue for libel could do so within three years of the offending article – one year is now the time limit – and so it came to pass that, some two years and three hundred odd days later, writs arrived at the *Guardian* from the eight officers who had been moved, seeking damages for libel. Alan Rusbridger, the *Guardian*'s editor, had decided to fight libel cases where he believed the paper was in the right and had recently won two high-profile actions brought by the Conservative politicians Jonathan Aitken and Neil Hamilton.

I was sent to see George Carman, the wiliest of libel lawyers, whose fee was £5,000 a day. I met him in his chambers and he effectively cross-examined me for an hour and then took on the case. He asked me about my background and when I told him I had a law degree he said it would better not to mention that in court as jurors did not like lawyers much.

The judge in the trial at the Royal Courts of Justice was the late Mr Justice French, whose last case it was to be. It was clear from the start that he was on the side of the police and our only hope was to convince the jury of our case. Carman told me that, when I was in the witness box, I should find a friendly-looking face amongst the jurors and deliver all my evidence to him or her, which I duly did. During the trial he would periodically ask for a brief break to clarify a point with his client. Outside the court, I would ask anxiously what the issue was only to be told amiably that he just needed a cigarette. Mike Taylor, the former head of the Flying Squad, and Peter Moorhouse of the Police Complaints Authority, gave evidence for the *Guardian*. The case was frustrating as we were not allowed to recount much of what had happened since we wrote our story – prisoners cleared, compensation for false imprisonment paid – and the judge would allow neither Rusbridger, nor the editor of the *Evening Standard*, Max Hastings, to give evidence as both wished to do. The five officers – three dropped out before the case came to court – and their relatives told the jury what a devastating effect on their lives the article had had. The judge summed up their evidence in great detail, told the jury they could award up to £125,000 per person in damages and ignored our arguments entirely. The jury went out overnight and returned the following morning with a judgement on our behalf. The police appealed and lost again in the Court of Appeal, ending up with a total bill for the Federation of around £600,000.

I was surprised to find that many of the people who contacted the *Guardian* afterwards to express their satisfaction with the verdict were police officers, including Federation activists, many of whom felt that media hostility to the Federation, which was often portrayed as obstructive and reactionary, stemmed partly from their aggressive attitude to the press. At the time the Federation's chairman, Fred Broughton, told the *Observer*'s David Leigh: 'the Federation is not engaged in any "campaign" to intimidate the media or suppress fair and accurate reporting by the threat of libel proceedings. That would be scandalous.' Not long afterwards, they lost a further, even more expensive, action brought against Channel 4's *Trial and Error* programme and further actions against the media dwindled in number.

15

They Got the Wrong One

Trial and Redemption by the Media

What part have reporters played over the years in highlighting the cases of the wrongly convicted? And what role have they also sometimes played in targeting or demonising the innocent?

In April 1815, Eliza Fenning appeared at the Old Bailey charged with attempted murder. She was a servant whose employers, Robert and Charlotte Turner, had become ill after eating the beef stew and dumplings she had prepared. Mr Turner suggested that Fenning had deliberately spiked the food with the arsenic he kept to deal with mice and rats and Mrs Turner suggested that she could have done so in response to being scolded for consorting with a couple of young apprentices. Fenning protested her innocence but the jury was unmoved and she was sentenced to hang, although food poisoning was the likeliest cause of the Turners' illness. William Hone, a radical writer, heard of her case, visited her in Newgate prison and launched a newspaper, *The Traveller*, specifically to fight for her release. It probably did no harm to her cause that she was young and beautiful and the artist Robert Cruikshank pictured her reading the Bible in her cell.

Others shared Hone's doubts about her guilt and a week before she was hanged she wrote to a Sunday-paper editor thanking him for his 'humane charitableness' in taking up her cause and adding that 'my dear parents and myself will feel in duty bound to pray for your kind interference in your paper as you have done'. The *Newgate Calendar* reported that 'thousands of persons, after examining the evidence adduced at the trial, did not hesitate to express their opinions very strongly on the case; and many of the lower orders, apparently convinced of the innocence of the sufferer, assembled in front of Mr Turner's house . . . hooting and hissing and otherwise expressing their indignation.'

Not all the newspapers were sympathetic. The *Observer* led the charge against Fenning, not least because she came from a Roman Catholic family. The campaign was to no avail and she was hanged. The well-meaning *Traveller* lasted only a year but Hone's investigation, which argued persuasively that she was innocent, could be seen as an early example of investigative reporting on such cases and of the way in which press can influence – or try to – the public as to someone's innocence or guilt.

Sir Arthur Conan Doyle also wrote in the press on more than one occasion on behalf of convicted men in whose innocence he believed. He campaigned in the *Daily Telegraph* and elsewhere on behalf of George Edalji, wrongly convicted on the bizarre charge of disembowelling a horse in Staffordshire in 1903. The Anglo-Indian lawyer served three years hard labour before being eventually pardoned, and concern about his conviction, contributed to the creation of the court of criminal appeal in 1907 and was the subject of a Julian Barnes novel, *Arthur & George*. Intriguingly, in 2015, it emerged that Staffordshire police fabricated evidence to try to discredit Conan Doyle's investigation. The chief constable, G. A. Anson, later admitted sending him a bogus letter signed 'A Nark, London'.

Conan Doyle was active, too, in the campaign to prove the innocence of Oscar Slater, a German Jew convicted of the 1908 murder of the elderly Marion Gilchrist, battered to death at her home in Glasgow, supposedly for her jewels. Miss Gilchrist's maid later named a respectable relative of the dead woman as the man who had fled the flat at the time of the killing but Slater, who had various aliases and was already en route for New York, was suspected because he had a pawn ticket for a jewel, despite the fact that the ticket predated the murder by weeks. Class and anti-Jewish prejudice clearly played a part in the police investigation and the initial press coverage. Slater was pursued to the United States, brought back to Scotland, convicted and jailed for life after narrowly escaping the death penalty.

The *Citizen*, which incidentally carried a photo of Slater's jury getting out of their omnibus on their way into court – unthinkable today – backed the verdict as 'just', as did the 7 May edition of the *Glasgow News*. Although disquiet was already being voiced about the case, by 18 May the *Scotsman* was dismissing it: 'Efforts most harmful and ill-advised, are being made to work up popular feeling and to receive signatures with the object of obtaining a reprieve for the man Oscar Slater who now lies under sentence of death. However amiable may be the sentiments that may have prompted some of those who have taken part in the movement it is one that cannot be otherwise than mischievous and futile.' Intriguingly, the *Weekly Record* has a quote from a juryman who disclosed that the verdict was reached by a show of hands without any debate as to innocence or guilt. 'The time was occupied by discussions that the Press should not know who voted one way or the other.' (Nine for guilty, five not proven, and one not guilty.)

William Roughead, the Scottish lawyer and chronicler of murder trials of the period, wrote first of the case in 1910 and was involved in it for many years. In *The Trial of Oscar Slater*, he described it as a 'long legal tragedy' and berated successive Scottish Secretaries for their failures to address it. He would later give evidence at the appeal. Roughead cooperated with Conan Doyle, and there is evidence of their correspondence on the subject in the Signet Library in Edinburgh: Conan Doyle even sent a telegram to Roughead as it looked as though their campaign would finally succeed and wrote that it was impossible to read the details of the case 'without feeling deeply dissatisfied with the proceedings and morally certain that justice was not done'. But it took many years before justice was finally done, despite the involvement of the press. On 20 May 1923, the headline in the *Sunday Mail* read: 'The Fate of Oscar Slater/Why He May Not Secure His Freedom/Sister's Longing for His Return' and the accompanying story recounted how 'the grim spectral figure of Oscar

Slater . . . is to come forth from his cell in Peterhead so that his case may be discussed again'.

On 15 February 1925 the same paper had a story of a fellow-prisoner who had smuggled out Slater's appeal written in 'tiny calligraphy' and hidden under his tongue. A Glasgow journalist, William Park, investigated further and published his findings in 1927. The *Daily News* added their weight by dispatching a special commissioner, E. Clephan Palmer, writing under the pseudonym of The Pilgrim, who filed twenty-four stories on the case. Finally, Slater was released pending his appeal after Conan Doyle had sent details of the case to Ramsay MacDonald, then leader of the opposition, who was clearly troubled by it. On 27 March 1928, Slater wrote in the *Daily Express*: 'I have seen and lived in hell . . . I am no longer the Oscar Slater of 1908, the swarthy foreigner who could hardly speak the English tongue and I am strong in body and purpose.'

When he finally appeared in court for his appeal, Conan Doyle described the scene in the *Sunday Pictorial* of 15 July 1928: 'One terrible face stands out among all the others. It is not an ill-favoured nor is it a wicked one but it is terrible nonetheless for the brooding sadness that is in it. It is firm and immobile and it might be cut from that Peterhead granite which has helped to make it what it is. A sculptor would choose for the very type of tragedy . . . It is Slater.' Slater was given a 'solatium' of £6,000 as compensation for his eighteen-and-a-half years inside. Not everyone was generous-hearted about the case. Edgar Wallace, in the *Morning Post* of 1 August 1927, wrote: 'He has served nineteen years for a crime of which anybody but a fool might know he is guiltless' but he added that 'there was nothing about Oscar Slater that was admirable. By the accident of birth he was a German Jew, by inclination he was a shady and immoral fellow.' Roughead, Conan Doyle, Park and 'The Pilgrim' all played a part in Slater's redemption. So what duty does a reporter have when he or she doubts a defendant's guilt?

Some crime reporters have rued the fact in retrospect that they did not do more to save the innocent. Harry Procter, who, as the *Sunday Pictorial*'s crime man, had the task of making a deal to pay for the legal costs of the serial killer John Reginald Christie, as we saw in Chapter Thirteen, was regretful of his role in that case. In his 1958 memoir, *The Street of Disillusion*, Procter reflected that 'it was unfortunate indeed that we, in Fleet Street – I was just as mistaken as the rest – regarded the Evans murder as what we professionally call "fish-and-chippy".' This was the expression given to run-of-the-mill domestic killings. 'None of us realised then that we were literally on the doorstep of the most horrifying crime story of the century.'

Procter chastised himself for failing to investigate further, although in those days crime reporters were still very trustful of the authorities. What was to trouble him right up to his early death in 1965 was his failure to subject Christie to the sort of robust questioning for which he was justly famous. Procter had covered Evans's trial but it attracted little attention at the time and the press box was empty for much of the case. The fact that capital punishment was still on the statute books obviously gave the issue greater weight and already some other crime reporters were demonstrating their concerns. Lindon Laing, of the *Daily Express* and later the *Daily Mail*, always left the press box before a death sentence was passed because he was so opposed to capital punishment.

Ludovic Kennedy, in his 1961 book *Ten Rillington Place*, investigated in greater detail how Evans came to be convicted. The book established a template for researching dubious convictions and played a major role in encouraging reporters to investigate alleged miscarriages of justice, a genre of journalism that would lead to many successful appeals in the last quarter of the twentieth century.

There remained for many years the feeling that such miscarriages of justice were still rare. Those who sought to question convictions in contentious cases were often reviled, as was the case some twenty years later in a very different type of crime. Journalist and author Chris Mullin was amongst those involved in campaigning against the conviction of the Birmingham Six, who had been jailed for the murder of 21 people in an IRA pub bombing in 1974. This persistence over the years by Mullin, who became a Labour MP in 1987, prompted the *Sun* to run the front page headline 'Loony MP Backs Bomb Gang' the day after the first appeal against the six men's conviction was dismissed in 1988. It would be some years before the 'loony' was proved right and the 'bomb gang' shown to be innocent victims.

Prisoners protesting their innocence still often contact the media, although the coverage of miscarriages of justice has dwindled since the demise of two television programmes, the BBC's *Rough Justice* and Channel 4's *Trial and Error*, both victims of austere times when reality television is cheaper than complex investigative documentaries.

Some inmates take drastic measures to highlight their cases. In 1993, Joe Steele escaped from prison in Scotland where he was serving a life sentence for the 1984 Glasgow 'Ice Cream Wars' murder of six members of the Doyle family. They had been killed in an arson attack between gangs controlling ice cream vans in the area. While he was on the run, I interviewed him in London and the story and his picture appeared in the *Guardian* under the headline 'Fugitive "killer" protests his innocence.' He assured me that he would give himself up once he had got publicity for his campaign: 'If I wanted to get away I would have gone abroad by now.'

The police arrived at the *Guardian* shortly afterwards. They wanted to know how and where I had met Steele and who arranged the meeting. On the advice of the *Guardian* lawyer, I replied 'no comment' to every question asked. A report was sent to the procurator fiscal in Scotland as the initial offence of escaping had taken place there. Shortly afterwards, Steele gave himself up, as he had promised, by climbing a pylon and hanging a banner from it protesting his innocence. No charges were ever brought against the *Guardian*. Steele and his co-defendant, Tommy Campbell, had their convictions quashed in 2004.

The veteran miscarriages-of-justice campaigner Paul May, who has been involved in a number of successful campaigns, from those of the Birmingham Six to that of young Sam Hallam, wrongly jailed for murder in 2005 but freed on appeal in 2012, reckons that press coverage can prove essential. 'Even cursory media attention can have a positive impact. In several cases with which I've been involved, new witnesses came forward after seeing media reports,' he wrote in *The Justice Gap*. He noted that sympathetic coverage had been given to the campaign by many newspapers and magazines and there had even been coverage on mainstream television, although that had been conditional: 'ITV made clear that, unless the actor Ray Winstone (whose nephew was a close friend of Sam) took part, it was unlikely the film would be made. In this celebrity-obsessed age, we were perhaps fortunate they didn't also insist on Ant and Dec appearing as co-presenters.'

The very way that cases are covered can, suggest campaigners on the issue, lead to a wrong verdict. 'My own view is that any miscarriage of justice is in part, at least, attributable to prejudicial reporting,' said Bob Woffinden, author of *Miscarriages of Justice*, the most comprehensive review of such cases published in book form. 'Generally, when people discuss matters of prejudicial reporting, they automatically but mistakenly begin talking about the national press whereas it is with the local press that the reporting may well be more dangerous.' Woffinden cited the case of Emma Bates, whom he believes was wrongly jailed in Birmingham for the murder of her boyfriend. Her family told Woffinden of their experience of coming out of court and seeing the newspaper placards of the *Birmingham Mail* effectively summarising the prosecution case and realised that the jurors would have had the same experience. 'You then need to consider that this never happens with the defence case, partly because there is not normally a defence opening as such, and partly because by the time it gets round to the defence, the papers have lost interest,' said Woffinden.

But if the press can highlight a miscarriage of justice that might otherwise have never come to light, they can also point the finger of suspicion in the wrong direction with grim results. Such was the case in the murder of Rachel Nickell, who in 1992 was killed in front of her two-year-old son on Wimbledon Common. It was a crime with all too many victims: her partner and father of their child, André Hanscombe; the young son, her family and many friends. But there was an additional victim in the shape of Colin Stagg, the man wrongly accused of killing her.

As with the Birmingham and Guildford pub bomb cases, the pressure on the police to make an arrest is intense, much of it fed by press coverage in the immediate aftermath and indeed for months or years afterwards. If the victim, as in Rachel Nickell's case, was an attractive young blonde woman, the chances of her case being heavily featured in the media were many times greater than if she had been less photogenic and from a different ethnic group. (Unsolved cases of winos beaten to death slip swiftly from public notice; they come under the heading of what some police forces and reporters used to call 'slag on slag' cases, where both victim and murderer were seen as of little social importance, whether they were junkies, dealers, winos, tramps or gang members. In Los Angeles, there is a vile equivalent, NHI, which was used informally by police to describe murders of young black men by young black men. It stands for 'no humans involved'.)

In the Nickell case, the pressure could not have been more intense. The twenty-seventh person arrested was Colin Stagg, a single man described at the time as 'the local weirdo', who was known to walk his dog on the common and in whose home police found a sheath knife, books on the occult and the walls painted black, meaning that he fitted a constructed profile of the killer. In a now infamous series of events, an undercover policewoman was instructed to make contact with him, pretending to be attracted to him and to be excited by the possibility that he might be the murderer. When she told Stagg: 'If only you had done the Wimbledon Common murder, if only you had killed her, it would be all right,' Stagg responded: 'I'm terribly sorry, but I haven't.' But the prosecution proceeded and to a great extent the press, anxious to see someone convicted for such a horrendous crime, accepted the police's version of events.

Stagg was held in jail for thirteen months while he awaited trial. He was fortunate in that Mr Justice Ognall, the judge in front of whom he eventually appeared, was robust enough to see the case against him for what it was – a mishmash of suppositions and mild coincidences, sprinkled with some fanciful psychological speculation. It was thrown out before it went to the jury. But even after Stagg was freed, the innuendos continued, with some members of the press still anxious to tar him with the brush of the 'man who got away with murder'. The drip-drip of misinformation about Stagg continued. While the public made clear their views with the graffiti near his home, the press continued to court any ex-girlfriends willing to sell their story about any 'weirdness'.

'A few days after an incredulous judge threw out the case against Colin Stagg in 1994, I saw the police descend into denial,' wrote the journalist Nick Cohen some years later. He had been working for the *Independent on Sunday* and with its then editor, Ian Jack, went for dinner with a senior officer at New Scotland Yard and the Stagg prosecution was raised. 'The senior officer looked at us as if we were fools. He could assure us that Stagg was as guilty as Crippen.' And many parts of the media continued to try their best to convict Stagg. The late television presenter and hoaxer, Jeremy Beadle, suggested that Stagg should face trial on television. Another high profile television character, the investigative reporter Roger Cook, got Stagg to take a lie detector test on television – which he passed. The *News of the World* ran a story about how the 'weirdo' demanded 'bizarre sex' with his 'terrified' girlfriend close to where Rachel Nickell was murdered. The *Daily Mail* quoted André Hanscombe as saying he was '99 per cent certain' that Stagg was guilty and the government should remove the double jeopardy law so that he could be tried again. It also serialised the book by the officer in charge of the case, Detective Inspector Keith Pedder, headlined 'How British Justice Betrayed Rachel's Son.'

Then, dramatically, in 2008, through compelling DNA evidence, it emerged that Robert Napper, a man already convicted for a double murder, was the real killer. He pleaded guilty at his subsequent trial and was jailed for life. To his credit, Stagg has always said that the real victims in this whole sorry saga are Rachel, André and her family but that did not stop another press furore over his being awarded £250,000 compensation for his ordeal. 'Anger as Colin Stagg's payout dwarfs that of Rachel Nickell's son,' was the *Mail*'s response.

Hanscombe wrote a very gracious letter of apology to Stagg for what he had gone through and described his own experience with the media. 'I am sorry for the ordeal that you have endured during virtually the whole length of this very sad affair, and any part that I might have had personally to make it worse,' wrote Hanscombe. 'I had been led to believe by officers of the Metropolitan Police that they considered you responsible for my partner's death. I know now that you were, and are, an innocent man who was mistakenly charged. I wish you a long, happy and productive life.' Hanscombe, whose new home with his son in France had been discovered by the press, characterised the reporters he encountered as 'callous, mercenary, unfeeling . . . cowardly, snivelling scum'.

Stephen Wright, who covered the case for the *Daily Mail*, was told in April 1996 by a very senior officer that he was 110 per cent certain that Colin Stagg did it. 'The whole mindset of the Met was this man did it and that filtered through to the media. Even when he was acquitted in 1994, a senior officer came out of the Old Bailey and effectively said "We're not looking for anyone else." That taught me a lesson. I went on to do very well on the case and won an award for it . . . I wrote the story that there had been a DNA breakthrough that meant that Napper did it. Stagg was a victim of a smear campaign by the Met. I put my hands up, I fell for it initially. Mitigation would be that virtually everyone fell for it – except for Paul Foot, he was a lone, sceptical voice early on.'

A case with an even higher media profile was the murder of television presenter Jill Dando, shot dead outside her home in Fulham in April 1999. There was much speculation as to why she had been killed. The 'golden hour', which detectives see as the chance to get the first vital clues that lead to a killer, passed with no indications of who had carried out the attack or why. There was no shortage of theories: a disgruntled criminal who had been caught as a result of a *Crimewatch* appeal which Dando presented; a spurned ex-lover; a case of mistaken identity; or a Serbian hit-man angered at her very recent television appeal for Kosovo.

Once again, the person arrested was a 'local weirdo' or, as the *News of the World* described him, a 'bug-eyed odd-ball'. Barry George, who had Asperger's and lived locally, was eventually convicted on slender evidence at the Old Bailey and jailed for life. The coverage of the trial in the press gave little indication that George might well be the victim of a miscarriage of justice. He was, as the spread in the *News of the World* described him, 'the imp who grew into the devil'. He spent more than seven years in jail before an appeal and a retrial in 2008 at which he was acquitted. The press had a particular if tangential role in the prosecution because of his obsessive collection of newspapers: part of the case against him was that he was obsessed with Dando, as evidenced by eight photos of her in newspapers found in his flat – but they were just a few of some 800 newspapers that he had collected, something that was given less prominence in the trial's coverage.

As with Stagg, some of the media were reluctant to accept George's innocence. After his acquittal, he agreed to be interviewed by *News of the World* reporters thinking, perhaps naively, that that might be the end of it. The article was headlined 'I didn't kill Jill Dando . . . I was stalking someone else at the time', something that George had never said. He successfully sued News International for libel. Not long afterwards, he left London for Ireland.

In 2010, came the murder of Joanna Yeates, a twenty-five-year-old Bristol landscape architect who disappeared in December of that year and whose body was found on Christmas Day at the edge of a quarry. She had been strangled. Initial suspicion focussed on her landlord and neighbour, a retired schoolteacher, aged sixty-five, called Christopher Jefferies. Detectives interviewed him for three days and he was released on police bail – a coded indication to reporters if not to the general public that the person is still of interest to the police.

This led to an orgy of speculation, fuelled by gossip and innuendo and his case tells us much about the dangers of too close cooperation between police and reporters: of leading details being given, off the record, leaving the press to draw their own conclusions. Another key issue was that, by 2010, Britain was now deeply into the twenty-four-hour news cycle with the constant pressure from news desks to keep updating stories. Jefferies' photo appeared on the front page of the *Daily Mail* with the headline: 'Could This Man Hold the Key to Joanna's murder?' You did not need to be Hercule Poirot to work out that, as her landlord, Jefferies certainly held the key to her front door. He was, said the *Mail*, 'the teacher they called Mr Strange' and he supposedly admired the poet Christina Rossetti 'who often wrote about death'. Later coverage noted that Jefferies had drawn his pupils' attention to Wilkie Collins's 'Victorian murder novel', *The Moonstone*.

The *Sun*'s front page featured a photo of Jefferies taken thirty years earlier, with blueish hair, and the headline, 'The Strange Mr Jefferies – Kids' nickname for ex-teacher suspect'. Inside, further heavy hints were dropped with the headings of 'Weird', 'Posh', 'Lewd' and 'Creepy' and references to his 'strange walk', the fact that he 'loved poetry, culture', had made 'sexual remarks' and was essentially a 'loner with blue rinse hair'.

'Jo suspect is Peeping Tom' was the *Daily Mirror*'s front-page headline alongside an assertion that 'arrest landlord spied on flat couple' and that he had a 'friend in jail for paedophile crimes'. He also became the 'Nutty Professor' – a minor change in itself as teachers accused of crimes are usually described as 'sirs'. The paper added that 'his eccentric manner and long-term bachelor status sparked unfounded school gossip that he was gay.'

In the *Daily Star*, Jefferies became an 'angry weirdo' with a 'foul temper' and 'a creep who freaked out schoolgirls'. The Sundays joined the hunt with the *Sunday Mirror* pointing out that he had taught pupils Oscar Wilde's 'The Ballad of Reading Gaol', which was 'the story of a man hanged for cutting his wife's throat'. The *Mail on Sunday* discovered that he had shown one class the 1961 Jack Clayton film, *The Innocents*, with its themes of murder and ghostliness.

Brian Cathcart is a professor of journalism at Kingston University, London and a founder of the Hacked Off campaign in 2011 which campaigned for greater press accountability. As he later noted in an article in the *Financial Times*, 'This hostile evidence was founded almost entirely on unnamed witnesses, with some of the most contentious quotations reproduced in several papers'. The Attorney-General, Dominic Grieve, eventually stepped in to remind editors of the Contempt of Court Act, which bans the publication of material relating to an arrested person that could prejudice a future trial. But by then the damage had been done.

Jo Yeates's partner, Greg Reardon, was one of a growing number of people dismayed by the coverage and issued a statement. 'Jo's life was cut short tragically but the finger-pointing and character assassination by social and news media of as yet innocent men has been shameful. It has made me lose a lot of faith in the morality of the British press and those that spend their time fixed to the internet in this modern age.'

Three weeks later a young Dutchman, Vincent Tabak, also a neighbour of the victim, was arrested and charged with the murder. Tabak admitted the killing, was convicted and jailed for life. Jefferies sued the *Sun*, the *Daily Mirror*, the *Sunday Mirror*, the *Daily Record*, the *Daily Mail*, the *Daily Express*, the *Daily Star* and the *Scotsman* and was awarded an estimated £500,000 in compensation. The *Sun* and the *Mirror* were found guilty of contempt of court on the basis that their reporting might well have derailed a future trial. It was also suggested that the coverage was damaging to the investigation in that potential witnesses might well have assumed from the coverage that the police already had their man. The *Sun* was fined £18,000 and the *Mirror* £50,000. Jefferies had never taught either Rossetti or 'The Ballad of Reading Gaol'.

16

True Crime

A Detective Takes Up the Tale

The headlines are worth a thesis in themselves. From 'The Doctor, the Torturers and the Lovestruck Kidnapper' to 'I Ate His Brains . . . It was Very Nice', *True Detective* and its sister publications, now based in south-east London, have been serving up the grisliest details of crime for nearly a century.

The original *True Detective* magazine appeared in the United States in 1924 and was swiftly followed by *Master Detective*. They were the brainchild of an eccentric American publisher called Bernarr Macfadden, who was a keen health and fitness promoter whose other publications included *Physical Culture* and *True Story Magazine*. He also launched the *Daily Graphic*, described by one of its staff as 'the world's zaniest newspaper' and nicknamed the 'Daily Pornographic' by its critics. It covered crime in a highly original way: they liked to stage photographic reconstructions of crime scenes such as, in 1926, the hanging of the gangster Gerald Chapman, which they shot in their art department, very nearly hanging a member of the art department by mistake. If a court case involved a woman having to disrobe in any way, the *Graphic*'s extremely graphic graphic team would helpfully reconstruct the scene.

The *True Detective* magazines tapped into the contemporaneous American fascination with lawlessness in the Prohibition era, which lasted from 1920 to 1933. It was a world of G-men and guns and hot dames and death row. The magazines ran details of famous murders, illustrated with mug shots and unsparing photos of dead bodies in morgues or at crime scenes. At its height, *True Detective* reached sales of two million and had writers like Dashiell Hammett and Jim Thompson as contributors, along with Alan Hynd, Manly Wade Wellman and Walter Gibson. Ann Rule, author of *The Stranger Beside Me*, about the serial killer Ted Bundy, wrote for the magazine under the pseudonym of Andy Stack. The cartoonist Charles Addams was briefly a staff lay-out artist charged with tidying up the grim photos of murder victims, although he has been quoted as saying that 'a lot of those corpses were kind of interesting the way they were'.

British crimes featured in the original *True Detectives*. In 1933, Leslie Randall of the *Daily Express* wrote 'The Astonishing Case of Elsie Cameron' for the magazine, 'a crime that was destined to shock the British Kingdom'. This was the story of Elsie Cameron, a twenty-six-year-old typist who went missing from her London home, to the distress of her parents. Her disappearance coincided with a shortage of human interest stories in Fleet Street, so a reporter was despatched to Crowborough in Sussex where her fiancé, a poultry farmer called Norman Thorne, lived, to investigate and to challenge the police's theory that she might have killed herself as she was known to suffer from 'nerves'. Thorne told the reporter that he was sure some dreadful fate had befallen her and Fleet Street's crime reporters duly descended en masse. Thorne was a supposedly upright young man, who had known Elsie from Sunday School days, had served in the RAF in the First World War, and belonged, along with Elsie, to the Alliance of Honour, an organisation of young people who pledged themselves to chastity.

What is interesting about the story is that Randall and his fellow crime reporters, clearly suspicious of Thorne, felt that the local Sussex police were not up to the job. A month after Elsie's disappearance, 'a party of us drove across country to urge upon the chief constable of Sussex, the necessity of calling in the Yard'. They had their way and 'ace' detective Detective Inspector Gillan was despatched from London. The reporters all

agreed that 'if Thorne is guilty, Gillan is the man to make him "squeak".'
Sure enough, the Yard man soon found a letter from Thorne to another
woman with whom he was having an affair, along with letters from poor
Elsie, who turned out to be pregnant and expecting marriage to the faith-
less Thorne. The police started excavating around the chicken run and
found Elsie's head in a biscuit tin.

Randall recalled of the police dig, supervised by Gillan in his trademark derby hat, that 'reporters, whose cigarettes glowed in the dark, were
the only spectators.' Thorne then claimed that Elsie had hanged herself
on his farm and he had then dismembered her body, a tale not swallowed by the police or the Old Bailey jury. Even after Thorne was charged
with murder, Randall had access to him and Thorne tried to sell his life
story – 'for a fabulous price' – to the *Daily Express*. The case attracted
much attention right through the trial, even Sir Arthur Conan Doyle, who
lived near where the murder took place, expressing a 'faint doubt' about
Thorne's guilt. Hard to imagine today that a group of crime reporters
could persuade a local chief constable that his or her detectives were not
up to the job and they should call in the Yard for help.

The success of *True Detective* led to an avalanche of imitators such
as *Dime Detective*, *Thrilling Detective*, *Startling Detective*, *Amazing Detective*,
Official Detective, *Complete Detective* and *Spicy Detective*, which sounds as
though it should have had a cocktail named after it. They all came with
suitably noir cover lines such as 'Once Over Lightly with Arsenic' or 'The
Slayer at the Foot of the Cross'. Many of the cover illustrations featured
young, scantily-clad women in vulnerable situations and carried headlines
like 'The Little Blonde Goes with Me' or 'They Left Her in the Desert to
Die' and had little to do with detective skills, either masterly or amazing.
'Dickbooks', as they were called, appealed to many, not least the head of
the FBI, J. Edgar Hoover, who had a subscription from the very first edition. But sales slipped as television started to provide its own form of true
crime tales and the American edition of *True Detective* finally embarked
on its own big sleep in 1995. Shiona McArthur, in the book *Crime: Fear or
Fascination?*, cites the attraction of the true crime formula: 'The narrative

voice, influenced by the American crime writing style, is always that of an investigating officer . . . The consumer is addressed as a privileged knowing subject, that is, someone who is something of an expert on murder and violent crime, the details and technical terminology used flatters the reader by implying they are being addressed as fellow experts.'

The format came to Britain in 1950 in the shape of *True Detective*, which now describes itself as 'the world's No. 1 true crime magazine' and its sidekick, *Master Detective*. They incorporated some American crimes – obviously a much richer field – along with local cases. In 1981, *True Crime Monthly* joined them and, in 1991, a quarterly called *Murder Most Foul*. The formula was, as the publishers described it, 'top-quality printing along with expertly crafted prose that described in lingering detail some of the more lurid scenes from modern life and all wrapped up in beautifully designed painted covers'. And the publisher's statement was clear: 'as readers of the dozens of detective magazines spawned by the *True Detective* knew full well, the perfect crime simply doesn't exist. If there was one thing the early detective magazines showed time and again, and month after month, it was that good will almost always prevail over evil.'

Early crimes covered included that of Donald Hume, who later boasted about getting away with the murder of the car dealer Stanley Setty; Thomas Ley, an Australian politician convicted in 1947 of the 'Chalk-pit Murder' in Wimbledon of a barman, John Mudie, whom he suspected of being his mistress's lover and whose body was dumped in a Surrey chalk pit; and Harold Dorian Trevor, a monocled con man with a dozen aliases who spent most of his life in prison, strangled a landlady who had seen him stealing and was hanged in 1942. For many years the magazines were seen prominently on the shelves of local newsagents alongside *Tit-Bits*, *Reveille* and *Woman's Own*, hitting sales of around 35,000 at their peak. As sales for most print publications declined, the True Crime stable, like the satirical magazine *Private Eye*, decided to stick to a purely magazine format and eschew the digital world.

The style for all the titles remained fairly standard: glossy colour cover with mug-shots of murderers and the traditional deathless cover lines like

'Hell's Kitchen Junkie Cooked Girlfriend Into Soup', 'Toy-boy Murdered His Elderly wife – Or Did He?', 'Slaughter in the Toilets' and 'Who Put Arsenic in the Salmon Sandwiches?' Inside were articles on past or present crimes, mainly murders, illustrated with photos of crime scenes, corpses and perpetrators. During Hume's trial at the Old Bailey, the judge held up a copy of the American edition of *True Detective* containing a story on the case and warned the jury to ignore anything they had read.

True Detective itself featured in a murder trial in 1956 when a bearded young pornographer called Leonard Atter was charged with killing a prostitute, Robina Bolton, who had been found battered to death in her flat in Paddington, west London. He admitted being a regular client and being in her company on the night of the murder but claimed that she had given him tea and sandwiches and asked him to leave before another visitor arrived. A copy of the magazine, which featured on its cover an illustration of a distressed woman being dragged into a car, was found in his flat and the suggestion was made that one of the cases reported in it, which also featured a murdered woman, contained 'remarkable similarities' to the killing of Bolton. Atter denied ever having read it, adding that it was not his kind of magazine. He was acquitted on the judge's direction and the murder remains unsolved.

What the genre perfected was a deadpan style that illustrated the banality of so many murderers. A typical example was 'Mansfield Shocker: Couple Buried Wife's Parents in the Garden', published in *True Crime* in 2014. This told the story of Susan and Christopher Edwards who murdered the former's parents, William and Patricia Wycherley, and buried them in their back garden where they lay undiscovered for the next fifteen years. Susan was a librarian and Edwards an accounts clerk, fitting the George Orwell definition of the ideal murderer, who was meant to be a 'little man of the professional class . . . living an intensely respectable life somewhere in the suburbs'.

It was a bizarre story. The couple killed the Wycherleys because they were in debt and to get access to their pensions, which they did successfully for the next fifteen years. It was only when William Wycherley was supposedly about to reach his 100th birthday that suspicions arose, as the Department of Work and Pensions finally decided they needed to interview him to confirm that he was still alive and the Centenarian society wanted to do the same in preparation for his telegram from the Queen. The arrival of the letter indicated to the Edwardses that the game was up so they fled to France where they ran out of money. They then appealed for funds to a relative who alerted the police. They were jailed for life with a minimum sentence of twenty-five years.

There is a staff of seven writers at the stable. Their readers, according to *True Crime*'s Philip Morton, are 'marginally more likely to be female than male, and likely to be aged 40 to 70. A recent small survey conducted via our weekly email bulletin seems to back up what we suspected: age range of respondents was 35 to 79, 60/40 female/male.' What interests their readers most is 'capital punishment and the crimes that led to it, from both sides of the Atlantic'. Their most notable famous reader was the late television presenter Jeremy Beadle, who once guest-edited an issue of *True Detective*. Morton says that the stories that provoke the greatest reader response tend to be 'the ones with connections to other cases – e.g., the observation that the officer who arrested Ruth Ellis – the last woman hanged – was the same officer who had previously arrested Styllou Christofi, the penultimate woman hanged . . . We also tend to receive more mail on modern cases where someone truly despicable (child-killers etc) gets their come-uppance. There seems to be a strong sense of justice, and even retribution, among our correspondents.' Letters from readers referring to particularly unpleasant criminals that conclude 'I hope he rots in hell' would seem to confirm this.

A rival publication, *Real Crime*, was launched in 2015 by the Bournemouth publisher Imagine, partly in response to the increased interest in true crime online, as evidenced by the enormous interest generated by the *Serial* podcast and *The Jinx* documentary mini-series, both of which looked in detail at puzzling murder cases. A glossy, high-quality magazine, it deals with both contemporary and historical crime and numbers among its contributors Seth Ferranti, a former LSD dealer from Virginia who became a writer while serving twenty-one years of a twenty-five-year sentence for drug dealing in the United States.

Real Crime's editor-in-chief, James Hoare, said that it had a readership of 27,000 and, while the staple remained the detailed cover of murder cases, a new readership was also interested in more contemporary subjects like drugs and the dark net. Research indicated, he said, that the new readership also went for in-depth true crime stories in online outlets like *Vice* and the *Huffington Post*. 'Cannabis, ecstasy and heroin are just a mouse-click away,' as one of their stories in 2016 put it. But murders on both sides of the Atlantic dominate the publications. As the writers who descended on a street in Gloucester in the 1990s discovered, the appetite for even the grimmest of murders remains undimmed.

17

The House of Horrors and the Garden of Evil

The West Case and its Legacy for the Press

Few cases in the twentieth century attracted as much media coverage as that of Fred and Rose West, the couple from Gloucester who ensnared, kidnapped, raped and killed at least ten young women and certainly many others over a period of more than twenty years. Never before or since had so many potential witnesses been approached by the press and never before had so much money been offered for their stories.

It was in March 1994 that the *Daily Mirror* published two brief paragraphs under the headline 'Dad Faces Death Case' after the bones of Heather West, the Wests' teenage daughter, had been found in the garden of 25 Cromwell Street. A few days later, when it became apparent that at least two more women had been buried there, the headline was 'Garden of Evil'. Howard Sounes of the *Sunday Mirror*, who worked on the story with the paper's crime reporter Chris House, and later wrote the first full account of the case, *Fred & Rose*, recalled being tipped off by a source in Gloucestershire that there were certainly more bodies buried in the cellar, so the story then moved from the back garden and became and remained 'The House of Horrors'. From then until the trial of Rosemary West, which ended in Winchester Crown Court in November 1995, the press was to play a major part in the case.

Fred West was a consummate liar, as was shown throughout the trial by the way in which he and Rose had managed to slip their way out of any inquiries about the missing women. He continued to lie to people who visited him in prison and whom he knew would pass on tit-bits to the press. He was envious of the amount of money – some of it highly exaggerated – that he had heard was being made by his relatives and acquaintances signing deals with reporters. A number of newspapers had placed ads in the local press asking anyone who knew the Wests to call a number if they thought they could 'help with enquiries'. This infuriated the detectives working on the case because it was phrased to sound as though it was the police asking for potential witnesses to come forward.

Before he could stand trial, on New Year's day in 1995, Fred West disobligingly hanged himself in his cell in Winson Green prison. He obviously knew he was going to be convicted and perhaps, in his twisted way, he thought that he might remove some of the pressure from his wife by absenting himself from the dock. His death did at least spare the relatives of the murdered women from having to hear the lies and claims he had made to the police after his arrest – that it was all their fault, that they had made advances to him and he had swatted them away and killed them by mistake.

There was fierce competition between the *Sun*, the *Daily Star* and the *News of the World* over the coverage of his funeral. The body was eventually removed clandestinely from Birmingham morgue and there was a tussle between photographers fighting to get pictures of the hearse.

When Rosemary West appeared for her committal hearing at Dursley magistrates' court the following month, children were handed eggs by reporters to throw at the van in which she was transported. Some of the camera crews and photographers missed the moment of her arrival so the jeering bystanders helpfully restaged it, although she was by now inside the court. At the hearing the defence counsel Sasha Wass argued that her client had little chance of a fair hearing because of the 'unremitting, sensational, inaccurate and misleading' coverage in the media. She suggested that the press had already accepted as fact the story of one of the Wests' victims, Caroline Owens, which had been published just after Fred's suicide, and that the public must already believe that her client was guilty.

Caroline Owens, who had worked briefly for the Wests as a nanny, was one of their early victims and might be counted as lucky to have escaped with her life. At the age of sixteen, in 1972, she was hired by the Wests, both of whom tried to seduce her. When she tried to leave they attacked and stripped her. Fred told her that if she did not agree to what he wanted he could 'keep you in the cellar and let my black friends have you and when we've finished we'll kill you and bury you under the paving stones of Gloucester'. She managed to escape and her mother called the police who arrested the Wests but, amazingly, they received only a fine when they appeared in the magistrates' court and there was only a very brief account of their case in the *Gloucestershire Citizen*; Rose West kept the clipping amongst her private possessions. After the Wests were arrested a second time, Caroline Owens contacted the police again.

Shortly afterwards, she was surprised to see two men in Wellington boots and Barbour jackets on her Gloucestershire doorstep. They informed her that they were from the *Sun* and were going to be writing her story. In *The Lost Girl*, her book on the case published in 2005 under her current name of Caroline Roberts, she says she told them she did not want her story to be in the papers but they said someone would do it anyway and she may as well take the *Sun*'s fee as compensation.

The *Sun*'s first offer of £500 quickly went up to £10,000 – and she agreed to it. The *Sun* informed her that other reporters had tracked her down and were on their way so she should come with them to the upmarket Chase Hotel near Ross-on-Wye, where they would hide her. She was not allowed to tell her family where she was in case they tipped off the pursuing pack. By the time she got back home, other reporters and photographers had arrived and camped outside her home, so she used a friend as a decoy to distract them.

The *Sunday Mirror* came in with an offer of £50,000 but by then she had signed a contract with the *Sun*. One photographer refused to depart, saying that his editor had told him he could not leave until he had a photo of her and he had children to support and needed the job. 'He was using emotional blackmail on me,' she wrote. 'I told him to tell his editor to go to hell and slammed the phone down.'

Thus the day after Fred West's suicide, the *Sun* ran a double-page spread under the headline, 'I Was Fred West's Sex Slave', complete with photos from Owens' modelling career. 'I was furious with them for publishing such a story without first telling me so that I would be forewarned and fore-armed.' She charged nothing for an interview with the *Guardian* in which she expressed her sadness that the police had not followed up her case more vigorously at the time as the Wests went on to carry out so many rapes and murders. She talked about the effect of the publicity: 'Blokes who've had a few come up and say, "You slept with Fred West, didn't you?" Other people go "Oh, there's Caroline, £75,000 richer," which is a load of nonsense.' She confronted one local newspaperman who made a big deal of the money. 'I said, "If I offered you £1 million to let your daughter go through what I went through would you accept it?" He said, "No."'

Apart from the publicity generated by the Caroline Owens story, Sasha Wass suggested that there was now a catalogue of factors that meant that Rose West could never receive a fair trial. For instance, the *News of World* had published the supposed confessions of Fred West that he had carried out abortions in the house. In addition, the suggestion in the *Daily Mirror* that there was a possibility that Rose West might make £10 million from selling her story – if acquitted, of course – was juxtaposed with a story that the mother of one of the murdered girls was unable to afford the costs of a proper burial for her daughter. Many of these cases were referred to the attorney general but he declined to intervene.

For the prosecution, Neil Butterfield QC argued that, in fact, the pros-ecution had suffered more from the pre-trial coverage in the media in that Fred West had supposedly told the *News of the World*, before he hanged himself in his cell, that his wife had nothing to do with the murders. The magistrate, Peter Badge, declined to delay proceedings.

The trial of Rosemary West took place in Winchester Crown Court in October that year. It lasted eight weeks and was attended by dozens of journalists from all over the world; more than 150 applied for accreditation. Such was the demand for places in court that there was an overspill room and reporters were warned that if they failed to take up their assigned place for a single day, they would lose it for the rest of the trial. I covered it for the *Guardian*.

As each witness appeared, I would make a note beside their names so that I could recall them afterwards. Most notes just had observations like 'fair hair/pony-tail/leather jacket' or 'smart/black hair/fringe/Welsh' but looking through seven notebooks from the trial, I noticed how often the phrase 'dead eyes' cropped up. These were the 'lucky' ones, the people who had been sexually abused, gagged with masking tape, tied up or raped by the Wests but who had escaped with their lives and were now having to relive the experience in front of the world's media.

It is a tradition that newspapers often send a 'colour' writer down to the big set-piece trials. Their arrival is usually resented by the reporter covering the case on a day-to-day basis as they take over the allotted seat in the press box and then write a piece of suitably purple prose – sometimes cheerfully inaccurate – before heading off into the sunset. There was no shortage of such writers for the West case, possibly the last time that the press, still in pre-digital days, would be able to marshal such a battalion of reporters able to work on nothing else for two months. What emerges in such a long trial is the mundane detail, such as that the Wests signed letters to each other with the words 'ever-worshipping'. They were not the traditional serial-killing 'loners', strange, remote characters like Dennis Nilsen, Peter Sutcliffe, Ian Brady or Colin Ireland – who had read in the press that you needed to kill at least five people to rate as a serial killer and duly murdered five men whom he picked up in gay bars. The Wests lived on a busy street, had children at the local schools and, to a young woman hitch-hiking in Gloucestershire, must have seemed like the perfect lift: a married couple with a couple of nippers in the back seat.

During the trial, the jury asked to be shown round the 'House of Horrors' – for once the cliché seemed appropriate. The judge, Mr Justice Mantell, said that one journalist could accompany them and mine was the name picked out of the hat. The deal in these situations is that the journalist concerned has to produce a 'pooled report' which he or she gives to everyone who wants it for use at the end of the trial. We had to don hard hats, no talking or dallying was permitted and we were not allowed to take notes, so the visit became like Kim's game – how much could you remember?

Was the mural in the room with the bar a Hawaiian or Caribbean scene? What struck me was how small the house was, how tiny the rooms, how close everyone must have been to the violence and how confident the Wests must have been to rape, kill and bury their victims when there were so many children and lodgers in such close proximity.

There were at least half a dozen authors covering the trial, among them the late Gordon Burn, Brian Masters, Geoffrey Wansell, Andrew O'Hagan and Howard Sounes. 'They were both so odd, in so many ways,' said Sounes of the Wests, looking back on the case in 2015. 'Not just wicked and bloodthirsty, but madly weird, even comically weird in the case of Fred, who had the appearance of a music hall maniac with his Marx Brothers hair, bug out eyes and gappy teeth. It dawned on me in the first couple of weeks that I was gathering too much material for use in the newspaper, even for the backgrounder after the trial. I had always wanted to write books, and here was the makings of a book. In that sense it turned into a fascinating and rewarding project, one that changed my life in that it allowed me to get out of newspapers and write full time, which I have ever since. Now almost twenty years later, I still have the mugshot photos of Fred and Rose the police handed out. I often think of having them framed, to hang in my flat as a reminder of what I owe the couple – but I suppose that would be considered bad taste.'

Once again, as in the committal hearing, the media's role in the case was prominent. The argument put forward by West's defence team, the dashing and charming Ulsterman, Richard Ferguson QC, and Sasha Wass, was that the offers of money to witnesses had poisoned the well: the witnesses concerned would know that their story would be worthless if Rosemary West was acquitted and so had every incentive to gild the lily. At one stage, Ferguson unsuccessfully requested the judge to order both the editors of the *Sun* and the *Daily Mirror* to attend court and to provide documentation of what the witnesses had told them, so that there could then be a comparison between what they had told the papers and what they would tell the court. Lord Wakeham, the then chairman of the Press Complaints Commission, said it was one of the most serious issues his organisation had faced. The prosecutor, one Brian Leveson QC, was getting a very early lesson in the ways of the press.

Caroline Owens was one of the most riveting witnesses. Described by Brian Masters in his book, *She Must Have Known*, as 'formidably attractive', he said that reporters covering the case 'felt like intruders on her intimacy just as her assailants had been'. She was asked about her dealings with the press and explained that she had contacted the police as soon as she heard of Fred West's arrest and had then been in negotiations with the press and was due to receive a total of £20,000 – the *Sun* had doubled their original offer. When, in re-examination, she was asked why she had agreed to give evidence if it was not for commercial gain through a newspaper story, she broke down in a way that affected everyone in court and said: 'I want to get justice for those girls who didn't make it because I feel it was my fault.' Masters noted that 'at that moment those of us who had doubted her felt ashamed'.

An even more remarkable witness, in some ways, was Janet Leach. She, then aged thirty-eight, had been called in by the police to be an 'appropriate adult' because Fred West was deemed to have learning difficulties and would need to have someone to explain things to him. 'Appropriate adults' were taken from a list of volunteers, prepared to sit in on police interviews with children or vulnerable grown-ups.

It transpired that she had a verbal agreement with the *Mirror* for £100,000 for her story. She was certainly well placed to spill the beans as she had spent a total of 400 hours listening to Fred West's grim confessions and boasts. Her story was turned into an ITV two-part drama in 2011, with Dominic West playing Fred and Emily Watson as Leach. Until then most film companies had shied away from touching the story.

When Anne Marie, Fred West's daughter, gave her devastating account of how she had been raped by her father with her stepmother, Rose, watching and making sarcastic remarks, there was a chill in the court. Should such details have been passed on to rattle around in people's heads? Was it pornography? 'We are none of us untainted,' Gordon Burn observed at the time. The Sky crime correspondent, Martin Brunt, described it as 'the grimmest, saddest story I ever covered'. I have never reported a case about which so many people told me that they could not read what I had written. At the end, I asked one of the prosecution witnesses, a woman who had had an affair with Rose, for her reaction to the verdict. She was with a minder and would not speak for less than £200.

Rose West continued to protest her innocence all the way to an unsuccessful appeal. Her lawyer, Leo Goatley, claimed that 'intrusive media activities' had blighted the trial. He said that 'The kind of money offered to some witnesses represents for them the source of their material well-being in the future which they could not otherwise have dreamed of.'

There were widespread political ramifications. The Lord Chancellor, Lord Mackay, announced that he had asked for a report into payments made by journalists to witnesses. The attorney general, Nicholas Lyell, said that 'more witnesses have been offered money than in any other modern case'. Tony Butler, chief constable of Gloucestershire, said that he and his officers were constantly fearful that the press coverage could have 'blown the case out of the water'. At one press conference, he asked, 'Are we running the criminal justice system as an entertainment business?' and suggested that the behaviour of some of the press had turned the case into a game of Russian roulette. There was talk of making it illegal to pay witnesses for their stories because there was no legal sanction against the press unless it could be shown that they intended to interfere with the course of justice. This would have meant that it had to be shown that the press was coaching the witnesses to exaggerate their tale.

This was not the first occasion when payments to witnesses had been an issue. In 1966, in the trial of Ian Brady and Myra Hindley, for the Moors Murders, it transpired that a key prosecution witness, David Smith, was due to earn £1,000 from the *News of the World*, who had already paid for him and his wife to holiday in France and had 'minded' him for months before the trial. The paper was not penalised as Smith's fee was not dependent on a conviction. This led to the Press Council, then under Lord Devlin, arriving at a principle that witnesses should neither be paid in advance of a trial nor interviewed until after the trial and that nobody involved in a crime should be paid, unless it was in the public interest to do so.

The subject was raised again when Peter Sutcliffe, the Yorkshire Ripper, was finally arrested for murdering thirteen women and stood trial in 1981. Roger Ratcliffe, who covered the case for the *Sunday Times*, recorded in a *Guardian* article in 2006 that the race for a media deal with his wife, Sonia, was 'the main sport in town for several months. The popular estimate of its worth at the time was £1 million.' Sutcliffe's father had already been bought up by the *Daily Mail* and the *News of the World* started bidding for Sonia at £80,000, with the *Mail* and *Express* offering her jointly £50,000. The *Express* topped that with £80,000 and the *News of the World* with £110,000. Sonia did not sell her story but passed on the many offers she received to the Press Council. She also sued *Private Eye* for suggesting she had taken money and was awarded £600,000 in damages, reduced on appeal to an agreed £160,000. She also successfully sued other publications.

At the bottom end of the scale was a camera-shy acquaintance of Sutcliffe's who told tales to the press through his letter-box in exchange for a tenner for every useable quote. The *People* was censured for paying £12,500 to a woman Sutcliffe met in Glasgow. The mother of one of the murdered women described all such deals as 'blood money' and there were many official pledges that this sort of behaviour must end.

After the trial, the Press Council stepped in again with a 70,000-word report published in February 1983, noting many acts in breach of the 1966 principles. 'Newspapers had fooled their readers by denying that they would ever pay the wife of a mass murderer,' wrote Roy Greenslade in *Press Gang*. 'They were prepared to go to extraordinary lengths to cover up their duplicity and they did so while knowingly defying the Press Council's strictures.' All this was forgotten in the frenzy created by the Wests.

In October 1996, Gloucester Council decided to demolish 25 Cromwell Street because it had become a macabre tourist attraction and doubtless, in a world of selfies, would be even more so today. The destruction was organised as a public spectacle as a symbol of the end of the Wests as part of the city. The actual contents of the house, including the Wests' fourposter bed, the bar and the 25 Cromwell Street sign, had already been removed, taken to RAF Quedgeley and destroyed in a bid to frustrate souvenir hunters. The entire house was demolished by a local firm, taken to a tip and crushed to dust. It was a farewell for the media to both the House of Horrors and the Garden of Evil.

Counselling was offered to reporters who had covered the case. One reporter, on being asked about it, lifted his pint of beer and said 'this is my counselling'. Stephen Wright, who covered the case for the *Daily Mail*, said, 'The evidence was very harrowing. I think we all self-censored. I think two or three journalists did take the counselling offered and I think there was a bit of sniggering about that because of the macho press pack. When I was in New York for 9/11 in 2001 there was a similarly macho attitude about the horrors that we, as journalists, witnessed. Personally I found the story difficult, people begging for help to find their missing loved ones, but it was years before I was open about that.'

A year after the trial, a group of reporters and writers who covered the case met in a London club for a reunion dinner. The instruction on the invitation was that there should be no mention of the Wests after ten minutes. It was not observed.

18
Crashing the Barriers
An Unsuitable Job for a Woman?

Sitting on the Old Bailey press benches for the trial in 1933 of a young man accused of murdering his father-in-law was a remarkable bohemian character called Fryn Tennyson Jesse, who was a pioneer for women crime reporters. Crime was then regarded – and still is to a lesser extent – as something that was carried out by men, investigated by men, prosecuted by men and reported by men, so the sight of a young, free-spirited woman covering the trial would have been remarkable to say the least.

'He is the only prisoner whom I have ever seen who wore a black tie and a black mourning-band round his arm as a sign of sorrow for the person he was accused of killing,' wrote Jesse of Reginald Hinks, a door-to-door salesman from Bath who had killed his father-in-law and tried to cover it up as a suicide by shoving his victim's head in the oven. It is one of many such observations she would make as she became a specialist in writing about murder cases.

Jesse cut her journalistic teeth at *The Times* where the editor, who employed her for a doomed 'feminine supplement', described her as the most beautiful woman he had ever seen. She had started taking morphine to treat the severe pain from an accident in which her hand was caught in a plane's propeller, and it became an addiction. She was also involved in compiling six volumes of *Notable British Trials*.

She was a fearless soul and, in 1914, aged twenty-six, persuaded the *Daily Mail* to send her to cover the early days of what would become the First World War. As Joanna Colenbrander describes it in her biography, *A Portrait of Fryn*, Jesse reported under such headlines as 'Girl in the Firing Line – the Advantage of Being Small' and left Antwerp only the day before the German army arrived.

Murder fascinated her and she wrote *Murder and Its Motives* in 1924, in which she suggested that the woman criminal was 'the panther of the underworld. She can follow relentlessly through the jungle day after day, she can wait her time, she can play with her victim and torture him in sheer wantonness, and she can pile cruelty upon the act of killing as does the panther, but never the lion.' This led to her being taken on by the publisher Harry Hodge for his *Notable British Trials* series and she developed an excellent relationship with the police as a result.

In 1939, the *Daily Mail* sent her to France to cover the trial, in Versailles, of serial killer Eugen Weidmann. Weidmann, a German career criminal who kidnapped and killed for money, was the last person publicly executed in France. During the case she met the novelist Colette, who, unusually for a novelist, was covering it for *Paris Soir*. Jesse, who had a troubled life punctuated by many suicide attempts, went on to write regularly for the *Manchester Guardian* and died in 1958.

She was indeed a rare sight on the press benches at the Old Bailey – it would take many years before women reporters were regularly covering murder cases. Nevertheless, there were some notable examples – and these were women who had to fight many preconceptions. In his novel *The Street of Adventure*, published in 1919, Philip Gibbs has a lively female reporter, Katherine Halstead, who turns down an offer of marriage by saying, 'I dare say it would be amusing for a little while, but afterwards the woman gets so tired of it all – women like me, I mean . . . selfish, restless creatures, who have got the poison of Fleet Street in their blood.' This remained the image, for many years, of the tough woman reporter.

Hilde Marchant, who wrote the memorable piece on the 'Murder Gang' for *Picture Post*, was also reporting trials from the Old Bailey during that period. One that she covered was that of Florence Ransom, sentenced to death in November 1940 for murdering her lover's wife, daughter and maid with a shotgun at their home in Kent; her sentence was commuted and she was sent to Broadmoor secure hospital. Marchant reported in the *Daily Express* that the trial was interrupted by an air raid siren and noted that there seemed little public interest in a case which would normally have been front page news, because there was already so much death around. One of her former editors, Arthur Christiansen, called her 'the best woman reporter that ever worked in Fleet Street'. In his memoir *Scoops and Swindles* another crime reporter, Alfred Draper, wrote sadly that Marchant, like too many of her colleagues, succumbed to the bottle and was found dying on the pavement, 'The lovely features that had turned many a reporter's heart ravaged by the demon that stalked The Street.'

Harry Procter, in his memoir *The Street of Disillusion*, talks about his coverage of the Craig and Bentley case and how he was helped by his colleague, Madeline MacLoughlin, who played a key role in gaining the confidence of the Craig family, befriending the killer's mother and sister. Procter said of MacLoughlin that she had 'a quality extremely rare in women; that of being liked by other women'. Her other function was keeping rival reporters at bay as they also sought interviews with the Craigs. In many ways, that reflected the period for both female reporters and police officers, the latter, still called 'WPCs' or even, disparagingly by some of their colleagues, 'burglar's dogs'; they were meant to stick to domestic subjects and leave the bloody murders to the chaps.

The first woman to become a daily newspaper crime correspondent in Fleet Street and the chairman of the Crime Reporters' Association was Sylvia Jones. She had arrived in London from Shropshire to start her journalistic career in the sixties with the *Hampstead and Highgate Express* and found her way to the old broadsheet *Sun* by upping her age from twenty-one to twenty-three – the minimum age at that time for a job in Fleet Street.

'I just wanted to be a reporter but initially I was on the *Sun*'s women's page, which was called Pacesetters,' said Jones. 'I hated it, having to take down copy from fashion shows in Paris. And they didn't like me going to the pub where the printers went, didn't think a young lady should be doing that.'

She left and became a general reporter with the Press Association: 'You covered fires and robberies. I started doing investigations there, including student sit-ins in 1968 at the LSE. It was the first time I was allowed to wear trousers to work! Women in those days were not even allowed to wear smart trouser-suits to work but I was allowed to so I would blend in more with the students. That was my first undercover investigation and I grew to love them.'

After her first child was born, she worked nights. 'That was when all the IRA bombs were going off in London and most of them were at night, so I probably covered more bombs in London than anyone else and they were always splashes.' She joined the *Daily Star*, working on the news-desk and also doing investigations into a 'Frankenstein Farm' where experiments were carried out on animals, and the 'Hostel Hovels', where homeless people lived and where some of the women were raped by the men who ran them. She moved from the *Star* after two years to the *Mirror*, again on the news-desk.

'I had a network of contacts and I was getting more stories than the two men who were doing crime. Then in 1983, I had a call from a contact at two in the morning saying, 'You had better get up to Cranley Gardens – it's another Christie.' I thought that they were talking about Stuart Christie [the young Scottish anarchist who had tried to blow up Franco in Spain]. I said, 'How many?' 'We think seven or eight and going up.' And I thought – whoops, it's mass murder!' This was the first news about Dennis Nilsen, subsequently jailed for life for the murders of young men whom he had taken to his home in Muswell Hill, north London, and killed.

She was persuaded by a senior *Mirror* executive, the late Richard Stott, who often edited the paper, to become Fleet Street's first female crime correspondent. The news of the appointment of a woman to the post sent shockwaves around the paper and the industry. 'There was huge anger, huge ructions inside the *Daily Mirror*. Some people gave me a really hard time. One of them later said, "I thought you'd sink but, by Jesus, you swam." That was the nearest he got to an apology.'

Some members of the Crime Reporters' Association did their best to exclude her from the organisation. 'They tried to find a rule in their constitution that would keep me out. Eventually Richard Stott wrote a legal letter saying they would take it to court. Even then they would try and exclude me from briefings.' When she got exclusive stories, rumours would be spread that she must have slept with a police officer to get them. 'Every time I got a front page story, there would be anonymous phone calls to my then husband saying, "She's over the side with him." It was really nasty. My marriage was falling apart anyway but you could do without that.'

When she became chairman of the CRA, some of the other members suggested that the chain of office – a large masonic-looking item – was not designed for a woman to wear. 'One of them even said that the chain was "made for a man with a constitution" and I said, "Don't worry, I don't have a beer belly but I do have quite a good cleavage." I had the chain shortened and wore it all the time with as low a neckline as I could get away with. The police were fine, the criminals were fine, the journalists were horrendous. Any time I was seen drinking with a police contact I would be very anxious about their reputation. Kenneth Newman, the then Met Commissioner, even asked me on one occasion if I was having "an improper relationship" with somebody and I never did. I made it a rule that I would only have lunch with people not a dinner – if I had got drunk like the men did, can you imagine the stories that would have floated round?'

There was, at the time, a huge drinking culture within both the press and the police, particularly noticeable at the seaside conferences of the Association of Chief Police Officers (ACPO), the Superintendents' Association and the Police Federation. 'At a Federation conference in Blackpool one year one crime reporter got really drunk and was banging on my hotel door in the middle of the night because he wanted to come in and screw me; he thought I was screwing everybody else so it was only fair. I had to have the hotel remove him to the staff annexe. It was just awful. It never occurred to them that I might have been a better journalist than them and that was why I was getting the stories.'

The Flying Squad used to have a boozy charity boxing night in which police boxers fought London boxing club members. The tradition was that the chairman of the CRA presented some of the prizes, so Jones was puzzled when she heard about the event but received no invitation. Roy Penrose was the commander of the squad at the time. 'I rang him up and said, "Roy, I haven't had my invitation." He was very embarrassed and apologetic and said, "I didn't think you'd want to come, it's a pretty all-male event" and I said, "the CRA chairman always comes" so he offered to send a car to pick me up which I didn't accept. I bought a slinky black evening dress and arrived at the top of the stairs (into the basement where the boxing was taking place) at this hotel in Kensington and there were hundreds of men and I could see them going "Wooo!" which was just the reaction I wanted. I sat at the top table with Roy – I had to dodge the blood from some of the boxers – and a lot of the cast from *The Bill* were there. I remember saying I just wanted to be treated as one of the lads.'

She found dealing with villains easier than dealing with some of the other reporters. 'I used to go out on drinking jags in the Great Western Hotel in Paddington with the Richardson crew after Charlie came out of prison. At first I was never allowed to buy a round so I would give the barman £25, quite a lot of money in those days, and say, "Give them a bottle of champagne when I've gone." Charlie described me as a "classy broad" and then let me pay my way.'

She also had what would have been rather unique experiences for a crime reporter at the time. In the wake of the big 1987 Knightsbridge Safety Deposit robbery, she went undercover using the name Sally Jones in Harrods because one of the women connected to the mastermind, Valerio Viccei, had allegedly operated as a hooker from there. 'I was there for about a month and I was still having to make a check call [to Scotland Yard's press bureau] in the coffee breaks. I had to get up really early to put on lots of make-up because I was about twenty years older than most of the girls. The fashion editor of the *Mirror* used to get clothes in and I swear she always got them a size too small for me. There was one black dress with a little frill at the bottom, like a tutu. I had a mini-cab to take me down to the pick-up joints near Harrods and he clearly thought I was a hooker and when I asked him for a receipt, he said he didn't have a book on him but "I'll bring it round to your house tomorrow"!'

After leaving the *Mirror* she worked as an investigative journalist for ITV's *Cook Report*, including one programme on Freddie Scappaticci, or 'Stakeknife', the IRA double agent. She also worked for the BBC and for independent television companies carrying out major investigations. She won a Royal Television Society award for a *Panorama* programme on Baby P.

Another pioneering woman reporter who specialised in crime was Shan Davies, who died in 2008. In an affectionate obituary for the website Gentlemen Ranters, Liz Hodgkinson described her as 'quite simply, the toughest female reporter ever known in the *Sunday People*'s long history. From the time she started working for the paper in 1976, she would enthusiastically undertake assignments that would make even the most hardened male reporters wince and shake their heads.'

A bank manager's daughter from Sheen, south-west London, she had always wanted to work in Fleet Street and made her way there after leaving school at 16, going to secretarial college and working at the *Kilburn Times*. When she joined the *Sunday People*, she was one of four women reporters out of around 150. She hung out with criminals and became friendly with Charlie Kray, the twins' older brother. On one occasion she was knocked out by the girlfriend of a criminal who had spotted Davies interviewing her boyfriend in a pub and had not realised she was a reporter.

Pretending to be a prostitute for an exposé of the porn industry, Davies was offered a part in a raunchy film. 'This time her cover was almost blown when she dropped her notebook on her way to the ladies', and it was picked up by the lighting cameraman,' wrote Hodgkinson, the author of *Ladies of the Street*, which celebrates women journalists. 'After leafing though the book, he handed it back to Shan, saying: "There can't be many prostitutes with perfect Pitman's shorthand." She quickly replied: "Oh, I used to be a secretary. But I couldn't make enough money at it."' She was also sent to walk in the footsteps of the Yorkshire Ripper, when he was still at large and she cheerfully regaled other crime reporters with what she got up to in the back of taxis with drunk detectives before her marriage. She died aged only fifty-five, one of many crime reporters to slip off early to the newsroom in the skies.

Jones and Davies were succeeded by others: Barbara McMahon at the *Evening Standard*, Lucy Panton at the *News of the World*, Andrea Perry at the *Sunday Express*, Rosie Cowan and Sandra Laville at the *Guardian*, Rebecca Camber at the *Daily Mail*, Fiona Hamilton at *The Times* and ITV's Ronke Phillips. Life had changed by the new millennium, although even in September 2015, when the Hatton Garden burglars pleaded guilty at Woolwich Crown Court, of the eighteen reporters on the press benches, only three were women.

Sandra Laville became crime correspondent at the *Guardian* in 2004. She started her career as general reporter with the *Northampton Chronicle and Echo* in 1991, then joined the *Telegraph* where she covered the case of Harold Shipman, the doctor convicted in 2000 of fifteen murders but suspected of many, many more.

'I was put onto it when they started exhuming the bodies so I was sent up to dig around in his life for a couple of weeks. It was hours in the library and trying to find his schoolmates – pre-internet! Going through microfiches of his old school rugby team photographs, I was one step behind the *Daily Mail* so I was quite pleased with myself when I found one of his friends who gave me the photographs from his school. Bingo! Also I found out that at his previous surgery he had been disciplined for stealing drugs.'

She covered his trial at Preston Crown Court. 'It was great fun, they don't seem to do trials like that now . . . On the day after he was convicted I went to the graveyard where lots of his victims were buried and there were relatives there re-laying flowers, it was really quite moving.'

Laville, whose partner Sean O'Neill was *The Times*' crime editor, also covered the case of Damilola Taylor, the ten-year-old boy murdered by a gang in London in 2000. 'It was horrific. I had to go and shake the news-desk because they weren't particularly interested at first. I eventually got the first interview with his parents, Richard and Gloria. It was the first time there had been two black people on the front page of the *Telegraph*. I found it a very emotional case to do. His father is lovely and I kept in touch with them for years.'

Had her gender made any difference to her life as a crime correspondent? 'As a woman, the police were a bit scared of me, partly because I was from the *Guardian* but I had known some of them for a long time, from the *Ham and High* and *Standard* days. I found on issues like rape and domestic violence they took me more seriously than the male reporters.

'For ages it was just me and Lucy Panton and then Rebecca Camber on the *Mail*. If we went to ACPO conferences, we would be the only women round the dinner table. The other crime reporters treated me perfectly normally although if they swore they would apologise which used to annoy me. I couldn't keep up with their drinking. There was a camaraderie but sometimes it would annoy me that everyone talked to everyone too much. There would be the "line" which everyone would agree on. I always chose to go a different way. Most of the ones I know – much as I love them – would always believe that the bloke in the dock was guilty. I think you always have to lift the stone and see what's there.'

The 2012 report on police-media relations carried out by Elizabeth Filkin for the Metropolitan Police warned police to watch out for crime reporters 'flirting' in order to get information. 'Lucy and I felt really offended because we were the only women and she [Filkin] said that crime correspondents 'cajoled and flirted'. It was all very sexist.

'Compared to some of the gnarled crime hacks I think I have a different way of approaching a family but I was off for six weeks because covering the child abuse cases all became too much. I did the Baby P case [the seventeen-month-old boy who died after suffering horrific injuries at his home in north London in 2007] and the Oxford trafficking case [a gang of abusers who subjected vulnerable girls in Oxford to years of rape, torture and extreme sexual violence and who were convicted at the Old

Bailey in May 2013]. That was the worst evidence I have ever heard, it was animalistic. You couldn't write most of it, it was self-censorship.

'I also did the Tia Sharp case [the twelve-year-old raped and murdered by Stuart Hazell in 2012; Hazell was jailed for a minimum of thirty-eight years]. They had this photo of her that he had taken on his phone that was shown blown-up in court . . . It was physically shocking, lots of us felt that it was too much. I felt I had had enough darkness so I took a break and I had some counselling and the counsellor said to me, "You know, if you were a police officer or social worker you wouldn't have done this for six or seven years without having some time out," which is probably true. Crime correspondents see a lot of nasty stuff.'

So what is the attraction of covering crime?

'You see all of life. It's the only reporting, other than going into a war zone, where you see people in extremis and how they respond to tragedy and violence. Extraordinary stories come out of a murder, people's lives get turned upside down.' And over the centuries, some of the most extra-ordinary stories have involved women as the accused.

19

Femmes Fatales, Molls and Madams

The Woman in the Dock

When a beautiful young woman was charged with a crime, she could be guaranteed lavish coverage of her case in the press. There would be no shortage of salacious prose used to describe her and to analyse her motivation.

In 1857, Madeleine Smith, a young Glasgow beauty, was charged with the murder of a Frenchman, Pierre Emile L'Angelier, with whom she had exchanged many love letters, some of them very explicit for the time. When she tried to end the affair and asked for the letters back, L'Angelier refused and threatened to show them to her father. The case against her was powerful: she had been seen at a chemist's ordering arsenic and soon afterwards L'Angelier died of arsenic poisoning.

The story enthralled not just Scotland but the whole of Britain. 'This trial will always rank among the causes célèbres of the world,' wrote the *Observer* on 13 July 1857, with some justification as it became a bigger news story than the Indian Mutiny with which it coincided. And from the earliest reports of murder trials, the female killer has frequently been portrayed as in many ways darker, more dangerous and dastardly than the male. By Victorian times, 'the popular press had, through its sensational treatment of such figures, defined the murderess as a cold-blooded monster who operated by stealth and was particularly attracted to poison as a weapon,' wrote Judith Knelman in 'Women Murderers in Victorian Britain', an article in *History Today* in 1998.

The women who killed were seen as traitors to their sex. 'Although the Victorian press was attempting to bridge the gap between the "otherness" of remote events and the everyday world of the reader, to expand reality to include what was seen and heard by others, it tended to treat crime as a fiction while presenting it as a fact.'

Certainly the case of Madeleine Smith had all the ingredients of a good noir novel: the beauty, the exotic foreigner, the passionate forbidden affair, the blackmail, the poison, the arrest, the trial and then – what verdict would the jury reach? The people of Glasgow, as *The Times* on 4 April reported, had been 'deeply moved by the report that a gentleman had been poisoned by his sweetheart, the daughter of a highly respectable family which moves in the better classes of society'. Key to many of the reports of women who committed murder were both their looks and their class. The report in *The Times* was in no doubt as to the shocking nature of the case and a possible motive.

'The thought that a highly and virtuously bred young lady could destroy her lover is too appalling for belief,' said the paper while passing on the rumour that 'a gentleman in a much more promising and prominent position in life than that occupied by L'Angelier had become a suitor for the young lady's hand' might provide a motive, while acknowledging that this was just 'the rumour of the day'. Smith's defence would argue that she had bought arsenic for use as a cosmetic and that L'Angelier might have poisoned himself.

It was a complex case held in the High Court in Edinburgh. No fewer than 89 witnesses were listed to be called and some 200 of the letters which had passed between the two lovers were to be given in evidence. Unsurprisingly, interest was intense. The press benches were expanded and hundreds waited outside to compete for the seats in the public galleries. The jury took only 25 minutes to reach a verdict of not guilty on one count and 'not proven' on the second and third counts. Madeleine Smith was a free woman.

The *Ayrshire Express* was in full flow: 'From the first moment to the last, Miss Smith has preserved that undaunted, defiant attitude of perfect repose which has struck every spectator with astonishment. She passes from the cab to the courtroom, or rather to the cell beneath the dock, with the air of a belle entering a ballroom. She ascends . . . with a cool jaunty air, an unveiled countenance, the same perpetual smile – or smirk, rather, for it lacks all the elements of a genuine smile – the same healthy glow of colour, and the same confident ease.'

The *Scotsman* reported that as they awaited the verdict, five minutes after the jury retired, 'a deep thrill of anxiety was visible throughout the court'. After the verdict had been delivered, 'instantly on the announcement of these last words, a vehement burst of cheering came from the audience, especially from the galleries, which was again and again renewed with increasing loudness in spite of efforts of the judges and officers of court . . . Her face broke into a bright and agitated smile . . . outside the announcement of the verdict called forth strong cheering from what seemed a majority of the great multitude collected.' The *Observer* of 13 July 1857 explained the 'not proven' verdict to its English readers: 'According to the Scotch law she may be again tried on the latter charges if at any time additional evidence is forthcoming. But this is not likely to be the case, as it must now for ever be locked up in her own breast whether she really did or did not see the deceased on the night of his death.'

The paper concluded that the fact it could not be proved that she actually saw L'Angelier on the night before his death, saved her. 'Madeleine Smith is, therefore, now free. But what a future must be hers! If she is guilty, conscience will ere long do its office, and her mind will be a perfect hell; and if she is innocent, the remainder of her days are blighted – the dark cloud of suspicion will envelope her; the shadow of a painful death by poison will precede her; she will be avoided as a pestilence; and wherever she goes she will be an object of distrust and dread.'

The Trial of Miss Madeleine Smith, published contemporaneously by D. Mathers, noted how the crowd outside the court devoured every fresh edition of the papers. 'The demand from news agents in all parts of the country was quite overwhelming and, although the managers of the various papers and the wholesale agents exerted themselves to the utmost, the inexorable railway trains had to depart in most instances without half of the required supply.' Another contemporary account by the advocate, John Morison, commented that, 'Whether they [the crowd] were right or wrong in this demonstration of joy we express no opinion; but shall only add in conclusion that the verdict has met with the approbation of nearly the whole press throughout the kingdom.'

Every publication on both sides of the border had an opinion about her. The *Spectator* wondered, 'Is she a Lucretia Borgia or is she only a boarding school miss led by a designing and theatrical Frenchman into a copy of Parisian romance?' The *Dundee Advertiser* pondered: 'within that melancholy form who can tell the pent-up woe'. Smith moved to London, married and had children and eventually emigrated to the United States where she died aged ninety-three, still a subject of much media interest.

Women accused of murder were not always treated kindly. Judith Knelman found that in the early nineteenth century the murderess was seen as cold, coarse, defeminised and unnatural. The Victorians were fascinated by the transgressive woman. 'To this audience,' writes Knelman, 'the murderess represented passion unleashed. She had spurned constraints imposed on civilised society, had given in to animal impulses.'

One 'femme fatale' who enthralled the press in the last century was Alma Rattenbury. She was a thirty-eight-year-old Canadian-born songwriter known as 'Lozanne' who was accused, in 1935, along with her much younger lover and chauffeur, George Stoner, of killing her sixty-seven-year-old architect husband, Francis, with a wooden mallet at their home, Villa Madeira, in Bournemouth. The press duly called it the 'Villa Murder' and it had everything: adulterous sex with a servant, the spectre of cocaine use and a touch of show business: while Alma awaited trial in Holloway prison, the *Daily Express* reported on its front page that she received a visit from Frank Titterton, the tenor, who sang one of her songs to her. The case against the couple was that they had been having an affair and had decided to get rid of Rattenbury.

By 8 a.m. on the opening day of the trial, 27 May 1935, the *Daily Mirror* reported that 100 people, mainly women, had formed a queue outside the public gallery, and some were offering their places in the line for sale. One unemployed man said that he had been outside the court since midnight because he was hoping to get married and by selling his place in the queue he could get enough money to set up a little business. 'A man I met yesterday told me he had sold his place for £2, and while I do not like doing this – my girl knows nothing about it – I am quite prepared to wait,' he told the *Mirror*. The opening day was covered for the *Mirror* by Barbara Back, who wrote in the first person and was attending an Old Bailey trial for the first time. She described Mrs Rattenbury as 'half hidden by her fur, and apparently quite unmoved. She is more than a pretty woman; her face is attractive with its large perfect eyes, short nose and thick-lipped mouth.'

The court heard that Alma had given a number of conflicting, drunken statements to the police, blaming Mr Rattenbury's son, then herself, then her lover. When the police arrived at the Villa, she supposedly told a Constable Bagwell: 'I did it with a mallet. "Rats" has lived too long . . . No, my lover did it. But I would like to give you £10. No, I won't bribe you.' She then claimed her husband dared her to kill him when they were playing cards, because he wanted to die. Stoner, however, took the blame. His counsel argued that he had been under the influence of cocaine on the fatal night and was thus suffering from temporary insanity. The *Mirror* reported this under the appropriate headline: 'Stoner confesses'. The jury took only fifty minutes to convict him and acquit Alma.

The *Daily Express* reported the summing-up under the headline: 'Judge's "regret" for Stoner – Position Due to Domination of That Woman.' In his summing-up, Mr Justice Humphreys recounted Alma's views on Francis Rattenbury 'that he was a very unpleasant character, for which I think we have no suitable English expression, but which the French call a *mari complaisant* – a man who knew that his wife was committing adultery and had no objection to it; not a nice character in this country or in any other civilised country'.

On Stoner, whose counsel had advised him not to give evidence, the judge brought things back to Alma in words given prominence by the press: 'It is the case for the prosecution, as I understand it, that this woman is a woman so lost in all sense of decency, so entirely without moral, that she would stop at nothing to gain her end, particularly her sexual gratification.' And he added: 'You remember she gave evidence that she was committing adultery with her husband's servant in her bedroom, and that in that bedroom, in a little bed, there was a child of six.'

The *Daily Express* dipped its quill pen in the purple inkwell and reported how the pair had sat 'in the confined glass cage of the Old Bailey dock, looking stolidly before them, never exchanging glances, parted by a warder and a wardress . . . yesterday at four o'clock both the passionate intimacy of the villa and the chilly association of the dock were alike ended as they separated for the last time – she for freedom, he for the death cell.' The day after her acquittal, Titterton, the loyal tenor, wrote a piece in the *Express* to try and salvage her soiled reputation. 'Lozanne wanted to be famous, but not so much for self gratification as for the sake of her two children, to whom she is so passionately devoted.'

Three days later, reported the *Daily Mirror*, 'Mrs Alma Victoria Rattenbury came down to Christchurch, within five miles of the scene of the crime of which she had been accused, smoked a final cigarette in a field of buttercups, and then committed suicide by stabbing herself to the heart and throwing herself into fifteen feet of water. This dramatic chapter in the history of the Bournemouth villa murder case was written last night in a lonely field half a mile from Christchurch.' The coroner's verdict was of suicide while of an unsound mind. Stoner's sentence was then commuted to life imprisonment and he served seven years before being released to fight in the Second World War and finally died in 2000. In his book *The Woman in the Case*, Edgar Lustgarten examined the story. 'A woman's uncontrollable lust is nymphomania,' he concluded. The fact that she was a songwriter was the key, he felt: 'the artistic temperament has always been curiously subject to that powerful impulse know as *la nostalgie de la boue* which may be freely translated as a craving – especially a sexual craving – for the dregs . . . she crucified herself on the pathetic altar of romantic love.'

Twenty years after the Villa Murder, 'Six revolver shots shattered the Easter Sunday calm of Hampstead and a beautiful platinum blonde stood with her back to the wall. In her hand was a revolver.' So ran the introduction to a spread in the *Daily Mail* the day after Ruth Ellis was committed for trial at the Old Bailey for shooting dead David Blakely, a 25-year-old 'dark haired and debonair' racing driver, as he came out of the Magdala pub. 'Model shot car ace in the back' ran the inside story about Ellis who had actually been a club hostess. For most of the five-hour hearing at Hampstead magistrates court, Mrs Ellis 'in an off-white tweed outfit with black velvet piping, sat in the centre of the crowded court calm and expressionless'.

Ellis, the mother of a three-year-old daughter and a ten-year-old son, pleaded not guilty but sealed her fate in what was described by the *Daily Mail* on 21 June 1955 as 'the shortest examination on record in any English murder trial'. After giving evidence for one hour and twenty-seven minutes, she was asked just one question in cross-examination by the prosecutor, Christmas Humphreys: what had she intended to do when she had fired the revolver at Blakely?

'Mrs Ellis, with her elbow resting on the side of the witness box, replied: "It is obvious when I shot him I intended to kill him." Mr Humphreys sat down. The cross-examination for the Crown was over.' Her complicated love life was reported, including Blakely's violence towards her: 'He only hit me with his fist or hands. I bruise easily.' Her description of her recent miscarriage was mentioned in the *Guardian*'s coverage: 'A few weeks or days previously, I do not know which, David got very violent. I do not know whether that caused the miscarriage or not. He thumped me in the tummy.'

The case for the defence was, as the *Mail* explained on 21 June, that 'the effect of jealousy upon a the feminine mind, upon all feminine minds, can so work as to unseat the reason and can operate to a degree in which in a male mind it is quite incapable of operating.' The trial lasted just over a day. A quick and unanimous verdict of guilty by the jury saw Mr Justice Havers don the black cap. Her legal advisers considered lodging an appeal on a new point of law – that of provocation brought on by jealousy. It was the only defence offered by her lawyers who asked for a verdict of manslaughter, according to the *Mail*. 'The appeal on the grounds that a woman thwarted by love is more irresponsible than a man could be taken to the House of Lords. It is the first time that such a point of law has been offered in a murder trial.'

On 12 July, the *Mail* deliberated on her plight: 'Ruth Ellis is a young and beautiful woman. Honest men will admit that this fact weighed heavily with them if they joined in the appeal for her life.' The article pointed out that the previous year, a Cypriot woman named Christofi was hanged for the murder of her daughter-in-law but 'there was no wave of sympathy for her . . . It is true that some MPs tried for a reprieve, but on the grounds of possible insanity. Yet it could be argued that the conflict between female in-laws is sometimes so great that either could be excused if in a fit of uncontrollable rage she killed the other. Such pleas have no place in our jurisprudence.'

In 1967, the femme fatale writ large appeared in the press in the shape of, as the *Daily Express* had it, 'blonde ex-nurse Valerie "Kim" Newell, aged twenty-three, who is expecting a baby in August'. This was very much from the noir school of murder, with similarities to the plot of *The Postman Always Rings Twice*. Newell had been having an affair with a married man, Ray Cook, and they decided to murder his older, richer wife so that they would get access to her £10,000 savings. Newell recruited a former lover, Eric Jones, who had performed an abortion on her when she was a teenager and could thus be blackmailed into taking part. The idea was to stage a car crash in which Mrs Cook would die. To this end she was plied with drink in a pub and then set off in her red Mini on a deserted country road where Jones was waiting, pretending that his car had broken down so that the Cooks could stop without alerting Mrs Cook. Jones then battered her to death with a car jack and the Mini was driven into a tree in a ham-fisted attempt to make it look like an accident. The police, led by Ian Forbes, were not convinced but did not have enough evidence to charge Newell. Crime reporters were alerted to the link and were calling so persistently at her home that she decided to come in voluntarily to the police.

At her trial for being an accessory to murder, at Oxfordshire assizes in June 1967, prosecuting counsel Brian Gibbens said that 'Lady Macbeth got her husband to commit murder while she remained aside. Like Lady Macbeth, this woman was urging her husband to "screw his courage to the sticking place". He was in her grip. Cook thought it was for marriage and love. She thought of nothing except money . . . In the witness box she presented herself to you with a wide-eyed innocence but did she finish up such an innocent maiden as at first she seemed?' Although Newell was only charged with being an accessory, while Cook and Jones were charged with murder, it was clear on whom the attention would focus.

After the guilty verdict, the *News of the World* splashed with an exclusive interview with Newell's mother, based on a letter Newell had written from prison, in which she professed her innocence. Inside, the story was of 'Kim, the wicked wanton', the 'vivacious villainess' and her 'dramatic reign of passion that brought brutal death to a wife and the downfall of two men who came under her spell'.

The paper's crime reporter, Charles Sandell, wrote a first-person account of his meeting with Newell – 'big-breasted in a green sweater which shielded the signs of her three-month pregnancy' – before she had been charged. '"I have nothing to hide," she said with a laugh, pulling firmly at the hem of her sweater and flashing her long legs as her trim grey skirt rose high.' He assured readers that 'men have long been putty in Kim Newell's pretty hands. Her power made them puppets on a string.' Her co-accused, reckoned Sandell, had clearly been 'besotted by her generous, nubile body'.

The investigating officer, Ian Forbes, wrote in *Squad Man*, his memoir, in a chapter entitled 'Woman of Evil', that 'crime reporters had said she was quite a siren, I couldn't fault that judgment.' He added: 'in different circumstances I would have been the first to admit that this twenty-three-year-old girl would have been a very attractive companion but I was looking at the most evil woman it was my misfortune to meet in my thirty-odd years as a copper.' She gave birth to a son in prison, served thirteen years and died of cancer in 1991.

Myra Hindley, who died in prison where she was serving life for the Moors Murders, was often regarded as the face of pure evil and a psychopath. In December 1995, after she had been described as the latter in an article in the *Guardian*, she wrote a 5,000 article for the paper, for which she was not paid. In it she said that 'I was corrupt, I was wicked and evil . . . without me those crimes could probably not have been committed. It was I who was instrumental in procuring the children, children who would more readily accompany strangers if they were a woman and a man than they would a man on their own . . . The *Sun* has described me, amongst thousands of other things, as "the symbol of the nation's revulsion at all those who prey on innocent children" in spite of hundreds of other females in the system who have been convicted of quite horrendous crimes . . . the tabloids have turned me into an industry, selecting me as the public icon / evil monster, Medusa-like image which holds the projected hatred, fear and fury of the nation's psyche.'

In 2014, Joanna Dennehy, aged thirty-one, became the first British woman to receive a whole-life tariff from a judge (it was Home Secretary Jack Straw who deemed that neither Hindley nor Rosemary West should ever be released). Dennehy, from Peterborough, was convicted of fatally stabbing three men and attracted attention by her attitude, posing in a photo with a knife and phoning a friend after one murder and saying, 'Oops, I did it again!' At her trial, the judge revealed that Dennehy had told a psychiatrist that she killed 'to see if I was as cold as I thought I was. Then it got moreish and I got a taste for it.'

Barbara Ellen wrote of the case in the *Observer*: 'It was as if she saw herself as some kind of fictional outlaw heroine, a Thelma without a Louise, or a cartoon psychopath, along the lines of Freddy Krueger or Hannibal Lecter – both of whom could be relied upon to be "witty" as they killed, a cut above the average psychopath . . . There's a palpable feeling of instant sexualisation about Dennehy's media profile that you just wouldn't see with a male murderer. In the same way that mentally-ill women often become eroticised, so, too, do female killers.'

But women didn't always have to kill to catch the attention of the crime reporter. In 1740, Mary Young, the nifty pickpocket who was better known under her alias of Jenny Diver, was executed. 'The name of this woman will long be celebrated in the annals of crime, as being that of a person who was the most ingenious of her class,' said the *Newgate Calendar*. And while the 'femmes fatales' – the murderesses – occupied the attention of crime reporters, there was also a place for the savvy female criminal, whether she was pickpocket, decoy, moll, getaway driver, international shoplifter, love-crazed kidnapper, saucy madam or 'tart with a heart of gold'.

By the twentieth century, the female thief had become an exotic creature in the press. On 27 November 1927, the *News of the World* introduced its readers to 'a Girl in the Toils – Beautiful Decoy of West-End Gang'. This was Josephine Gordon, aged nineteen, who had found herself in court along with a gang of Soho wide boys, not the first young woman from an upper-class family to enjoy the frisson of the underworld. 'Well bred, educated, and certainly good-looking, she unconsciously drifted from a life of ease and happiness to the society of the most accomplished gang of forgers, swindlers and confidence men in London.'

The case against her was that she worked with a team of con men who, in the gentler days before photo-ID, credit cards and online banking, cut a swathe through the more trusting shops and businesses in London. What was obviously most interesting to reporters was the decoy herself: 'She has the face of the ingenue – oval regular features, large expressive eyes, a tiny mouth and an abundance of soft brown hair. But the most striking thing about her is her clothes. They are cut in the riding-habit fashion, and she affects the soft collar and long tie generally accepted as the masculine mode.'

Gordon had been born in the Wye Valley and then gone with her family to India. She had married young, in Buenos Aires, where she had a 'topping time' before returning to England. The marriage broke up and one day in a Piccadilly cafe she got chatting to a group of smartly dressed chaps, led by 'an aristocrat by birth but a rogue by profession'. The group were later joined by a 'villainess' who had 'a mania for long jet earrings' and who persuaded her to use her charms to facilitate the forgeries. She eventually came unstuck when she tried to use a dud cheque for £25 to buy a 'leopard cat coat'. She was lucky. The magistrate took a lenient view and bound her over for two years on the understanding that a 'gentleman and his wife' had agreed to accept her as one of their family. After the case, Josephine told the *NoW* reporter that 'since my police-court experience I have been called "the beautiful decoy" but the boys used to say I was their lucky mascot.'

Maggie Hill, who was active at the beginning of the twentieth century, was known as the 'Queen of the Forty Elephants' and operated a team of shoplifters. Stanley Firmin, the *Daily Telegraph*'s crime correspondent, later suggested that the name of the gang came from a combination of a connection with Elephant and Castle and the fact the shoplifters were 'mainly large women, some nearly six feet tall'. Maggie Hill was a mischievous soul; as it was reported, when she was sent down on one occasion she told the judge, 'You didn't say that last night when you were making love to me!'

Maggie was to remain the best-known female shoplifter in the press until the postwar arrival of Shirley Pitts, the 'Queen of Thieves', who was credited with introducing 'team shoplifting', where a group of eight women would descend on a large shop, with many of them acting as decoys. Having learned her trade at the age of seven from some of Maggie Hill's old gang, she was an expert at disguise. She also took her teams across Europe and was celebrated in a book, *Gone Shopping*, by Lorraine Gamman. Her fame guaranteed her a spectacular south London funeral, reported in the *Guardian*, when she died of cancer, aged fifty-seven, in 1992. The words 'Gone Shopping' were spelled out beside her grave in a six-foot-long floral arrangement, alongside a Harrods' shopping bag made of flowers.

One of the most remarkable members of the small band of female professional criminals was Lilian Goldstein, something of an enigma to the reporters who first came across her in the same year that the 'beautiful decoy' had captured their attention. Goldstein came from a middle-class family from Wembley Park in north London, and on 6 June 1927 she was charged with being in unlawful possession of a handbag, a gramophone and a record case. More intriguingly, she was described in court as being wanted in connection with a Birmingham hold-up in which a woman had been killed.

Unlike Gordon, Goldstein was not prepared to retreat from crime at the first sound of gunfire. She would soon act as a getaway driver to the best-known smash-and-grab man of the time, 'Ruby' Sparks, who had won his nickname by stealing a maharajah's rubies and then giving them away under the mistaken belief that they were fakes. Thirteen years after her first press appearance, Lilian Goldstein was back in the news. Sparks, who had escaped from Dartmoor, had been recaptured and was back in court with his lover alongside him. On 19 July 1940, the *Daily Mail* reported on the jailing of Goldstein and Sparks and described how Sparks – 'completely unrecognisable from his published photograph . . . he had spent much of his freedom sunbathing and golfing' – made a gallant plea on behalf of Goldstein, now 37, telling the Old Bailey judge that 'she is a young woman but has gone grey worrying about me. She begged me again and again not to go near her.' As the *Daily Express* reported it, he told the court that she was too frightened to turn him in: 'I am a dangerous man and would stop at nothing. She knew that.' The judge, Sir Gerald Dodson, told her: 'I suppose it is a woman's nature to protect what she has loved but it is an offence for people to obstruct the law.'

A teenager at this time was the woman who would later become known as Gypsy Hill, so called because her mother's Gypsy friend decided that she must be of Romany stock. A striking beauty, Gyp initially attracted the attention of Billy Hill, the 1950s 'Boss of the Underworld', by belting three women with a high heel after she had seen them mocking a deaf mute person in the street. When Hill masterminded the famous 1952 Eastcastle Street robbery of £230,000 from a Post Office van, she was one of his getaway drivers. The police were unlikely to suspect a woman in a car in those days and the pair divided up their money in a suite at the Dorchester hotel.

In 1955, the couple tried to move to Australia but, by the time they reached New Zealand via the Pacific, it was clear Australia would not admit them because of Hill's record. 'It makes you sick when you think we have come this far – and then for this to happen,' Gyp told the reporter from the *Daily Express*, who had been following their progress. 'If only we had known sooner, we could have got off earlier – in Tahiti.' She moved to Tangier, where Hill had a club called Churchill's, kept a chimpanzee as a pet and eventually moved back to Britain and retired from the fray. Her son Justin told the *Guardian* that he remembered her enjoying a spliff while watching *Widows*, the 1980s ITV series about gangsters' wives who carry out a robbery.

Then in the seventies came allegations of a very different kind of crime, involving an American couple in Britain. He was 'the Manacled Mormon' and she was, forever, the woman who would have 'skied down Mount Everest in the nude with a carnation up my nose' to win his love. The man was Kirk Anderson, a bashful Mormon missionary, and the woman Joyce McKinney, a former beauty queen with an IQ of 168, a raunchy past in Los Angeles and an unrequited passion for Kirk. The combination made for what was described as the 'tabloid scoop of the decade', a tale which saw rival newspapers hurling money and bodies into battle.

McKinney, originally from North Carolina, had come to Britain from California in 1977, apparently intent on winning back Kirk, with whom she had a previous brief liaison in Utah. To this end she recruited a friend, the devoted Keith May, to help her and they grabbed Kirk at gunpoint from outside his church near Kingston-upon-Thames and took him off to Devon where he was, in his version of events, tied to a bed and spread-eagled while sex took place. McKinney would later claim that all the sex was consensual and it was only after brainwashing by the Mormons that Kirk changed his tune.

When McKinney and May appeared at Epsom magistrates court ten days later, McKinney managed to pass a note to reporters saying: 'I am innocent. Please help me.' As anyone who ever watches television news will know, whenever a high-profile prisoner arrives at or leaves a court hearing in a prison van, hopeful photographers pursue the vehicle, snapping furiously in the hope of catching that one vital haunted image from behind the tiny windows. Why, people sometimes wonder, do they bother? At her next court appearance, McKinney showed that all that effort was sometimes worthwhile. Behind the bars in her van she held up a Bible, open at the Book of Job, on which was scribbled: 'Please tell the truth. My reputation is at stake.'

Anthony Delano, in his book on the saga, *Joyce McKinney and the Case of the Manacled Mormon*, recounted the scene in court: 'The reporters were utterly engrossed. People simply did not behave in English courts like this self-possessed pink-blonde stranger determined to bare the most intimate details of her life.' The story was too big to leave to crime and court reporters alone. When McKinney made her naked, carnation-enhanced skiing pledge in court, Jean Rook, doyenne of the *Daily Express*, weighed in, suggesting that 'in 12 poetic words, Miss McKinney snatches your icicled breath and paints your perfumed world a passionate pink'.

McKinney was remanded to stand trial at the Old Bailey and the newspaper cheque books were at the ready. The *Sun* was supposedly offering £70,000 for a nude picture plus skis plus carnation. Strangely, McKinney and May were granted bail and, during this pretrial period, the *Daily Express* entered the field, with their dashing reporter Peter Tory squiring McKinney to the West End premiere of *The Stud*, a soft-porn film starring Joan Collins, who was duly upstaged by the arrival of the defendant in a low-cut dress.

But, within two days, McKinney and May had vanished, blagging their way onto a flight to Canada with false passports and a claim that they were part of a deaf-mute theatre company. With her were no fewer than 13 suitcases crammed with press clippings. It was that big a story. Scotland Yard did not seek to extradite the couple, no doubt dreading the circus of an Old Bailey trial, and she was eventually sentenced in absentia to a year's jail. But the story did not end there.

Both the *Daily Mirror* and the *Daily Express* were still on the case. For the *Mirror*, their veteran photographer Kent Gavin had acquired a trove of nude and bondage pictures of McKinney from a former friend of hers in Los Angeles. The 'friend' was swiftly smuggled across the border to Mexico to keep him safe from rival papers. McKinney, unaware of the fact that she had been betrayed in this way, had meanwhile negotiated a £40,000 deal for her story with the *Express*, who flew out Tory and a photographer for a clandestine meeting with her and May in Atlanta. There they found the fugitive couple disguised, first as Indians and then as nuns, and set about writing the gospel according to McKinney: essentially a romantic story of an innocent beauty queen who had loved and lost a young Mormon and tried to win him back.

On 22 May 1978, the two papers produced their competing front page stories. While the *Express* had McKinney, dressed as a nun, begging 'Please God Help', the *Mirror* had her lying naked on a rug under the headline 'The Real McKinney'. There was much more from both sides over the next week under such headlines as 'Temptress in the Garden of Evil'. Tory was with McKinney when the *Mirror* story broke and it was relayed to her by phone from London. In *Tabloid*, the 2010 Errol Morris documentary about the whole affair, Tory recounts how 'she just went absolutely crazy. She clung on to the curtains and then she went for the balcony and I grabbed her by the ankles. I didn't know if she was going to jump off. It would have been very embarrassing to say the least.'

Even then, the story was not over. After her beloved pit-bull 'Booger' died, she spent a small fortune having him successfully cloned into five puppies in a South Korean lab in 2008. In the documentary, McKinney explained to Morris than any suggestions of her raping Kirk were nonsense and impossible – 'like putting a marshmallow in a parking meter' – and concluded that 'there are tabloids in England that are filth'.

Sex of a rather different but also unconventional variety was behind one of the biggest stories the same year that McKinney did a runner. In 1978, police raided the Streatham, south London, 'disorderly house' run by Cynthia Payne to provide 'personal services' for her mainly elderly clients. By the time she was convicted at her trial in 1980 she had become a household name thanks, once again, to the wide coverage she was granted both during and after her court appearances.

The reason that her case attracted so much attention was twofold: her clients and the method of payment. The former were said to have included a peer, vicars, barristers, ex-police officers, politicians and bank managers, not to mention a cross-dressing former RAF squadron leader who remained loyal to the end. She charged punters £25, which included a 'luncheon voucher' – a token that entitled the bearer to have sex with any of the women in the house who agreed. 'Madam Sin', as she had become by now, was sentenced to eighteen months, later reduced to six on appeal. Her barrister, Geoffrey Robertson, asked for a non-custodial sentence, assuring the court that no 'beardless youngsters [were] initiated into the fleshpots'. This did not prevent much speculation in the press as to which rumoured politician and senior copper had been part of her 'naughty but nice' activities. On the day she started her sentence, the press were given a conducted tour of her premises by the former squadron leader, and had their attention drawn to a sign in the kitchen that read: 'My house is clean enough to be healthy . . . and dirty enough to be happy.'

When she emerged from prison, she was met by a Rolls-Royce and a battalion of the press whom she obliged by posing for photos. She later wrote to her friends that, 'The reporters were all surprised that I stopped the car to allow my photo to be taken, as I could have put a coat over my head but, as I thought the press had been so good to me, plus the fact that they had waited for four hours for a glimpse, I thought I'd make their wait worthwhile. They all cheered when I posed for them, blowing kisses.' When she met journalists she gave them her business card, a laminated luncheon voucher on the back of which she would write, for men: 'to [reporter's first name], thank you for past custom!' and for women: 'sorry to lose one of my best girls!'

In 1987, she was back in court again. This time she was acquitted, a verdict widely welcomed by the press. The *Guardian* ran a front page story: 'When she arrived at the court yesterday, Mrs Payne was already in good spirits. She posed for photographers holding a policeman doll which laughed when she pulled a string hidden in its bottom.' A *Guardian* leader captured the mood: 'Is there anybody out there who isn't, even itsy-bitsy secretly under covers, pleased at the acquittal of Mrs Cynthia Payne? It's not just that the chirpy concierge of Ambleside Avenue has charmed her way into the nation's hearts over the years . . . It's not just that the local police, dressed to kill in rouge and sequins for the raid, have been made to look wonderfully silly . . . Good for her. Good for the jury. And what a shame it had to come to an end.'

Women famous for their criminal partners were also a subject of fascination for the press although few of them might actually describe themselves as 'gangster's molls'. One who was happy to was Marilyn Wisbey, daughter of the great train robber Tommy Wisbey, and partner for a number of years of 'Mad' Frankie Fraser about whom she wrote in her memoir, *Gangster's Moll*. In 1998, she explained in the *Independent* series, 'How We Met': 'I've been out with nine-to-five people, electricians, turf accountants, accountants, you name it. Once they find out whose daughter I am, they don't like that sort of thing. So I feel more comfortable with guys who've been out of prison, they understand me.'

Kate Kray, who married Ronnie Kray in 1989, was very media-friendly and very quotable. She talked about Ron as 'him inside' – as opposed to 'her indoors' – and the 'Smiling Viper'. She parlayed her fame as a 'Kray-by-marriage' into a successful writing career, with true crime books like *Ultimate Hard Bastards* and *Lifers* and novels like *The Betrayed*, the story of a beautiful young actress who falls in love with a gangster. Asked in 2000 by the *Independent* what made her want to be the wife of a bisexual paranoid schizophrenic murderer serving life in Broadmoor, she replied: 'Maybe it was a mid-life crisis. Men buy Harley Davidsons and get a young bird – I married a Kray.'

Roberta Kray, who married Reg Kray in Maidstone prison in 1997, when he was still hoping for parole, was hardly the typical gangster's moll. Her parents were both teachers, she studied classics at North London Polytechnic and worked in academic publishing and media research.

When I met her in her home in Norfolk, I noticed that the main books on her shelves were those of Virginia Woolf, Vita Sackville-West, Primo Levi, Saul Bellow and Dorothy Parker. The Women's Press imprint was the most obvious. She was conscious of the fact that, by marrying a Kray, she had entered the media spotlight: 'It scares me. You are always aware that you might say something wrong.' She objected to the way she was portrayed in the press as someone who had 'sacrificed' herself and suggestions that, because her father had died when she was eleven, 'her husband's twenty-five years older than her so that must mean she's looking for a father figure'. Like Kate, she has made a successful writing career under the Kray name, with eleven crime novels with titles like *Bad Girl* and *Villain's Daughter*.

In the twenty-first century, 'gangster's moll' would remain a handy term to describe anyone associated with a professional villain, just one of the many time-honoured clichés in the crime reporter's lexicon that has developed over the years.

20

They Made Their Excuses and Left

The Language of Crime Reporting

I n 1790, the London press was convulsed by the behaviour of a man universally described as 'the Monster', whose exploits were eagerly reported and lubriciously illustrated. The use of an evocative nickname to describe a criminal or suspect was soon to become a standard tool in the crime reporter's kitbag.

The Monster in question was accused of attacking women in the street with a sharp instrument, often cutting their clothes and stabbing them in the buttocks. To protect themselves, some women even went out wearing copper pots under their dresses. 'The Monster', as he soon became in headlines and ballads, was often described as having a long nose, leading to a suggestion in *The Times* on 8 May that he might be wearing a disguise: 'we would advise all those hardy English Hercules's who are determined to rid London of such a wretch to pull him hard by the nose!' A young Welshman called Rhynwick Williams was eventually arrested, tried and jailed for six years, although in her book *The London Monster*, Jan Bondeson argues persuasively that this might well have been an early miscarriage of justice.

The 'Monster' has since become a staple of crime reports, as have other handy monickers, not least the prefix 'Mad'. Crime is perhaps the only profession where being known as monstrous or mad is a good career move. The late 'Mad' Frank Fraser, who spent more than forty of his eighty-nine years inside, found that the nickname stood him in good stead when it came to collecting debts and settling arguments. Frank 'the Mad Axeman' Mitchell, and 'Mad Teddy Smith' were two Kray associates murdered in the 1960s.

One of the most famous of prison escapers was Walter 'Angel Face' Probyn, who was given his nickname at the age of fifteen by the press who had been fed it by the police. Probyn reckoned that the police and press collaborated on fancy nicknames for villains because it made any arrest sound more heroic and made life easier for headline writers. He was relieved that another monicker the police tried to give him – the 'Dimpled Demon' – did not stick, although sometimes he was referred to as the 'Hoxton Houdini'. Brian Wright, the very busy cocaine smuggler jailed at Woolwich Crown Court for thirty years in 2007, was known as 'the Milkman' because he 'always delivered'. This ensured that, when he was on the run and hiding out in Northern Cyprus in the early years of this century, he attracted the kind of media attention that someone without a nickname might have avoided. Valerio Viccei, who masterminded the 1987 Knightsbridge safe deposit robbery and had a string of glamorous girlfriends, became 'the Italian Stallion' and later 'the Wolf'.

Some nicknames carry no threatening baggage: Jack 'the Hat' McVitie, who was killed by Reggie Kray in 1967, was sensitive about going bald and thus always wore his trademark headgear. John Moriarty was a north London armed robber active in the seventies who was known as 'The Target' because he had been shot so many times. Micky Cornwall, shot dead in 1977, was 'the Laughing Bank Robber' because of his permanent grin.

Freddie Foreman, jailed for his part in McVitie's death, became 'the Managing Director of British Crime', a title dreamed up by the publishers of his 1996 memoirs, *Respect*, and to which he objected; they had originally wanted to call him 'the Enforcer' but he put his foot down on that. He was also unhappy that the press referred to him, when he was on the run in Spain, as 'the Mean Machine', as that title already belonged to bare-knuckle fighter Roy Shaw. 'Unfortunately, it sticks,' he told me of the nickname. He was also known as 'Brown Bread' which happily rhymed with both Fred and dead. The old cat burglar Peter Scott, who died in 2013 aged eighty-two, was the 'King of the Cat Burglars', 'Burglar to the Stars' and the 'Human Fly', although he described himself as a 'master idiot'. The most famous smash'n'grab thief of the last century was 'Ruby' Sparks who earned his nickname by stealing a maharajah's jewels. He was also known as 'Rubberface' because he contorted his features when the police tried to take mug shots. His getaway driver, Lilian Goldstein, was always referred to as 'the Bobbed-Haired Bandit'.

In 2014, an armed robber called Michael Wheatley and nicknamed 'Skullcracker' absconded from Standford Hill open prison on the Isle of Sheppey in Kent and became a major news story along with the traditional 'members of the public are warned not to approach this man'. Had he not been known as Skullcracker would there have been such a hue and cry?

Nowadays, if a woman criminal is given a nickname by the press it is often the misogynistic 'Black Widow'. A nurse of either gender accused of killing patients becomes 'the Angel of Death'; over the last two decades, around half a dozen of them have been so described in Britain, the United States and Italy.

Many nicknames have been borrowed from American gangsters: Philip 'Little Caesar' Jacobs was jailed at the Old Bailey 1972 for various gangland activities; Victor 'Scarface' Russo was a Glasgow wide-boy of the fifties, who also operated in London and whose own face had been redecorated many times in the period when criminals used cut-throat razors rather than guns.

Peter Manuel, the Scottish serial killer, was 'the Beast of Birkenshaw'. Another notorious Scottish criminal, the robber and drug dealer Tam McGraw, who died in 2007, was known as 'the Licensee'. The *Daily Telegraph* crime correspondent Neil Darbyshire and his colleague Colin Adamson came up with 'the Stockwell Strangler' as the name for Kenneth Erskine, who was jailed for life in 1988 for seven murders and sexual assaults of elderly people in south London.

The Great Train Robbery started life as the more prosaic Cheddington Train robbery before it got the name with which it is associated, which came from the 1903 American film of that title. One of the robbers, Charlie Wilson, who told the police nothing, was known as 'the Silent Man', not to be confused with the two journalists, Brendan Mulholland and Reg Foster, known as 'the Silent Men' for their refusal to name their sources in the Vassall case. The great train robber Bruce Reynolds, in his memoir *Crossing the Line*, noted that when Wilson was shot dead in Spain in 1990, 'the hacks were clutching at straws and outdoing each other with catchy labels. Chas was the "Silent man", "the King", "the Brains" . . . then he became an "Aristocrat of Crime", "Mr Big of the Costa drug runners", "the Commander in Chief of Crime".'

When the Hatton Garden safe deposit boxes robbery took place over Easter in 2015, the *Daily Mirror* got access to CCTV footage of the thieves and swiftly named them as though they were characters in the film *Reservoir Dogs*: 'Mr Ginger,' 'Mr Strong', 'the Gent' and so on. When it emerged that those involved included some septuagenarians, they immediately became 'Dad's Army' as well as 'the Diamond Wheezers'.

Police officers have also gloried in their own press-donated nicknames. There was Fabian of the Yard – the Yard being a useful handle – the title adopted by Superintendent Robert Fabian, who left the police in 1949 but had a successful subsequent career as a writer. Commander Wally Virgo, who was part of the Obscene Publications Squad in the 1960s and later jailed for corruption, was known to villains, because of his busts of porn shops, as 'Wally Vibro'. Sir Robert Mark, the Met Commissioner who cleaned up the Yard was described, somewhat tortuously, as 'The Lone Ranger of Leicester' because of his mission and his roots.

The Metropolitan Police Commissioner, John – later Lord – Stevens, who was regarded as one of the more successful holders of the post, was known both as 'Captain Beaujolais' and, within the Yard, as 'Champagne Charlie'. Interestingly, it emerged during the Leveson Inquiry that Stevens had been assisted by former *News of the World* deputy editor Neil Wallis, when he applied for the top job in policing, which he held between 2000 and 2005. 'I advised Lord John Stevens throughout the application and interview process in which he was ultimately successful,' Wallis told the inquiry in his written evidence. 'My input in this process was that he would be well advised to emphasise that he was a "copper's copper" or 'thief-taker' – in other words he was a man of action, rather than rhetoric.' In fact, the 'copper's copper' – usually a way of distinguishing an officer from the more liberal graduate-intake officers – was a popular monicker for any aspiring chief. To the possible dismay of his successor, Lord Blair, Stevens went on to write for the *News of the World* under the name of 'The Chief'. One of his predecessors was the upright Scotsman, David McNee, who was known as 'the Hammer', a nickname he was given by the *Sun's* crime correspondent, George Hollingbery, after a Scottish friend had told him that McNee had 'hammered' the local crooks. Among other detectives with nicknames was the affectionately named 'Nipper' Read, who hunted the train robbers and the Krays.

Crime reporters themselves have had fewer nicknames, the most famous being Jimmy Nicholson's 'Prince of Darkness', a title which was to be handed on to Greg Miskiw, the head of news at the *News of the World* when the scale of hacking skullduggery at the paper emerged. In 2015, a contrite Miskiw suggested to *Channel 4 News* that 'Duke of Darkness' might be more suitable. In Glasgow, the veteran crime reporter, Stuart McCartney was known as 'the Bullet'; the name supposedly came from the speed with which he embarked on stories as a young man.

When Andy Coulson and Rebekah Brooks stood trial for phone hacking and conspiracy in 2012, their appearance at the Old Bailey was described as 'the trial of the century'. Every century has had many such trials. In 1892, the case of Dr Thomas Cream, the Glasgow-born serial killer known as 'the Lambeth Poisoner', was described as 'the greatest criminal trial the century has seen', but only three years later Oscar Wilde's appearance at the Old Bailey in 1895 was 'the most sensational trial of the century'. Still, at least the writer of that headline could claim that it was possible to make such a claim as 1900 was just around the corner. Other trials that have since competed for the title were those of Dr Crippen,

(1910), Neville Heath (1946), John Haigh (1949), John Christie (1953), Peter Manuel (1958), Stephen Ward, (1963), the Krays (1969) and Jeremy Thorpe (1979). The Moors Murderers, Rosemary West, Peter Sutcliffe and the killers of Jamie Bulger have all since had the phrase attached to their cases. It has been used more frequently in the US, attached to such cases as the Rosenbergs, Leopold and Loeb, Charles Manson, Patty Hearst and O. J. Simpson, while the murder trial of the athlete Oscar Pistorius in South Africa in 2014 was also thus named.

Many people have been promoted as 'Public Enemy Number One' over the years, a term borrowed from the FBI which used it from the 1930s onwards after it had first been employed by the Chicago crime commission to describe Al Capone and his associates. The FBI did not actually introduce its Top Ten list until 1950. Nowhere can we find reference to Public Enemy Number Two.

Criminal jargon was also often used in news stories. 'Crime is the backbone of slang,' according to Jonathan Green, author of the *Oxford Dictionary of Slang*. 'It represents a larger proportion of the vocabulary than even sex. The vocabulary of lowlife and underworld has always been sexy. Then and now, whether in penny-dreadful, film noir or graphic novel, it conferred authenticity and atmosphere, underlined the writer's insider knowledge, and, again, seemed to initiate the reader into a forbidden world.'

Who came up with the phrase 'I made my excuses and left'? That form of words became the traditional signing-off point for a reporter from the 1950s onwards exposing a vice scandal in which he – almost always a he – had to bow out before finding himself in a compromising situation. There seem to be three contenders as excuse-making author: Sam Campbell, the editor of the *People* in its pomp; Duncan Webb, that paper's crime reporter, who exposed the Soho vice rackets of the period; and Webb's legman, the Australian journalist, Murray Sayle. Roy Greenslade suggests that Campbell might have been the man. Ed Glinert, in his book *The London Compendium*, attributes it to Webb, while some of Sayle's contemporaries credit him with the phrase.

There are many words and phrases that feature regularly in crime reports. An offender or suspect who lives alone is a 'loner', even though this description would now fit 34 per cent of Britons. On the day after a murder or kidnapping, the local residents are 'trying to come to terms' with it or, indeed, 'trying to make sense' of it, although how this is achieved is never quite explained. This is partly because, after a major crime or tragedy, there is inevitably demand for a follow-up, often when nothing new has happened. A news-desk still wants an update and report-ers far from home must justify their reason for being there. There are other conventions: graves should be 'shallow', robberies become 'heists' and, if it isn't a sunny day for the funeral of a police officer killed on duty, the sky should be of 'gun-metal grey'.

A murder victim or murderer who didn't speak much to the neigh-bours on either side of him is someone who always 'kept himself to himself'. This is essentially shorthand for 'I couldn't find out a damn thing about him.' It wasn't just the reporters: once in Hertfordshire, reporting on the hit-man murder of Robert Magill – for which I believe the wrong man, Kevin Lane, was later convicted – I knocked on the door of a neigh-bour of the victim, who had been shot that morning while walking his dog. A young reporter from another paper was with me and as we waited, I muttered: 'I bet they say "he kept himself to himself"'; the unwitting woman who answered the door and gave us the phrase verbatim was understandably baffled by my colleague's loud guffaw.

Robert Hutton, the UK political correspondent at Bloomberg News, compiled a list of such phrases in a pocket-sized book called *Romps, Tots and Boffins . . . the Strange Language of News*. Hutton, who previously worked for the *Mirror* and *Financial Times*, listed and defined all those odd words that appear in newspapers but rarely in real life. He found no shortage of crime clichés and hyperboles. 'Drug kingpins', 'vile thugs', and 'Jekyll and Hyde characters' all feature. 'Sex fiends' must be 'caged'. There were some helpful translations for the lay reader. 'Named locally', which often refers to a suspect under arrest, means 'the cops aren't saying who it was but fortunately everyone in the pub knew.'

Many murder victims unconnected to their killers are said to be 'in the wrong place at the wrong time'. But shouldn't that cancel out – they should surely have been either in the wrong place or in the right place but at the wrong time? Anyone convicted but given a suspended sentence, probation, a community service order or fine is often deemed to 'walk free', regardless of what restrictions are placed on them. When we have no idea what has happened, 'mystery surrounds' a case.

'Blood on Their Hands' is another popular headline. It was used to attack the social workers and those associated with them in the case of Peter Connolly, 'Baby P', who died after suffering horrific injuries at his home in north London in 2007, and again by the *Daily Mail* to attack Facebook for failing to spot that one of the murderers of the soldier, Lee Rigby, in 2013 had been boasting and posting about planning to kill a soldier. One phrase that was common in Northern Ireland during the Troubles was that of ODC – 'ordinary decent criminal' – used to differentiate career criminals from those suspected of terrorist offences. It is now used to distinguish professional villains from paedophiles, rapists and murderers.

When a major trial finishes at the Old Bailey, a senior detective often makes a statement to the assembled media just outside the court. Look carefully and you will see that some crime reporters have positioned themselves at the detective's elbow, usually scribbling conscientiously into their notebooks and clearly visible to television viewers. Sky TV correspondent Martin Brunt, who describes it as 'video bombing', is used to it: 'Some reporters are quite shameless. If it's live, then their editors know that they're there doing their job.' It is also known as the 'Old Bailey doughnut', a term borrowed from the House of Commons after proceedings there were televised, whereby MPs would cluster beside a speaker to give the impression that the chamber was fuller than it was and which led to the neologism 'doughnutting'.

The police have their own euphemisms, which they have passed on to the media, although they have changed over the years. One of these was to describe a woman who had suffered a sexual assault or rape as having been 'interfered with'. A dimly remembered sketch from the 1960s went something along these lines: 'Police said that they had recovered the body of the murdered woman who had been stabbed fourteen times, beaten around the body and beheaded. She had not been interfered with.'

People arrested for crimes are still routinely described as 'helping with inquiries' when usually it is the opposite of what they are doing. A more recent addition to the vocabulary of arrest is 'a person of interest', which is to say a suspect but without quite enough incriminating evidence yet available. Not that there would ever be a shortage of 'people of interest' as one of the biggest cases of the twenty-first century would demonstrate.

21

The Leveson Leviathan

How Hacking Damaged Hacks

On 5 July 2011, the headline in the *Guardian* read: 'Missing Milly Dowler's voicemail was hacked by *News of the World*'. The report, by Nick Davies and Amelia Hill, revealed that when the thirteen-year-old Milly, later found murdered, had gone missing in 2002, the *News of the World* had hacked – gained illicit access to – her phone messages. The story, accompanied by further revelations of the reluctance of the police to investigate the hacking, led to a firestorm which would have dramatic and lasting ramifications for the entire media and for crime reporting in particular.

One of the first effects of the story was the closure of the *News of the World* by its owner, Rupert Murdoch. Two weeks later, the Metropolitan Police Commissioner, Sir Paul Stephenson and the assistant commissioner, John Yates, resigned over their own roles in the saga. In the wake of the revulsion felt across the political spectrum about the hacking, the prime minister David Cameron announced that he was appointing Lord Justice Leveson, the man who had successfully prosecuted Rosemary West, to head an inquiry that would examine 'the culture, practices and ethics of the press in its relations with the public, with the police, with politicians and, as to the police and politicians, the conduct of each'. For the media in general and crime reporters in particular, the world now became 'BL' and 'AL' – Before Leveson and After Leveson.

Much of the response to the initial *Guardian* revelations about hacking, from both the police and the rest of the media, was dismissive. The Mayor of London, Boris Johnson, who had responsibility for setting policing priorities for the capital, described the early stories as 'codswallop' that 'looks like a politically motivated put-up job by the Labour Party'. As a damage-limitation exercise, the management standards committee of News International, which owned the *News of the World* and the *Sun*, handed over to the police millions of emails which revealed the contacts and sources of many of their journalists. In one of the subsequent trials of journalists charged with hacking, a defence counsel, Nigel Rumfitt QC, told jurors that the police had been 'spoonfed' evidence 'by a mighty multinational desperate to save its own skin'. He described News International as 'a copper's nark – a grass, and like all grasses gives a mixture of inaccurate and misleading information to the police'.

Meanwhile, the police launched three inquiries in quick succession: Operation Weeting, into phone hacking; Operation Elveden, into allegations of paying money to police officers and other public officials for leaks and tip-offs; and Operation Tuleta, into computer hacking. Between 2011 and 2015, a total of sixty-seven journalists were arrested. Operation Weeting led to the arrest of twenty-nine journalists of whom nine were convicted or pleaded guilty. Under Operation Elveden, thirty were arrested, twenty-nine charged and only one convicted. Under Tuleta, one journalist pleaded guilty and was cautioned.

Two former editors of the *News of the World*, Andy Coulson and Rebekah Brooks, appeared in the dock of the Old Bailey. After an eight-month trial, in July 2014, Coulson, who had been the Prime Minister's communications director, was convicted of conspiring to intercept voicemails and jailed for eighteen months. Brooks was found not guilty. In separate cases, the paper's former chief reporter Neville Thurlbeck and former news editors Greg Miskiw and Ian Edmonson, all pleaded guilty; the former two were jailed for six months and the latter eight months. Many of the subsequent cases, in particular those resulting from Operation Elveden, resulted in acquittals for the journalists concerned and considerable bitterness about the prosecution process, aimed at the police and the Crown Prosecution Service (CPS).

In April 2015, many of the Elveden prosecutions were abandoned by the CPS before they even came to trial. The former *News of the World* crime correspondent Lucy Panton, who won her appeal against conviction for conspiracy to commit public misconduct by paying a prison officer, was one of those against whom further charges were dropped. She had been on bail for more than nineteen months before being charged and described the experience as a 'hellish ordeal'.

There was widespread condemnation of the prosecutions. Michelle Stanistreet, the general secretary of the National Union of Journalists, described Operation Elveden as 'a £20-million fiasco. What was so damaging for the journalists was that they were forced to breach the most basic tenet of the profession – that you always protect your source.' Indeed, the NUJ's code of conduct states clearly that a journalist 'protects the identity of sources who supply information in confidence and material gathered in the course of her/his work'. She blamed Rupert Murdoch 'and his henchmen and women' for handing over reporters' emails and contacts to the police and concluded that 'we must never have a situation where journalists are abused in this way. If they have no guarantee they can do their jobs safely and can protect their sources and journalistic material, we will not have a functioning free press.'

In May 2015, Anthony France, the crime correspondent of the *Sun*, was found guilty over payments to a public official and received an eighteen-month suspended sentence. France was convicted because he had, over a period of more than three years, given £22,000 to a PC Timothy Edwards who worked at Heathrow airport as part of the counter-terrorism unit. Sentencing him, Judge Timothy Pontius described him as of 'hitherto unblemished character' and 'essentially a decent man of solid integrity'. He was also sentenced to complete 200 hours of unpaid work and ordered to pay costs of just under £35,000, on the understanding that News UK would foot the bill. France, who told the court he had inherited Edwards as a contact, was widely regarded as very unlucky to be convicted.

The fullest account of the events that led to the Leveson Inquiry and the arrests of journalists can be found in Nick Davies's book *Hack Attack*. Davies suggests that illegal hacking was regarded within News International as justifiable provided it didn't 'go Main Street'. The hacking of the parents of Madeleine McCann, the three-year-old who disappeared in Portugal in 2007, and of Milly Dowler was 'Main Street'. He also suggested that no action was initially taken over the hacking of Milly Dowler's phone because, as one officer put it, the press were 'untouchable and all-powerful'. The original suggestion in the *Guardian*, that messages on Milly Dowler's phone had been deleted, thus giving her parents and the police false hope that she was still alive, turned out not to be the case.

The Leveson Inquiry, held in the Royal Courts of Justice and televised live, took oral evidence from 337 witnesses, including eleven chief constables and twenty-five journalists, digested nearly 300 statements, cost £5.4 million and produced a 2,000-page report on its findings and recommendations. With evidence given by journalists, police officers and victims of press malpractice, such as the Dowler family and the parents of Madeleine McCann, it threw open a window on the dark arts of investigations and the effect they had on their subjects. The Home Affairs Select Committee calculated that at least 12,800 people had had their phones hacked but the true figure will never be known.

Lord Justice Leveson published the first part of his inquiry on 29 November 2012. It examined, amongst many other aspects of reporting, 'public concern that the police had become too close to the press in general, and News International (NI) in particular, with the result that the investigation of phone hacking had not been conducted with the rigour that it deserved and calls for re-consideration of the allegations were ignored.' The NI influence at the Yard was major: ten out of forty-five press officers had come from there.

High on the list of Leveson's recommendations – and perhaps the most controversial suggestion – was that an independent regulatory body, backed by law, be set up with the power to investigate serious ethical breaches and to sanction newspapers. This was vigorously opposed by most newspapers who argued that it would give the state too much power and they duly set up their own body, the Independent Press Standards Organisation (IPSO) in 2014 with the backing of all the national press with the exception of the *Guardian*, the *Independent*, the *Observer* and the *Financial Times*. The report explored the various ways in which the press behaved and portrayed itself.

Leveson considered 'the arguably over-cosy relationship between the police and the press' and he pointed to five potential features cited in a summary by the high-profile counsel for the inquiry, Robert Jay QC: inappropriate hospitality; off-the-record briefings; leaks; press attribution of 'police sources'; and the press turning up at incidents because they had been tipped off by a police officer.

Jay suggested that the frequently used expression 'police sources' was 'a term which is redolent of impropriety, or at the very least carries with it the possibility of inappropriate behaviour, either because the police officer has indulged in gossip or leaks, or because the term is in truth a cipher or fig-leaf for an invented story because the source does not in fact exist'. He also suggested that the presence of the media at 'incidents or newsworthy occasions, because they have been tipped off by a police officer . . . is indicative of an unhealthy relationship'.

On the issue of hospitality offered by journalists to the police, the former Met Police Commissioner, Lord Condon, was quoted as suggesting that 'hospitality can be the start of a grooming process which leads to inappropriate and unethical behaviour'. Evidence was given of police officers being entertained at expensive restaurants and given bottles of champagne 'which did nothing to enhance the reputation in the public mind of the MPS or the officers involved'. Leveson noted in passing that the Chief Constable of Avon and Somerset, Colin Port, had cited the so-called 'blush test' and had said in evidence, 'I trust and rely upon the discretion of my staff. They make life-and-death decisions day in and day out, and if I can't trust them to decide that a cup of coffee or a glass or wine or a pint of beer at the appropriate time is not appropriate, then I've lost the plot.'

As far as senior officers dealing with the media were concerned, Leveson found that 'the distinction between endeavouring to improve the standing of the Service on the one hand, and working in the pursuit of self-interest on the other, may be a fine one.' And as regards high-profile arrests and the British equivalent of the American 'perp walk' – when an arrested person is filmed or photographed by the media – Leveson concluded that 'the professionalism required of police officers must be sufficiently robust to instill the mindset that such leaks about forthcoming arrests or the involvement of the famous in the criminal justice system are not in the public interest . . .' He also urged that, except in exceptional circumstances, the names or identifying details of people arrested or sus-pected of a crime should not be released to the press. His suggestions were soon to be cheerfully ignored as high-profile figures in the entertainment industry – many of them completely innocent – were arrested during investigations into historic cases of sexual abuse.

One side-effect of the inquiry was to shine some shocking light on the murder of Daniel Morgan, a private investigator who was killed with an axe to the head in the car park of the Golden Lion pub in south London in 1987. It has been suggested that Morgan was about to blow the whistle to the press about police corruption in the area. No one has ever been convicted of his murder, despite five police inquiries into his death and an unending and dogged campaign by his loyal brother, Alistair, to get to the truth. A new investigation was launched under Dave Cook, a dedicated and conscientious detective who finally gave the Morgan family hope that the truth of what had happened might finally emerge. Morgan's former partner, Jonathan Rees, who worked extensively on assignments for the *News of the World*, and a former police officer, Sid Fillery, stood trial in connection with the murder at the Old Bailey in 2011 but the case against them collapsed.

What the Leveson Inquiry learned was that, in 2002, Dave Cook noticed two vans hanging round near his home and following him and his wife, another police officer called Jacqui Hames, who was a presenter of the BBC's *Crimewatch*. Both vans had been leased to the *News of the*

World. 'The *News of the World*'s alleged justification for this surveillance was that it was suspected they were having an affair together, a position that lacked any credibility given that Ms Hames and Mr Cook had been married for some years and had two children.' Here was an uncompromising detective trying to solve a shocking murder being hounded by the *News of the World*, one of whose freelancers had been charged with the very same murder.

Amongst some of the most intriguing and frank evidence was that from Richard Peppiatt, formerly of the *Daily Star*, who shone a light on the reporting of crime figures for his paper: 'if there's something that comes out saying crime has gone down, you then go look for the statistic which says knife crime has gone up 20 per cent but the rest of crime – well, we'll just focus on knife crime. Because there is an overwhelming negativity and it runs throughout the tabloid press. You know, a story is simply not a story unless it's knocking someone, or knocking an organisation or knocking an ethnic group, whatever it may be.'

On the issue of 'sources', Peppiatt said that 'although unnamed sources are a valuable journalistic tool to protect sources, often in my experience of tabloids they are simply made up by the reporter to increase the word count and add a veneer of legitimacy to something that is speculation, at best.'

Running in tandem with the Leveson Inquiry was a separate report, entitled The Ethical Issues Arising From Relations Between the Police and the Media, which was commissioned in 2011 by the home secretary, Theresa May, and the then Commissioner of the Metropolitan Police, Sir Paul Stephenson, in the wake of the initial revelations about phone hacking but before the Leveson Inquiry got underway. It was headed by Dame Elizabeth Filkin, the former parliamentary commissioner for standards, who seemed to take as her creed the wonderful poem by Wendy Cope, 'How to Deal with the Press', which recommends that you should never confide in a journalist.

Her report, published in 2012, suggested that officers watch out for 'late-night carousing, long sessions, yet another bottle of wine at lunch

– these are all long-standing media tactics to get you to spill the beans. Avoid.' The report continued: 'Mixing the media with alcohol is not banned but should be an uncommon event.' She suggests that drinking with officers 'may be seen as inappropriate hospitality'. She also advised the police to watch out for reporters 'flirting'.

The Filkin Report received a warm welcome from the then newly appointed Commissioner of the Met, Sir Bernard Hogan-Howe. 'There should be no more secret conversations,' he said at the time of its publication. 'There should be no more improper contact and by that what I mean is between the police and the media – that which is of a selfish, rather than a public interest. Meetings will no longer be enhanced by hospitality and alcohol.' Reporters were in no doubt as to the effects of the Filkin Report, the Leveson Inquiry and the arrests and prosecutions. Sean O'Neill, crime editor of *The Times*, said that the combination of the events had 'created a culture of fear reinforced by a set of rules and regulations that have left sensible officers worried about the impact on their careers of having conversations with journalists'. The end result of the high-profile arrests, he said, was 'a press that is all too willing to bash the police at every opportunity because it has now seen bully-boy policing up close'.

As a sign of the cooling relations between police and reporters, since the Leveson Inquiry the traditional CRA Christmas party, to which police officers were always invited, was cancelled as few of the officers now turned up. 'On the eve of the publication of the Leveson report we went to the Barley Mow – one detective who was coming had a text saying "you are not to go",' said John Twomey, chairman of the CRA. 'They thought that we would photograph senior police officers going into the pub and then publish it on the day that the Leveson report was published. No one would have done that. Hopefully, eventually, the police will come to a better understanding. You don't want to go out and get slaughtered every lunch time with them or go to the Ritz and have a £500 bottle of Cristal but just normal social interaction – you'd have a couple of glasses of wine over lunch or a couple of beers before you go home and they had trust in reporters that they knew.'

As for the lasting effect on the police, here is the response of a senior serving detective in March 2015 whom I had asked to interview about media/police relations: 'Much as I would like to, I cannot speak to journalists without a senior press officer present and they only give permission to comment factually on jobs. The world is a very different place. Sorry.'

22
Still the Best Job in the World?
The End of an Era

The old cosy relationship between crime reporters and the police was already coming to an end by the time Leveson reported and with it the nights of booze and nicotine and the days of imaginative expenses and newspaper deadlines as the 24-hour online news culture arrived. And perhaps nobody was better placed than Chester Stern to judge the relationship between the police and crime reporters as the twentieth century came towards its end and a new generation of crime correspondents took over from the Sultans. For sixteen years he worked in Scotland Yard's press bureau and, for the next nineteen years, he was the *Mail on Sunday*'s crime correspondent. The gamekeeper turned poacher.

His own entry into the world of crime came as a result of a policeman fitting up a peace campaigner in 1963. Harold 'Tanky' Challenor, who became a policeman after wartime service in the SAS, was charged with conspiracy to pervert the course of justice after he had planted a half-brick on Donald Rooum, a cartoonist and member of the National Council of Civil Liberties, who was protesting against Queen Frederika of Greece. 'There you are, me old darling,' Challenor told Rooum as he produced the half-brick. 'Carrying an offensive weapon.' Challenor was found unfit to plead on mental health grounds but the scandal led to a Royal Commission which recommended that Scotland Yard should have a professional public relations and press set-up. The head of PR at Schweppes, Bob Gregory, was appointed and, for the first time, he recruited press officers with a background in journalism rather than the civil service. Stern was at the time an editorial assistant on a food industry magazine. 'A colleague said, if you ever want to be a crime reporter, this is a wonderful way in. I saw it as a glorious opportunity to work at world-famous Scotland Yard.' He stayed for the next sixteen years and ended up as head of the press bureau. 'Challenor gave everyone a huge shock because the service image at the time was Dixon of Dock Green and the police were consistently top in all polls of public esteem,' said Stern.

'The CID were totally in control and, although the public didn't realise it, totally and utterly corrupt. Crime reporting up to then was very glamorous – we had only just lost the death penalty – and there was a little group who formed a caravan, travelling round the country on murder inquiries for which the Yard was still routinely called in. There was no spin, no PR, no proactive stuff. Police officers you asked questions of simply lied if it was inconvenient for them and at a lower level, because corruption within the CID was a way of life, lesser corruption – being paid by reporters – was equally acceptable and understood as a routine.'

The arrival of Robert Mark as Commissioner changed everything, not least when he released his famous 'General Memo 11/72', which called for far greater openness with the press. 'It was almost like a bible to me. It became a blueprint for the country but nobody adheres to it any more. The basic principle was that, if the police are to be accountable to the public they serve then, with a few obvious exceptions, the public have the right to know everything that the police are doing on their behalf.' The new approach had some unforeseen consequences: 'It led to media groupies – a lot of senior officers suddenly got a taste for seeing their name in the papers, which led eventually to that unacceptable cosiness between New Scotland Yard and News International.'

Stern decided to cross over to the other side of the street when he heard that there was a crime reporter's job going at the soon-to-be-launched *Mail on Sunday* in 1982: 'I looked at some of the crime reporters at the time and, without mentioning any names, I thought if they can do that, I can do that.' He was nervous at first because of loyalties to the Met that he still retained. In his first month, this loyalty was tested when he was asked to use his inside knowledge over the shooting of Stephen Waldorf, a film editor who was shot several times after being mistaken for the wanted armed robber David Martin. Stern was under pressure from his new editor, Stewart Steven, to come up with the inside story and did so with a scoop about the Blue Berets, the specialist firearms unit. Other front page stories followed and his editor took him out to lunch and told him that 'I thought you were a disaster, you were imposed on me from Scotland Yard and I was ready to sack you but I know now that crime is very important to our readers and you're very good, would you like to be an executive?' Stern demurred and was told by Steven: 'Correct answer. In Fleet Street there are only two good jobs: what you do now – reporter/specialist; and what I do. The in-between is a nasty slippery slope.'

As a crime reporter, he was taken on a number of raids by the police on the grounds that it was in their mutual interest as it gave the police an independent witness that they had done everything right. On one occasion he was taken, along with a photographer, on a drugs raid in south London. The detectives were thrilled that they had finally captured a 'Mr Big' and duly celebrated, taking a Union Jack off the wall and dancing around as Mr Big sat handcuffed on the floor with his hands cuffed behind him, watching all this. 'He got his lawyer to force us to disclose the photos which they then used to suggest that this was a press stunt and that the officers had planted the whole thing. So it was chucked out, much to the chagrin of the whole drugs squad.'

His old contacts in the specialist squads unit stood him in good stead, not least because they dealt with many cases that had a foreign element to them. 'I used to say: "What have you got? I've got the money, the time, no legal constraints, I can go and investigate something for you and you can follow it up or whatever." I got a lot of stories and trips that way.'

One of his most intriguing journeys came about through them. As was the case for many of his contemporaries, the murder in 1974 of the nanny Sandra Rivett and the subsequent disappearance of her employer Lord Lucan, the chief suspect, was a major story. 'Two years after the murder, one of Lucan's drinking buddies got wiped out by a car and a PC got an address book out of his pocket which said "Lord Lucan, Hotel Ambassadeurs, Beira, Mozambique" so I went out there. I showed them a picture of Lucan and they said "You friend? English?" "Where did he go?" "Hotel Estoril." I looked at the register there – what did I expect to find? It said in April 1975, for nine or ten days, John and Susan Maxwell-Scott (the last known contacts made by Lucan in England before his flight) had stayed there. I went to see Susan Maxwell-Scott when I returned and she changed her version of the story many times.' Stern has his own theory as to what might have become of him: 'He was a Nazi fanatic, a huge Hitler fan – they raided his flat and he had a full set of Hitler's speeches on tape – and he was a fluent German speaker. There is a German community in Mozambique and I would have thought very easy to take up a new life as a German.'

Another journalist who covered crime in this period was the South African Garth Gibbs, of the *Daily Mirror*, who died in 2011 at the age of seventy-five. As his obituary in the *Press Gazette* recorded, he also managed to spend much of his time hunting for Lord Lucan, who was the subject of bogus sightings which placed him everywhere from Kenya to Colombia, Gabon to New Zealand. As recently as 2003, he was supposedly tracked down to Goa in India, although the man identified as Lucan turned out to be a blameless folk singer from St Helens. Gibbs did not mind that Lucan was never tracked down.

'As that brilliantly bigoted and crusty old columnist, John Junor, once cannily observed: "Laddie, you don't ever want to shoot the fox,"' he wrote. "Once the fox is dead there is nothing left to chase."' He added: 'I regard not finding Lord Lucan as my most spectacular success in journalism . . . I have successfully not found him in more exotic spots than anybody else. I spent three glorious weeks not finding him in Cape Town, magical days and nights not finding him in the Black Mountains of Wales, and wonderful and successful short breaks not finding him in Macau either, or in Hong Kong or even in Green Turtle Cay in the Bahamas where you can find anyone.'

Other crime reporters came to the job by more traditional routes. Jeff Edwards, crime correspondent of the *Daily Mirror* from 1993 to 2008 and chairman of the CRA, started work at the *Leytonstone Express and Independent* in 1967, in the days when local papers still covered all the courts and police cases. The newspaper's office was 100 metres from the local police station so officers would often come round if they needed bodies to put on an ID parade. His first interaction with the local police was memorable. He was waiting at the front counter on the other side of which were some bound books. 'I was eighteen and a mod – I looked like Bradley Wiggins – and there was a sergeant there – he looked like PC Dimbleby from [satirical television puppet show] *Spitting Image*. He suddenly growled at me: "I'll teach you to read my books over the counter!" and he put one hand on the counter, vaulted it, hit me with a forearm smash and pinned me against the wall with his face in my face. I saw a couple of PCs with their jaws hanging open and one said, "Sarge, put him down!"' Back at the office, the editor called Edwards in and said that he had been told that he had been looking at the officer's books. 'I said, "No, I wasn't," and he said, "You should have been, that's what I'm paying you for." I began to realise there was a strain of violence running through the British police.'

He joined the *Newham Recorder* in 1970 and 'I realised quickly that the fount of much information was the CID. I was talking to DCs of around my age. I was single, I liked girls, I liked football and cricket, I liked going to pubs and I liked talking to people who had interesting lives so I started getting invited: "Meet me round the Spotted Dog at seven and we'll have a chat." So I got inveigled into the police pub culture and started to get terrific results. One stunt for the police in those days was to pretend the photocopying machine was a lie detector; a gullible suspect would be asked to place his hand under the flap and answer questions as the light flashed. They got clear-up after clear-up through that . . . As I said when I gave talks at Bramshill [police training college], Gene Hunt in *Life on Mars* is a pale imitation of what it was like.'

Another tale of the era, said Edwards, was when an east London solic-itor who had a client in custody came in to the police station and left a *Daily Mirror* and a toothbrush for him with the detective. 'Between pages 24 and 25 of the *Mirror* he had written "Charlie, under no circumstances say anything." So the detective went next door to the newsagent, got another copy of the paper and wrote "Charlie, it's all right, I've straight-ened everything out for you. Tell them everything they want to know". The lawyer came back four hours later and said, "Can I see my client?" and was told, "Yes, you can but he's admitted the offence and fifteen other TICs [taken-into-consideration]!" Some of the police were violent, drunk on duty and corrupt but also thoroughly decent, nice people.'

Throughout his career, which included time at the broadcaster LWT on the programme *Crime Monthly*, the *News of the World* and the short-lived *London Daily News*, Edwards kept in touch with officers he met early in his career. 'Cops talked to me because they trusted me. One of the most flattering things I've ever had said to me was, "You're as well known for what you don't write as what you do write." It was a question of, "I'll tell you anything you want to know, just don't let it come back to my door." In today's climate many people would look askance at that, but I had good personal friends and you could have that late night dialogue along the lines of, "If I did something seriously wrong, you'd have to arrest me and if you did something seriously wrong, I'd have to write about it."'

On one occasion, while at the *News of the World*, he found himself covering a crime on his own doorstep. Many newspaper employees were still paid in cash in the eighties so their offices became the targets of armed robbers. The paper was still based in Bouverie Street, near Fleet Street. 'I had just got in when Stuart Kuttner, the assistant editor, an eccentric character in every way, appeared in the doorway of the office and said, "Ah, Jeff, can you pop down to the wages office. I'm told there's a man down there with a gun." And then he disappeared.'

Edwards found a clerk tied to a chair, a huge reinforced safe door wide open and money all over the floor. 'The clerk said, "Four blokes come in, one put a gun to my head." Six months earlier we had hired, as head of security, Bert Wickstead, an old-school detective with a trilby who had been given the job as a part of a deal for the serialisation of his memoirs, *Gangbuster: Tales of the Old Grey Fox*. When he sees me in the room, he says, "What are you doing here?" I said, "Doing my job." He said, "Fuck off, you are contaminating a crime scene."' Wickstead refused to tell him how much had been stolen until the editor, Derek Jameson, called them both to his office and told Wickstead, "We're going to look a right bunch of cunts if our rivals have got a better story than we have. Tell him what he wants to know." Wickstead had to give me a full breakdown. About £1 million had been stolen.'

Amongst Edwards' friends and contacts was John Donald, a detective who was jailed for eleven years for corruption in 1996. 'He was, I thought, a nice guy. In 1993, he got in touch with me because he knew I'd been around LWT and said, "There's a rumour that *World in Action* have set up a camera in a derelict shop opposite our offices in Surbiton." I thought he was giving me information as background. Later he got back in touch and said he thought it was *Panorama* so I asked *Panorama* because I thought, if they were doing something, I'd like to have a head's-up and do something in the paper. That night on *Panorama* it was, "We expose corruption," and there was footage of John Donald . . . *Private Eye* had a story a couple of weeks later saying something along the lines of, wasn't it strange that a very good friend of Donald's should ring *Panorama*, but I had no idea that he would be the one under investigation. Even after all this time, I am upset that there were people who thought I was trying to find information which would help him. The truth is, it never occurred to me that he was corrupt. He gave off no lifestyle signs of being bent and I always thought of him as a decent, likeable man who wouldn't have had the balls to get involved in anything bad. I – voluntarily – told CIB [the anti-corruption branch then under Ian Blair, later to become Commissioner] that he had never asked for, nor been offered, a penny by me and I think Blair accepted it as true. I still see him occasionally, he's a self-employed chauffeur and a pub musician and, despite his crimes, I like him.'

Other officers have sought his help on more honest grounds. 'In 2004, Mike Todd [chief constable of Greater Manchester, who died of exposure on Mount Snowdon in 2008 after taking a mixture of alcohol and sleeping tablets, possibly out of fear of tabloid exposure in connection with affairs with female colleagues] rang me and said "Can you help me out? An organised crime man from Manchester has been accidentally released in mistake for someone else. We have intelligence that he has a gun. He thinks we've arranged to have him released so we can bump him off. Can you write a story about this – dangerous man released in a cock-up – we want him to know that it's a cock-up and we are not intending to shoot him. What I am trying to avoid is a bloody confrontation – I'm concerned some of my people could get shot." That was agile thinking on Todd's part. How many Chief Constables will have that kind of contact with crime reporters nowadays? They're not allowed to. Will they give out their private numbers? No, they'll think they're going to be hacked.'

There have been frustrations for Edwards, too. In November 1983, 'I had a wonderful exclusive story one weekend. I met a police officer at midnight under a darkened railway bridge in south-west London. The story was that [Conservative party grandee and minister of state] Cecil Parkinson had fathered a child with Sara Keays, his then secretary, and the officer said that there had been a burglary at her house. Nothing had been stolen but a locked filing cabinet had been sprung open and her papers and documents had been gone through. Most people thought MI5 did it, though they may have sub-contracted out the work to a PI or pro. The paper said, "We'll splash on that." The next morning Brink's-Mat happened [a £26-million bullion robbery at Heathrow] and that was mine, too. They said, "You'll have the whole front page: Brink's-Mat down the right hand side, Sara Keays down the left." Then the printers walked out and the paper was never published!'

John Weeks covered crime for the *Daily Telegraph* from 1964 to 1989, having started his career with *West Essex Gazette* and the *Chingford Express*, and recalled that, in his very early days, the Krays were a subject of great interest. 'I went to Esmeralda's Barn [their gaming club in Knightsbridge] and they would say, "What do you want to drink?" If I was drinking gin-and-tonic, they would bring a whole bottle up. When I left after a few drinks they would mark the bottle with a big black line and when you came back six weeks later you would have your bottle returned to you. Didn't pay for it of course. They knew who we were, they quite liked the press. I knew Nipper Read, who investigated the Krays, and the only time I saw him get annoyed was when I asked about them doing good for the OAPs, taking them to the seaside in charabancs. He said, "That's the biggest load of crap. They did nothing at all."'

He was the first reporter on the scene when three police officers were shot dead at Shepherd's Bush in west London in 1966, a story that shocked the country and for which three men were jailed for life, one of them, Harry Roberts, being finally released in 2014. 'The police arrived from all over London and Surrey. I knew quite a lot of them. The bodies were still under the car when I got there. The *Telegraph* sent me a team of five including a new reporter and he was listening to me talking to one of the officers and he got his notebook out and starting writing and asking the officer "What's your name?" It's one of the few times I've lost my temper. He's the only reporter I've threatened to punch.'

The press culture in those days was still one of heavy drinking and smoking. 'Some bright spark worked out that the average crime reporter in those early days drank about eight pints a day in half pints of bitter but it was quite a long day and there was no breathalyser then!'

Weeks also covered the Lucan case. 'There were different theories about what happened to him, that he hid in a ditch and died or committed suicide. I was quite well in with the people investigating it and Tom [Sandrock] and I had a ten-hour lunch with them, which must be an all-time record. Tom had a phenomenal memory and we would both go to the loo at different times and make a note so we got a whole page in the paper. I went to Mauritius where he was supposed to have been and I spent a nice week there. Nothing to report.'

In the 1960s, he was persuaded to take a detective from the Obscene Publications Squad [known as the Dirty Squad] home one night. 'He lived in a huge house which had everything in it and these were the days when people didn't even have fridges. He was a detective inspector and there was no way on earth he could have afforded that on his wages. I was warned off him and he ended up going away for seven years. But I think the talk of corruption was overplayed, it was thought that there were only about forty of them [corrupt officers] and that the level of corruption was about 0.5 per cent which is very low by international standards.'

When the phone-hacking scandal finally blew up in 2011, John Twomey was the chairman of the Crime Reporters' Association and crime correspondent at the *Daily Express*. 'The idea of covering crime was attractive because national newspaper crime reporters seemed to have a great time,' he said. 'Whether the economy is blowing up or there's a scandal at Westminster or a royal baby on the way, if you get a big crime – like Lord Lucan, for instance – that's going to wipe everything off the front pages.' He started his career on the *South London Press*, which traditionally covered crime in a big way.

'Our bread and butter in those days was armed robbery. Part of the job was getting to know CID officers and they were happy to talk – I know it sounds like an old record with the needle stuck – but once they trusted you in the 1980s, they would talk to you. I went out with the drug squad on one occasion – they even sat me in a room where they brought in a supplier and they just invited me to ask him questions. You would be in constant contact with them, having drinks with them and you would ask questions in a certain way that didn't sound like you were just about to rush to the phone and put it in the paper.' He worked for the *London Daily News* and the *People* before joining the *Express* in 1987.

Covering police corruption was difficult. 'Some of the older reporters would discourage you from writing about it and would say, "Don't put your name to that." It made sense in a very limited, short-sighted way but it was quite disgraceful. We were always the cheerleaders for the CID because they were the people who would give us stories.'

Twomey has had a few threats over years. The wife of one north London gangster about whom he has written sent him a fax from Spain to say 'those lies you keep on printing, you must be getting them from all the bent coppers you used to know on the *South London Press*.'

Stewart Tendler became crime correspondent at *The Times* after he had been working there on stories about the drugs world and the case involving Jeremy Thorpe, the former leader of the Liberal party acquitted of conspiring to murder his former lover, Norman Scott, in 1979. 'In those days, the press room at the Yard was open to reporters 24 hours. You simply walked in and turned right at reception. There were some chairs, a table and a filing cabinet which usually contained a half-eaten cheese roll, someone's porn magazine and documentation for the CRA. A truncheon had been left on one of the desks. The air was filled with cigarette smoke and the clatter of typewriters. In the press room you would find relics of the golden days, several who dressed like the senior detectives of the 1950s and 1960s, with a brown trilby and a military-style overcoat – "The British Warm". Drink lubricated the day.'

Neil Darbyshire, who covered crime for the *Evening Standard* and the *Daily Telegraph* in the eighties and nineties, started his career on local papers in south London before joining the *Standard* in 1979, where he acted as a legman for the paper's chief crime reporter, the colourful John Stevens. Stevens, famous for his handlebar moustache and addressing everyone as 'my dear fellow', died in 2016, aged eighty-six. He was known by many colleagues to meet his police contacts weekly in the bar of the Britannia hotel in the West End where he gave them envelopes stuffed with cash, depending on what stories they had supplied that week. At the time, relations between the police and the press were mainly amiable.

'Crime reporters had their contacts and they kept them very close to their chests,' said Darbyshire, now assistant editor at the *Daily Mail*. Stevens had a full contact book and Darbyshire recalled that, when there was a series of arrests of corrupt officers, 'I remember the contact book with red lines put through names as they went to prison or retired on health grounds . . . There was certainly a degree of protection given by crime reporters to their contacts but I don't think they tried to prevent other journalists from writing a story if it broke, but they wouldn't write it themselves.'

Darbyshire was involved in much of the early coverage of the Yardies, Jamaican criminals involved in drugs and gun crime in London, and was allowed access to the special squad that pursued them. When he first wrote about the issue he was called at home late at night by a very senior Met Police officer and told that his story was sensationalist. 'Then, as the problem continued, I suspect as a sort of "sorry-about-that" gesture, they allowed me access to the squad. I went on the first raid of a Yardie crack house – belonging to Rankin' Dread [DJ and musician Errol Codling]. What would happen before you went on a raid was that you would go to the police station and sit in on the briefing. It would be very early in the morning – although with quite a lot of the Yardies they could have left it a bit later.'

Justin Davenport has been covering crime at the *Evening Standard* for around twenty years, reporting on everything from the murder of television presenter Jill Dando in 1999 and the mistaken shooting of Jean-Charles de Menezes in 2005, to the arrival of the eastern European gangs. During that time and in the wake of the hacking scandal and the Leveson report he saw many changes.

'When I first started the job around twenty years ago it was accepted practice at Christmas to reward people with cases of wine or bottles of whisky,' he said. 'That would never happen now . . . The idea that detectives were always telling stories out of turn over a drink was a bit of a fallacy. It may have happened but more often than not you would take someone out and drink huge amounts of alcohol and never get a thing from them . . . There were often stories that you were told but asked not to run and you didn't. That built trust between police and reporters and it helped relations.'

Davenport has attended dozens of police raids with the Met: 'They used to be much more open and accessible. I remember several when you ended up in the suspect's living room. You could be three or four back behind the cop with the sledgehammer and you all charged in and you stood around while this guy was cuffed. On one occasion I was standing there and the guy who was arrested said, "Who the fuck's he, then?" and the big detective just said: "He's with us," and nothing more was said about it. These days they have to ask permission for us to go into a house and the raids are rarely as exciting as they used to be, when you were much closer to the action. I have been out with the Met's surveillance teams and once on an undercover operation targeting suspected corrupt banking officials. I could not imagine that happening now.'

Stephen Wright, the *Daily Mail*'s crime specialist for fifteen years from 1996, would agree. He worked on the paper's famous front-page naming of the Stephen Lawrence killers. 'The other really satisfying story for me was the corrupt police commander Ali Dizaei [jailed for perverting the course of justice and misconduct in a public office in 2012], which I spent ten years writing about. That was a vicious battle, and I and the *Daily Mail* were the only paper to take him on. He had elements of Fleet Street and the broadcast media in his pocket. People thought it was a duel between him and me but it wasn't – although it was a relief when he was convicted because it was seen as a vindication of my journalism. I am so glad that I didn't go to court to see him led down to the cells because I didn't want to make it look personal.'

Like his colleagues, he noticed the sea change in relations with the police in the wake of the hacking scandal. 'My view is that the Metropolitan Police currently doesn't respect journalists,' he said. 'I said to Leveson, I didn't like the commissioner's monthly briefing to crime reporters. I felt it was an attempt to control us. I thought it was a control mechanism – "keep your friends close, keep your enemies closer". It's good to be respected by senior officers but to be taken seriously you mustn't be afraid to give them a slap from time to time, when they deserve it.'

Martin Brunt is Britain's longest-serving television crime correspondent and has also witnessed the changes in the job. He had wanted to be a reporter as a teenager at the school in Soham where, many years later, the murderer Ian Huntley was the caretaker. His first job was with IPC and the *Power Laundry and Cleaning News* where he worked for two years. 'The novelty of writing about laundry machines wore off eventually,' he said with understatement. He worked in local newspapers and agencies in Plymouth and Exeter before moving to London to work for Ferraris, the news agency which specialised in coverage of courts and crime. Soon he became chief reporter at the *Sunday Mirror*. He joined Sky when it started in 1988 and he became their crime correspondent in 1994.

'For me it was brilliant, coppers in those days were rather flattered by the attention of a TV reporter, something they hadn't really encountered before,' he said. 'It's changed now out of all proportion (after the hacking scandal, Leveson and restrictions on police talking to journalists). Coppers won't even meet me now to talk about stories.'

In the 1990s, trust between the media and the police was such that Brunt was invited along when detectives went to Italy to interview Valerio Viccei, the mastermind of the Knightsbridge safe deposit robbery of 1987. Viccei was technically still serving his sentence. 'The two cops went off to do their business and the next morning I went to a restaurant on the beach and Valerio turned up, with his Rolex watch and rather refined clothes, looking every bit the glamorous figure and charming with it. I liked him a lot. I asked about the money and he just smiled and tried to give me the impression that it had all gone and the jewels had been sold at knock-down prices. I remember him saying that, "You have to remember, we had Fabergé eggs which were melted down – a travesty, I know but that's what we had to do to get rid of them, they went for 10 or 20 per cent of the true value." I said, "There must be some buried somewhere for when you come out of jail?" He said no – but he said it with a smile.' Two years later Viccei was shot dead by the carabinieri while on day release from jail.

Brunt also covered in detail the story surrounding the disappearance of three-year-old Madeleine McCann in Portugal. This led to him much later, in 2015, exposing Brenda Leyland, an internet troll who had been attacking the McCann family anonymously, sending more that 400 abusive tweets about the case. Two days later, Leyland killed herself. In the wake of that, Brunt was himself subjected to abuse on Twitter. 'We were encouraged as reporters when Twitter became established to tweet and I used to do quite a lot but, since the Brenda Leyland thing, if I put a tweet out now, I would get bombarded by people who say "remember Brenda Leyland". Occasionally I'm accused of being a murderer. "You've got blood on your hands." Generally I can rise above all that. I understand twitter trolls for what they are, rather sad people with nothing better to do. I have this image of them sitting there waiting to be outraged. It doesn't really bother me but I am aware of it and, to be honest, it does become a bit wearing. I think it will be something that will follow me to the end of my career.'

Brunt is perhaps unusual in that he has many contacts amongst villains and spoke at the train robber Bruce Reynolds's funeral. 'There is a tendency to accept everything the cops tell you and do things from their perspective so I quite like the challenge of doing things from the other side. It was easier talking to those old-fashioned villains – Frank Fraser, Freddie Foreman, Bruce Reynolds – because a lot of them had books coming out and I was quite keen on where art met crime. It's not quite as easy to get alongside and be friendly with Kosovan drug dealers and the crime lords of today.'

Danny Jones, one of the burglars who took part in the spectacular Hatton Garden safe deposit theft in 2015, wrote to Brunt from Belmarsh jail saying that he wanted to show the police where he had hidden his share – in a cemetery in Edmonton. In his letter, Jones said: 'I'm not crying Martin, I did it. I can't talk for other people, only for myself and whatever I get on judgment day I will stand tall, but I want to make amends to all my loved ones and show I'm trying to change. I no [sic] it seems a bit late in my life, but I'm trying.' The police duly went to the cemetery and, to Jones's dismay, found not only the stash of gold, jewellery and precious stones hidden in a relative's grave that he had told them about, but another stash of more expensive jewels in the same cemetery that he had somehow neglected to mention.

For Mike Sullivan, crime editor of the *Sun*, fascination with crime started early. 'Believe it or not, for me it started with reading True Crime magazines at a very young age. I was quite paranoid and I remember, when I was about seven, reading about a woman who had poisoned her own children and being wary of my mother poisoning me!' He had also become curious about the Great Train Robbery, which took place in the year he was born. 'This is probably wrong – but its challenge to the establishment was quite appealing. The other thing I associated with crime reporting was a gritty glamour, like the James Cagney films which I used to love as a kid. It's such an interesting subject – and you don't have to commit a crime or be a policeman to be involved.'

His father was a scrap metal dealer and the nature of the job meant that there was no shortage of a presence of both police and crooks. His uncle Jimmy, also in the same business, had been the target of a hit-man in a scrap metal feud. Sullivan took a journalism course in Sheffield, worked for two years on local papers in St Albans and joined the National News agency where he covered sieges and robberies. One of his earliest stories was the murder of Donald Kell, who saw a robbery happening at Lloyds Bank in Swiss Cottage in 1989, tried to 'have a go' with a piece of wood, and was shot dead.

Sullivan joined the *Sun* in 1990 and there were soon a series of high-profile cases to cover: the murders of Alison Shaughnessy, in Battersea, south London in 1991, for which two sisters were convicted then cleared on appeal, and of Rachel Nickell on Wimbledon Common; and the death of Stephen Milligan, the Conservative MP found dead wearing a bin-liner and with an orange in his mouth, through auto-erotic asphyxiation. Sullivan got a tip-off about what had happened to Milligan while the police were still trying to keep it under wraps. Sullivan noted how dramatically relations with the police have changed since he started work. 'In the early nineties, the police weren't these anonymous characters that they are forced to be now. You had some of the old school and you could go into certain bars around the Old Bailey and meet and drink with them at length. There were lawyers on the make, clerks and even the odd judge or two in the mix. Legal reports and documents flew around like confetti at the Wine Press in Fleet Street on Friday nights – nowadays it's a Tesco Metro. There were people who just wanted stories to get out or who just liked the craic.' It was well known that some officers were happy to leak stories to the press.

As to how the *Sun* was regarded by the police, 'The lower ranks were perhaps more comfortable with someone from the *Sun*. I didn't enjoy going to ACPO [the Association of Chief Police Officers, now the National Police Chiefs' Council] conferences and I can remember how some of them – not all – would look down on you.' The *Sun* was at that stage sponsoring the annual Police Bravery awards, a relationship that ended after many News International journalists were arrested. 'The idea was that we were the force's paper, the idea was to ingrain ourselves as the police canteen paper – and look what happened!'

Sullivan has had to experience the effects of the very worst of crimes himself. 'The most difficult period for me was after my own sister was murdered in 1992. She was stabbed 14 times by someone who was mentally ill. I was in Norwich on a story when it happened. I can't describe it in a professional way. I was asked at the time by my office, "Do you want to still be a crime reporter?" I had no hesitation about it. If anything, it gave me more insight into how people feel in those situations and in respecting the process of grief. We are a bit like funeral directors, doctors and jewellers because we're there for the most dramatic – sometimes the worst – part of a person's life and, if you have a personal insight, it's probably beneficial. The only thing I don't do is look at PM [post-mortem] pictures and sometimes, when the physiological details are being read out in a trial, I quietly leave court. And watching gratuitous violence on television is very hard to deal with.'

Some crime stories get greater prominence than others. 'I remember being despatched down to south London by the news-desk because a fourteen-year-old had fallen off a bridge or been thrown off it onto a busy road and died. On the way down I got a call from the news-desk asking "What colour is she?" I remember thinking, "What does it matter?" I was told to check it out. Sure enough she was Asian and I was told to come back and not worry about it. I thought, fuck that, and carried on, did the story, and it did make a bit in the paper which pleased me. One thing I would take some pride in is that we have done a lot of stuff trying to make sure that every murder counts. Like the detective, Harry Bosch, in Michael Connelly's novels, says: "Everybody counts or nobody counts." It's a good phrase for a crime reporter.'

However, the reality remains that some murders are more newsworthy than others, as Mike Sullivan recalled, in the case of the lawyer Tom ap Rhys Pryce who was discussing wedding plans with his fiancée on his mobile on his way home when he was fatally stabbed by two muggers in Kensal Green, north London, in 2006. The Met Police issued a major appeal for information and a senior officer attended the scene. 'On the other side of London, Balbir Matharut tried to stop two people stealing his car, fell under the wheels and subsequently died but the Met provided next to nothing on that and I think we got three paragraphs in while there was a great big page on ap Rhys Pryce,' said Sullivan. 'The same day a guy called Billy Robinson and his wife, Flo, got chopped up by hoods in Tenerife. That again made two paragraphs. It's the middle-class City lawyer who gets the publicity. I don't know what that says about us, the police or society in general.'

But life was about to change at the *Sun* for other reasons. 'You had this ticking time bomb in the background, the hacking at the *News of the World* which, until Clive Goodman [the royal correspondent jailed for phone hacking] was arrested, I hadn't really heard of; we were all rather old school on the *Sun*. It meant nothing, even at the time. I think the police, who were dealing with 7/7 [the aftermath of the 2005 bomb attacks in London] at the time, probably felt the same.'

The scandal broke at the time of the trial of Levi Bellfield, who was convicted in February 2008 of murdering Marsha McDonnell and Amelie Delagrange and, in June 2011, of the murder of Milly Dowler. 'The story was one of the highlights of my career. I had done the background piece explaining how he came under suspicion and had gone round the country interviewing a number of his victims. Then he is convicted and a few days later you are learning that Milly Dowler's phone had been hacked. I have to say all of us working in the *Sun* office felt a collective sense of shame that someone working in the same company had done that in the name of journalism. The *Guardian* got an important part of the story wrong and Milly's voicemails were never deleted but it doesn't detract from the revulsion of what happened. Sadly, the Met and the CPS then lost the plot and tried to burn as many tabloid journalists at the stake as they could, aided and abetted by our company lawyers in New York. To them we were all criminal scum. To us, they were Stasi stormtroopers.'

The scandal had many ramifications. 'It all came about as a result of a few journalists losing their souls and doing the unthinkable. I know it's not the same thing at all as putting someone to death in a concentration camp, but it's still someone who has done something where the abhorrent becomes normal. I won't say it's been the death of crime reporting because crime reporting will always exist, but it's done so much damage.'

Sullivan's employer, News International, which changed its name to News UK in 2013, handed over all the company's emails to the police and reporters were asked if they had ever paid the police money or hacked phones. 'It's the worst thing that ever happened to me as a journalist – the company handing over everything.' Sullivan was one of those arrested in 2012 and was on bail for fourteen months before being told he would face no charges. 'I thought: it's going to take ages to sort this out and then they'll find there's nothing there. That's largely what happened . . . Almost the entire office was nicked and it became a very difficult area to operate as a crime reporter. It's changed everything. Everything is controlled. I still get the odd story but it's not like it used to be, although I'm sure every generation of crime reporter has probably said that.'

As Sullivan noted, race could often be behind a decision as to what cases were covered and how. Indeed, race has always been an underlying issue in the coverage of crime, not least because, until very recently, the world of reporting was not only very male but very white. It was only in 1999 that Tony Thompson became the first black crime correspondent on a national newspaper, the *Observer*, where he held the post until 2005.

Now he is one of the most prolific of authors on true crime with nine books to his credit. Other black, Asian and minority ethnic crime reporters have followed, notably Anthony France at the *Sun*, Vikram Dodd at the *Guardian* and ITV's Ronke Phillips.

Thompson started his career writing for *Your Computer Magazine*, free-lanced for the *Sunday Mirror* and *Evening Standard* and branched into music journalism – 'so vacuous and boring' – before an investigation of the security industry, which involved applying for jobs undercover, pointed the way to a life of crime reporting. It was the time of 'Florida Phil' Wells, the security guard who stole £1 million of foreign currency from Heathrow in 1989 and fled abroad. Thompson found the challenge enticing and, after freelancing for *Time Out*, became the magazine's news editor in 1995. He was commissioned to write his book *Gangland Britain* in the wake of an article on the subject for *GQ* magazine. 'Relations with the police varied,' he said. 'I once wrote a satirical piece for a free-sheet called *Midweek* about possible careers in crime like "drug dealer" or "hit-man" and one of them was "bent police officer". I got called in by the Yard and told that they didn't take it as a joke. My speciality was talking to criminals and I never had great mates in the police that I would go for a drink with, like many of the previous generation of crime reporters.' He knew one reporter on a Sunday paper who told him that, in the old days, one day a week was spent giving money in envelopes to police officers for the stories they'd provided.

'In terms of the job, being black hasn't been a problem for the most part,' he said. 'It sometimes helped – most of the time it made no differ-ence and occasionally it made things more tricky.' He cites the fact that he was able to gain the sort of access to stories on the Yardies that a white reporter might not have had and that his appointment coincided with a time when there was a growing number of black officers.

Regarding his dealings with criminals, 'I've had a few threats. I had one guy who told me he'd been asked to beat me up by people who didn't know that he was actually my informant.' The Hell's Angels on whom he has written extensively and critically had his photo pinned up on the wall in their Wolverhampton headquarters. Following the 1995 Rettenden shoot-out case in which three drug dealers were shot dead in their Range Rover in Essex, he was approached by the supergrass involved, Darren Nicholls, who gave crucial evidence against the men convicted of the shootings and who wanted his help to write his story. The book, *Bloggs 19*, appeared in 2000. 'There was no police involvement, as has been suggested,' said Thompson, 'it was between him and me.'

Vikram Dodd, who has covered crime for the *Guardian* since 2007, knew that he wanted to be a journalist from when he was a thirteen-year-old schoolboy in Birmingham. The son of first-generation Punjabi immigrants, his family had wanted him to find a job with a good pension, stability and social standing. 'None of which applied to journalism, but to be fair to them, they put up with it.' At school, the careers adviser laughed at the idea and said maybe, if his exams went well, he might find a job in a bank. He did work experience for the *Birmingham Daily News* and local radio stations and freelanced for the *Voice* before studying politics, philosophy and economics at Oxford University where he co-edited the student paper *Cherwell*, taking it to its first student journalism prize for best paper award for twenty-five years. He followed this with a course in journalism at City University London.

Why someone so well qualified was not snapped up, as his white Oxford contemporaries were, by a regional daily, is a matter of valid speculation. 'I don't think anyone could prove a chain of causality but there was quite a strong correlation between the way the media was then and their coverage of certain issues,' he said. Of the changes in crime coverage, he said: 'In the past, the story had been "cops v robbers". Now it became "cops v communities".'

Dodd believes that the case of Stephen Lawrence, both in the way it was investigated by the police and reported by the press, was highly significant. And he cites the murder of Ashiq Hussain, who was fatally stabbed in a Birmingham petrol station in 1992 after going to the aid of another driver who was being racially abused, as another example of 'a blindingly obvious race attack but the investigation got messed up'.

He joined the *Guardian* in 1998 and, in 2000, unmasked the seventy-eight-year-old Nazi war criminal Alexander Schweidler, who lived in a council flat in Milton Keynes and who had been a member of the SS 'death's head' unit at the Mauthausen concentration camp in Austria. Four days later Schweidler died. 'When you're asked, "What story of yours has ever had an impact?", I can say, "There was this geezer, we wrote a story about him and he died,"' said Dodd.

Had his ethnic background made a difference to the way he was able to do his job? He recalled at the turn of the century when he had a story connected to the case of Ali Dizaei. 'Someone at the Yard said, "We know how you got that story." The insinuation was that I got the story because I had been sleeping with a woman [from an advising group] who I don't think I had ever met. They had confused me with another Asian reporter whose first name began with V.'

As to how race and crime are dealt with in the media, 'the coverage is less explicitly racist but it's still very much there. People don't use the "N" word. They don't say "all blacks are criminals", they talk about "street populations" – it's coded. Race ethnicity and what are called "community issues" are now very much the fault line of policing and the criminal justice system, both for the Caribbean communities and, post 9/11 and 7/7, for the Muslim communities. The call a commissioner might have dreaded in the fifties or sixties would have been about a big bank heist, in the seventies or eighties about an intruder in the Queen's bedroom and, as of this morning, it's a gun attack by those claiming to act in the name of religion.'

Post-Leveson, Dodd has also noticed a sea change in relations with the police. 'Every time I pick up the phone to call someone, I am potentially putting them in a position of a disciplinary offence or a criminal offence. The cops are trawling through stuff to find who's talking . . . It is a mistake for the police to believe that a) they are meeting their democratic duty to be accountable and b) doing the service and public justice, if all they do is try to communicate by press release and the odd press conference.'

But despite all the difficulties, the appeal of the job remains intact. 'Who would want to be covering health or education when you can cover crime?' said Martin Brunt. 'It's that old adage of all human life is there. I wake up looking forward to going to work. I'm sixty and I don't know how many of my contemporaries feel the same thing.'

And whatever local difficulties crime reporters in Britain have to face they can hardly be compared to the risks faced by their colleagues elsewhere in the world. In Mexico, in Russia, in Honduras, in Pakistan, in dozens of countries around the world, reporters pay with their lives or their freedom for the crimes and corruptions they reveal. Nor is Western Europe immune. In Ireland, Veronica Guerin was shot dead in 1996 because of her investigation into drug gangs. And Roberto Saviano, the courageous Italian journalist who exposed the Camorra in his book *Gomorrah* in 2006, has had to live a life in the shadows ever since. In 2015 he wrote in the *Guardian*: 'For the last eight years I have travelled everywhere with seven trained bodyguards in two bullet-proof cars. I live in police barracks or anonymous hotel rooms, and rarely spend more than a few nights in the same place. It's been more than eight years since I took a train, or rode a Vespa, took a stroll or went out for a beer . . . After all these years under state protection, I almost feel guilty for still being alive.'

23

The Crime Reporter in Space

What the Future Holds

The date is January 2016, the place is court two of Woolwich Crown Court, and the trial of the men accused of carrying out the most spectacular British crime of the decade: the theft of around £14 million of jewellery, gold and cash from the Hatton Garden safe deposit company over the Easter weekend of 2015. The ringleaders, Terry Perkins, Brian Reader, Danny Jones and Kenny Collins, have already pleaded guilty and the four men in the dock are accused of playing minor parts. This is, in prosecuting counsel Philip Evans's phrase (repeated in every daily newspaper), 'the largest burglary in English legal history'.

This is the sort of crime story that doesn't come along very often; a 'project' crime, one that requires planning and cunning and offers a massive reward. Part of the fascination is that this is 'old school'. Old being the operative word. Perkins is sixty-seven, Reader seventy-six, Jones sixty and Collins seventy-four. Hence their nickname, the 'Diamond Wheezers'. There are witnesses with Runyonesque nicknames like 'Billy the Fish' and 'Jimmy Two-baths', and hidden police tape-recordings of the protagonists chortling about 'the biggest robbery in the fucking world we was on'. But there is puzzlement, too, that the thieves seemed unaware that their mobile phones and computers could help incriminate them. It is as if they are trapped in a sort of criminal aspic. The end of the trial prompts massive press and television coverage but

261

there is a feeling amongst the crime reporters in court that this is an end-of-an-era event.

The twenty-first century has presented the criminally inclined with new opportunities that were quickly seized and developed: the cyber-thief who hacks into bank accounts and transfers the money to foreign banks; the menacing troll who threatens and blackmails; the online con artist with promises of profit or bogus pleas for help; the people smuggler, taking advantage of fleeing refugees; the sex trafficker, exploiting vulnerable women; the anonymous internet dealer in drugs and pornography on the dark net. The days of the high-profile blags are numbered. Bank robberies and break-ins declined, as security and technology advanced, down from 847 nationally in 1992 to 108 by 2012. In London, the numbers fell from 291 to 26 in the same period.

At the same time, technology and the digital age has not just influenced the nature of crime, but the methods of reporting it. Crime reporters, like all journalists, are now under pressure from above to show that their words are being read, something that their editors can now monitor, even to the extent of telling how long readers linger on a particular story. The twenty-four-hour news cycle, initiated towards the end of the twentieth century by rolling news on television, became de rigueur as newspapers were transformed into 'news providers' in an online world. In late 2014, the Telegraph group noted that four key skills for their reporters would be 'social, video, analytics and search engine optimisation'. What about 'journalism' asked one online wag, and you could almost hear the bodies of W. T. Stead and Duncan Webb turning in their graves. Too often 'search engine optimisation' means shoving the name of a celebrity into a story to snare the casual browser. No time to research and delve deep when the demand is for measurable internet hits.

The opportunities created by new technologies have been harnessed to some effect by journalists but the digital age, and the ubiquity of the mobile phone, has also presented new pressures. In 2014, for example, it transpired that nineteen police forces in England and Wales made more than 600 applications to uncover confidential sources of journalists in the previous three years. Requests to use anti-terror legislation to access reporters' communication records were made in thirty-four police investigations into suspected leaks by public officials, the Interception of Communication Commissioner's Office (ICCO) found. Sir Anthony May, the then interception of communications commissioner, said that police forces 'did not give due consideration to freedom of speech' and that the Home Office guidelines did not sufficiently protect journalistic sources. How secure would a confidential source – a police officer, a lawyer, a criminal on the run – feel when they make contact with a crime reporter in the future?

So where is crime reporting heading? Will crowd-funded reporting feature more heavily in the future? The journalist Peter Jukes, for example, successfully explored this to allow him to tweet the big 2014 Old Bailey hacking trial in its entirety. A year later he and Alastair Morgan, the brother of Daniel Morgan, the private eye murdered in 1987, started a crowd-funded podcast in Britain to explore 'the most investigated unsolved murder in British history'. They had taken their cue from *Serial*, the amazingly popular American podcast to re-examine a 1999 murder.

As for the future methods of crime reporting, these are unlikely to stand still. The drone, for example, 'is a wonderful tool for getting above a crime scene', according to Martin Brunt of Sky News. 'I think the authorities are very keen to stop us doing that . . . but I am sure they will become part of our tool box simply because they can get vision footage where we can't. They will become the norm.'

So – will all reporters have drones to monitor crime scenes? Will trials be streamed live? Will juries vote online? Will detailed reporting be crowd-funded? Will blogs and podcasts replace the crime bureaux of old? Will police forces and security services be able to intercept every email and text message so that reporters will once again have to meet their contacts down shady lanes? Who will Hold the Front Page when there are no more front pages to hold? Who will be the crime correspondent to report the first murder in space? And if it bleeds, will it still lead?

Of course it will.

Bibliography

Archibald, Malcolm, *Bloody Scotland: Crime in 19th Century Scotland* (Edinburgh: Black and White Publishing, 2014)

Arnold, Catharine, *Underworld London* (London: Simon & Schuster, 2012)

Babington, Anthony, *The English Bastille* (London: Macdonald and Co., 1971)

Bailey, Paul, *An English Madam* (London: Jonathan Cape, 1982)

Barker, Revel, *The Last Pub in Fleet Street* (London: Palantino Publishing, 2015)

Bates, Stephen, *The Poisoner: the Life and Crime of Victorian England's Most Notorious Doctor* (London: Duckworth, 2014)

Binyon, T. J., *Murder Will Out* (Oxford: Oxford University Press, 1990)

Biressi, Anita, *Crime, Fear and the Law in True Crime Stories* (London: Palgrave Macmillan, 2001)

Bondeson, Jan, *The London Monster* (Stroud: Tempus, 2005)

Boran, Anne, *Crime: Fear or Fascination?* (Chester: Chester Academic Press, 2002)

Brake, Laurel and Demoor, Marysa (eds), *Dictionary of Nineteenth Century Journalism* (Ghent: Academia Press, 2009)

Brewer, John, *Sentimental Murder: Love and Madness in the Eighteenth Century* (London: Harper Perennial, 2004)

broadsides.law.harvard.edu

Brooke, Alan and Brandon, David, *Tyburn: London's Fatal Tree* (Stroud: Sutton Publishing, 2004)

Burden, Peter, *How I Changed Fleet Street* (Leicester: Matador, 2011)

Byrne, Gerald, *John George Haigh* (London: Headline Publications, 1950)

Cameron, James, *Point of Departure* (Stocksfield: Oriel Press, 1978)

Campbell, Duncan, *That Was Business, This Is Personal* (London: Secker & Warburg, 1990)

Campbell, Duncan, *The Underworld* (London: BBC Books, 1994)

Chandler, Charlotte, *Nobody's Perfect: Billy Wilder, A Personal Biography* (London: Simon & Schuster, 2002)

Chibnall, Steve, *Law-and-Order News* (London: Tavistock Publications, 1977)

Clark, Neil, *Stranger Than Fiction: the Life of Edgar Wallace* (Stroud: The History Press, 2014)

Cockburn, J. S. (ed.), *Crime in England 1550–1800* (London: Methuen, 1977)

Colenbrander, Joanna, *A Portrait of Fryn* (London: Andre Deutsch, 1984)

Collins, Philip, *Dickens and Crime* (London: Macmillan, 1965)

Cook, Andrew, *The Great Train Robbery* (Stroud: History Press, 2013)

Cope, Wendy, *If I Don't Know* (London: Faber & Faber, 2001)

Cressy, David, 'Literacy in Seventeenth Century England', *Journal of Interdisciplinary History*, MIT Press, Vol. 8, No. 1 (1977), pp. 141–50

Crew, Albert, *The Old Bailey* (London: Ivor Nicholson and Watson, 1933)

Curtis, L. Perry Jr, *Jack the Ripper & the London Press* (New Haven: Yale University Press, 2001)

Daly, Max and Sampson, Steve, *Narcomania* (London: Heinemann, 2012)

Davenport-Hines, Richard, *An English Affair* (London: William Collins, 2013)

Davies, Andrew, *City of Gangs* (London: Hodder, 2013)

Davies, Nick, *Hack Attack: How the Truth Caught Up with Rupert Murdoch* (London: Chatto & Windus, 2014)

Defoe, Daniel, *Moll Flanders* (London: Vintage Classics, 2010)

Delano, Anthony, *Joyce McKinney and the Case of the Manacled Mormon* (London: Revel Barker, 2009)

Dickens, Charles, *Oliver Twist* (London: Penguin Classics, 1985)

Draper, Alfred, *Scoops and Swindles* (London: Furnival Press, 1988)

Eckley, Grace, *Maiden Tribute: A Life of W. T. Stead* (Bloomington: XLibris, 2007)

Edwards, Owen Dudley, *Burke & Hare* (Edinburgh: Birlinn, 2010)

Edwards, Robert, *Goodbye Fleet Street* (London: Jonathan Cape, 1988)

Engel, Matthew, *Tickle the Public* (London: Indigo, 1996)

Emsley, Clive, Hitchcock, Tim and Shoemaker, Robert, 'The Proceedings – Ordinary of Newgate's Accounts', Old Bailey Proceedings Online (www.oldbaileyonline.org, 12 November 2014)

Fabian, Robert, *Fabian of the Yard* (New Delhi: Cedar Books, 1956)

Fabian, Robert (introduction), *The Boy's Book of Scotland Yard* (London: Clerke & Cockeran, 1958)

Fabian, Robert, *London After Dark* (London: Naldrett Press, 1950)

Firmin, Stanley, *Crime Man* (London: Hutchinson, 1950)

Flanagan, Maureen, *One of the Family: 40 Years with the Krays* (London: Century, 2015)

Flanders, Judith, *The Invention of Murder* (London: Harper Press, 2011)

Forbes, Ian, *Squad Man* (London: W. H. Allen, 1973)

Frost, George 'Jack', *The Flying Squad* (London: Rockliff, 1948)

Gay, John, *The Beggar's Opera* (London: Penguin Classics, 1986)

Gibbs, Philip, *Adventures in Journalism* (London: Heinemann, 1923)

Goodman, Jonathan (ed.), *The Daily Telegraph Murder File* (London: Mandarin, 1993)

Greenslade, Roy, *Press Gang: How Newspapers Made Profits from Propaganda* (London: Pan Books, 2005)

Grey, Isabelle, *Good Girls Don't Die* (London: Quercus, 2015)

Hill, Justin and Hunt, John, *Billy Hill Gyp and Me* (London: Billy Hill Family Ltd, 2012)

Hitchcock, Tim and Shoemaker, Robert, *Tales from the Hanging Court* (London: Hodder Education 2006/Bloomsbury, 2010)

Hitchcock, Tim; Shoemaker, Robert; Emsley, Clive; Howard, Sharon; and McLaughlin, Jamie, et al., *The Old Bailey Proceedings Online, 1674–1913* (www.oldbaileyonline.org, version 7.0, 24 March 2012)

Hobsbawn, Eric, *Bandits* (London: Pelican, 1969)

Hodge, Harry, (ed.), *Famous Trials 1* (London: Penguin, 1941)

Hodge, James H. (ed.), *Famous Trials 5* (London: Penguin, 1955)

Hodgkinson, Liz, *Ladies of the Street* (London: Revel Barker, 2008)

Holmes, Richard, *Defoe on Sheppard & Wild* (London: Harper Perennial, 2004)

Howson, Gerald, *Thief-taker General: The Rise and Fall of Jonathan Wild* (London: Hutchinson, 1970)

Hutton, Robert, *Romps, Tots and Boffins . . . The Strange Language of News* (London: Elliott & Thompson, 2013)

Innes, Brian, *Crooks and Conmen* (Leicester: Blitz Editions, 1992)

Ireland, Thomas, *The West Port Murders* (Edinburgh: Thomas Ireland, 1829)

James, P. D., *Talking About Detective Fiction* (London: Faber & Faber, 2009)

Johnson, Graham, *Hack* (London: Simon & Schuster, 2012)

Knelman, Judith, *Twisting in the Wind: the Murderess and the English Press* (Toronto: University of Toronto Press, 1998)

Knelman, Judith, 'Women Murderers in Victorian Britain', *History Today*, Vol. 48, August, 1998

Kohn, Marek, *Dope Girls* (Lawrence and Wishart, 1992)

Kohn, Marek, *Narcomania* (London: Faber & Faber, 1987)

Leslie, David, *Crimelord* (Edinburgh: Mainstream, 2005)

'The Leveson Inquiry', webarchive.nationalarchives.gov.uk/ 20140122145147/http://www.levesoninquiry.org.uk/ (January 2014)

Linebaugh, Peter, *The London Hanged* (London: Penguin, 1993)

Linebaugh, Peter, 'The Ordinary of Newgate and his Account', in Cockburn, J. S. (ed.), *Crime in England 1550–1800* (London: Meuthen, 1977)

Lustgarten, Edgar, *Defender's Triumph* (London: Pan, 1957)

Lustgarten, Edgar, *The Woman in the Case* (London: Great Pan, 1958)

Lustgarten, Edgar, *One More Unfortunate* (New Jersey: Gregg Press, 1980)

McKay, Reg, *The Last Godfather* (Edinburgh: Black and White Publishing, 2006)

McKenzie, Andrea, *Tyburn's Martyrs* (London: Hambledon Continuum, 2007)

Mair, John (ed.), *After Leveson? The Future for British Journalism* (Bury St Edmunds: Abramis, 2013)

Marks, Amber, *Head Space* (London: Virgin Books, 2009)

Marks, Howard, *Mr Nice* (London: Vintage, 1998)

Mawby, Rob, *Policing Images* (London: Willan Publishing, 2002)

Meaney, Joseph, *Scribble Street* (Beaufort: Sands, 1945)

Millen, Ernest, *Specialist in Crime* (London: Harrap, 1970)

Morton, James, *Gangland: London's Underworld* (London: Little Brown, 1992)

Morton, James, and Parker, Jerry, *Gangland Bosses: The Lives of Jack Spot and Billy Hill* (London: Sphere, 2005)

Mulpetre, Owen, 'W. T. Stead Resource Site', www.attackingthedevil.co.uk/pmg/tribute/

Nicholas, Sian and O'Malley, Tom (eds), *Moral Panics, Social Fears and the Media* (London: Routledge, 2013)

Olden, Mark, *Murder in Notting Hill* (London: Zero Books, 2011)

The Ordinary of Newgate (Eighteenth Century Collections Online print edition), oldbaileyonline.org

Payne, Chris, *The Chieftain: Victorian True Crime through the Eyes of a Scotland Yard Detective* (Stroud: The History Press, 2011)

Pearson, John, *Notorious: The Immortal Legend of the Kray Twins* (London: Century, 2010)

prisonvoices.org

Procter, Harry, *The Street of Disillusion* (London: Revel Barker, 2010)

Ramsey, Winston (ed.), *Scenes of Murder Then and Now* (Old Harlow: After the Battle, 2011)

Randall, David, *The Great Reporters* (London: Pluto, 2005)

Reynolds, Bruce, *The Autobiography of a Thief* (London: Bantam Press, 1995)

Ritchie, Jean (ed.), *True Crime Stories from the News of the World* (London: Michael O'Mara Books, 1993)

Roberts, Caroline, *The Lost Girl* (London: Metro, 2005)

Robinson, W. Sydney, *Muckraker: the Scandalous Life and Times of W. T. Stead* (London: The Robson Press, 2012)

Root, Neil, *Frenzy!: The First Great Tabloid Murders* (London: Preface, 2011)

Roughead, William, *In Queer Street* (Edinburgh: W. Green and Son, 1933)

Roughead, William, *Knave's Looking Glass* (London: Cassell & Co, 1935)

Roughead, William, *Trial of Deacon Brodie* (London: Forgotten Books, 2012)

Roughead, William, *Twelve Scots Trials* (Edinburgh: Mercat Press, 1995)

Rowbotham, Judith; Stevenson, Kim; and Pegg, Samantha, *Crime News in Modern Britain: Press Reporting and Responsibility, 1820–2010* (London: Palgrave Macmillan, 2013)

Schlesinger, Philip and Tumber, Howard, *Reporting Crime: the Media Politics of Criminal Justice* (Oxford: Clarendon Press, 1994)

Sell, Henry, *Sell's Dictionary of the World's Press* (London: Sell's Ltd, 1888, 1902)

Shaaber, Matthias A., *Some Forerunners of the Newspapers in England 1476–1622* (Philadelphia: University of Pennsylvania Press, 1929)

Sharpe, James, *Dick Turpin: the Myth of the English Highwayman* (London: Profile, 2004)

Skirball, Aaron, *The Thief-taker Hangings* (Guilford, CT: Lyons Press, 2014)

Slipper, Jack, *Slipper of the Yard* (London: Sidgwick & Jackson, 1981)

Snoddy, Ray, *The Good, the Bad and the Unacceptable: the Hard News About the British Press* (London: Faber & Faber, 1992)

Stephens, Mitchell, *A History of News* (Oxford: Oxford University Press, 2007)

Storey, Neil R., *London: Crime, Death and Debauchery* (Stroud: Sutton Publishing, 2007)

Stratmann, Linda, *Cruel Deeds and Dreadful Calamities: The Illustrated Police News 1864–1938* (London: British Library Publishing, 2011)

Thatcher, George, *Fitted Up* (Stroud: The History Press, 2014)

Tietjen, Arthur, *Soho: London's Vicious Circle* (London: A. Wingate, 1956)

Thurlbeck, Neville, *Tabloid Secrets* (London: Biteback Publishing, 2015)

Tomalin, Claire, *Charles Dickens – A Life* (London: Viking, 2011)

Wallace, Edgar, *The Feathered Serpent* (Looe: House of Stratus, 2001)

Webb, Duncan, *Dead Line for Crime* (London: Frederick Muller, 1955)

Whittington-Egan, Richard, *William Roughead's Chronicles of Murder* (Isle of Colonsay: Lochar Publishing, 1991)

Williams, Kevin, *Get Me a Murder a Day* (London: Bloomsbury Academic, 2010)

Woodhall, Edwin T., *Secrets of Scotland Yard* (London: The Bodley Head, 1936)

Zec, Donald, *Put the Knife in Gently* (London: Robson Books, 2003)

Acknowledgements

I am grateful to many people who have helped directly or indirectly: first and foremost, Hélène Mulholland, for her invaluable and diligent research work; my agent, Andrew Lownie; Jennie Condell and Pippa Crane of Elliott and Thompson, and also, in no particular order: Roy Greenslade, Kate Macleod, Mark Olden, Alistair McClure, James McClure, David Jenkins, Karen Payne, Matthew Engel, Amber Marks, Jonathan Green, Stuart Christie, Ferdinand Dennis, Stella Coradi, Julia Quenzler, Clare Longrigg, the late Bobby King, Richard Adams, Alan Campbell, Peter Clark, Jason Rodriques, Luc Torres, Katy Stoddard, Lorna Macfarlane, the late Professor Andrew Huxley, Nick Davies, John Lloyd, Mark Sullivan, Christopher Sheppard, Bob Woffinden, Richard Norton-Taylor, Nick Reynolds, Ruby Crystal, Bruno Vincent and, particularly, all those who agreed to be interviewed on the record or off the record (a term that Lord Justice Leveson understandably found confusing – I always thought it meant that you could use the information but make sure it was untraceable; others believed it meant not for use at all. Too late and too bad if I got it wrong).

I am also grateful to the staff of the British Library, to James Hamilton of the Signet Library in Edinburgh, and the staffs of the National Archives, the Scottish National Library, the British Museum, the Wellcome Collection, the Guardian Library, the British Newspaper Archive, the Dickens Museum, the BBC Archives, the oldbailey online, *History Today*, the Broadway Bookshop, Harvard University, Wikipedia, Murderpedia. org, *Press Gazette* and Gentlemen Ranters. My thanks also to the *Guardian*,

Observer, *New Statesman*, the *Oldie*, *Esquire*, *British Journalism Review* and the *Journalist* for whom I wrote about some of the subjects addressed in this book. I have tried to credit any information that I have found in books – see the Bibliography – and articles. If anyone has been omitted, my apologies; all I can suggest is that they buy many, many copies of this book to ensure its republication which would then, of course, include suitably amended attribution.

Index